D1231652

Abraham Lincoln

A NEW PORTRAIT

ABRAHAM LINCOLN. One of several photographs taken by Alexander Gardner on April 10, 1865. After his return to Washington from City Point, Lincoln visited Gardner's studio to have a picture taken. Four days later he was assassinated. *Courtesy of the Library of Congress.*

Abraham Lincoln

A NEW PORTRAIT

Edited by *HENRY B. KRANZ*

G. P. Putnam's Sons   New York

Contents

PART II

Preface

————⌁————

ABRAHAM LINCOLN has been portrayed in more books than any other American, in more essays, in more countries and in more languages. A book devoted to telling his absorbing and inspiring story again can hardly promise to open up much fresh and surprising material. It can, however, use a different, untried approach in drawing the image of the man who created a new America and became its mirror. Here the approach is different and new because a number of distinguished historians who have spent the greater part of their lives in studying and probing Lincoln and his times, and in writing about him, were asked to join in one effort; each of them is now viewing in a short, succinct and analytical essay a single aspect of Lincoln's singular personality.

Abraham Lincoln is unique in his fascination. The more often we look at him, the more different facets we perceive. He was not one but many men. He was the first American after Franklin and Jefferson whose thinking and whose talent covered an amazing number of human affairs. But in many respects he was unlike these men. He was more complex. He was statesman and poet, economist and inventor, politician and military strategist, lawyer and philosopher, farm hand and businessman, revolutionary theorist and conservative legislator, friend of the laborer and protector of vested interests. He surpassed in grandeur and majesty all the panegyrical orators of his day and he knew how to voice in a few unstudied, homespun words the wisdom of a prophet. He was deeply religious but not a member of any Christian church. He did not indulge in any youthful pleasure but seemed to be more satisfied with his life than his young friends. He fought one of the most murderous wars of history and desired peace more ardently than the men who advised him against calling the nation to arms. He was rigidly honest and did not care for financial success or personal comfort but knew well how to take advantage of his interests and died a rich man. He was, as Carl Sandburg has said, "hard as a rock and soft as a drifting fog, who holds in his heart and mind the paradox of terrible storm and peace unspeakable and perfect." He had infinite faith in democracy and stoical confidence in the ultimate justice of the people but appeared to a great many as an autocratic tyrant. He was patient and excitable, shy and brash, sad and gay, taciturn and eloquent, lonely but a passionate public speaker and storyteller, "apart from all but alienated from none," as John Drinkwater phrased it. He was humble and ambitious, guileless and astute, a natural unquestioned leader, yet confessed that events had controlled him. Some saw him as humble, some as arrogant. His first biographer, Josiah G. Holland, noted: "He rarely showed more than one aspect of himself to one man. He opened himself to men in different directions." Lincoln was, and perhaps will always remain, enigmatic.

It seemed to me that if men who had studied Lincoln for a long time were to discuss only one single phase of his personality, a new multicolored image of him in mosaic form would emerge and explain some of his enigma. I hope the reader will accept this as a reasonable motive for adding another Lincoln volume to those that made their appearance in this Sesquicentennial year.

To amplify and strengthen some of the points made in the essays, a limited selection of Lincoln's letters, speeches and most significant thoughts is presented. Many important speeches, letters and other historical documents may be missed, but this was unavoidable in preserving the character of the book. I also felt that a profile of Lincoln as conceived by some of his eminent contemporaries in prose and verse would be of benefit. The volume is designed to display the enormous range of Lincoln's arresting personality and to interpret some of its puzzling, paradoxical features. His life of high purpose, his moral strength and firmness, and his merciful struggle for the rights of men wherever they might be, secure for him a lasting place in the history of mankind.

While the opinions and conclusions of the authors are their own, the editor is responsible for the choice of subjects.

The editor is indebted to the contributors who have drawn upon a rich body of scholarship and experience; he is deeply grateful to Dr. David C. Mearns for his interest in the project, his advice on numerous occasions and his critical assistance.

The Lincoln documents in this book have been selected from *The Collected Works of Abraham Lincoln* (8 volumes and index), edited by Roy P. Basler, with Marion Dolores Pratt and Lloyd A. Dunlap as assistant editors, and published in 1953 by Rutgers University Press.

Washington, D.C. HENRY B. KRANZ

Part 1

LINCOLN, PLAIN MAN
OF THE PEOPLE

By Bell Irvin Wiley

Dr. Bell Irvin Wiley, Professor of American History, Emory University, Atlanta, is a member of the President's Civil War Centennial Commission and a former President of the Southern Historical Association. Among his books are: The Life of Johnny Reb: The Common Soldier of the Confederacy *(1943);* The Life of Billy Yank: The Common Soldier of the Union *(1952); and* The Road to Appomattox *(1956).*

I WAS BORN and have ever remained in the most humble walks of life," wrote Abraham Lincoln in 1832 when he was making his first bid for public office. Twenty-eight years later, while seeking the Presidency, he replied to a biographer's request for material about his early years: "It is a great piece of folly to attempt to make anything out of my early life. It can be condensed into a single sentence and that sentence you will find in Gray's Elegy—'The short and simple annals of the poor.' "

Thus did the man who was destined to lead the American nation through its greatest crisis identify himself with the plain people. There was no pretension in his claim to humble beginnings. He was born in poverty. While yet a boy he toiled in forest and field with ax, hoe, and plow. As he attained maturity he worked as a hired hand, splitting rails, building a flatboat, and transporting cargoes of farm goods from his home country to New Orleans. Later he clerked in a store, served as village postmaster, and practiced surveying. He then read law and rode

the circuit as a country barrister. Until he moved to Springfield
in 1837—and to a large extent thereafter—his most intimate associates were the plain working people of the American frontier.
He ate the simple fare and wore the unpretentious clothing to
which they were accustomed. He shared their superstitions, enjoyed their rough humor, entered heartily into their song fests,
and excelled in their manly sports. He sat with their sick and
helped bury their dead. He was one with them in thought, word,
and deed.

These early associations and experiences impressed on Lincoln the solid virtue, individually and collectively, of the common people and instilled in him a deep desire to promote their
welfare. He developed a profound conviction that the hope and
future of America depended on the security, progress, and
loyalty of the ordinary folk. America was "a new nation, conceived in Liberty and dedicated to the proposition that all men
are created equal." Its strength reposed ultimately in the character of the masses. "It is upon the brave hearts and strong arms
of the Country," he said to a group of common soldiers during
the Civil War, "that our reliance has been placed in support of
free government and free institutions."

The influence of Lincoln's humble background and associations is apparent in his often-expressed belief in the worth and
dignity of labor. About the time he took his seat in Congress he
wrote: "In the early days of the world the Almighty said to the
first of our race, 'In the sweat of thy face shalt thou eat bread,'
and since then, if we except the *light* and the *air* of heaven, no
good thing has been or can be enjoyed by us without having
first cost labor: And inasmuch [as] most good things are produced by labor, it follows that all such things of right belong
to those whose labour has produced them." In a speech at Cincinnati in September 1859, Lincoln declared that "Labor is the
great source from which nearly all if not all human comforts
and necessities are drawn." And in February 1861, while en
route to Washington, he told a Pittsburgh audience that "Labor
is the true standard of value."

Lincoln was deeply concerned that those who toiled should be
fairly compensated and should have full opportunity to improve
their status. He opposed the subtreasury scheme in 1840, because

he thought it would reduce the amount of money in circulation and thus work to the disadvantage of the laboring and debtor class. He favored the Homestead Law, because he wanted the public domain to be disposed of in such a way "that every poor man can have a home." One of his reasons for opposing the extension of slavery into the territories was the handicap which the introduction of forced labor would impose on free laborers seeking to establish themselves by their own toil.

The right of laborers to strike, Lincoln specifically defended on a number of occasions. In commenting on a strike among Massachusetts shoe workers in a speech at Hartford, Connecticut, on March 5, 1860, he declared: "I am glad to know that there is a system of labor where the laborer can strike if he wants to. I would to God that such a system prevailed all over the world." To a New Haven audience he declared the next day: "I *like* the system which lets a man quit when he wants to and wish it might prevail everywhere."

One of his basic objections to slavery was that the system prevented the worker from bargaining with his employer as to the conditions of his labor, and denied to those who toiled any hope of lifting themselves in the social and economic scale.

Lincoln was in no sense opposed to capital. He was firmly committed to a system of free enterprise. But he believed that those who worked for wages should have a full and free opportunity to attain a position where they in turn could hire the services of others. "There is no such thing as a freeman being fatally fixed for life in the condition of a hired laborer," he said on one occasion. "Labor is prior to and independent of capital . . . capital is the fruit of labor . . . labor can exist without capital, but capital never would have existed without labor."

In his speech of March 6, 1860, at New Haven, Lincoln stated: "I take it that it is best for all to leave each man free to acquire property as fast as he can. Some will get wealthy. I don't believe in a law to prevent a man from getting rich; it would do more harm than good. So, while we do not propose any war upon capital, we do wish to allow the humble man an equal chance to get rich with everybody else."

During the Civil War, Lincoln on several occasions manifested an interest in the laboring classes and in their support of the Union cause. In July 1864 he requested Secretary of War Stanton to investigate a reduction in the wages of women workers that had come to his attention, and to see if the pay could not be restored to at least the original rate. In March 1864 he "gratefully accepted" honorary membership in the New York workingmen's Democratic Republican Association and congratulated that organization on its realization that the conflict between North and South was "in fact a war upon the rights of all working people." He also expressed to this association his regret that in the draft riots of the prior summer some working people had hanged other working people. "The strongest bond of human sympathy outside of the family relation," he added, "should be one uniting all working people of all nations, and tongues and kindred." Early in 1863 he sent messages to the workingmen of London and Manchester, thanking them for their expressions of sympathy for the Northern cause. To the latter he wrote: "I know and deeply deplore the sufferings which the workingmen at Manchester and in all Europe are called to endure in this crisis. . . . I cannot but regard your decisive utterance upon the question as an instance of sublime Christian heroism [and] reinspiring assurance of the inherent power of truth and of the ultimate and universal triumph of justice, humanity and freedom."

As he climbed the ladder of success Lincoln showed no inclination to forget or deplore his humble origins. In his New Haven speech of March 6, 1860, he stated: "I am not ashamed to confess that twenty-five years ago I was a hired laborer, mauling rails, at work on a flatboat—just what might happen to any man's son." His acquaintance with poverty and hardship gave him an abiding sympathy for the needy and the oppressed. He advocated liberal policies of immigration, so that people of other lands threatened with political persecution or ground down by poverty might share in America's "new life." And he also urged humane and generous treatment of foreigners after they reached the American shore. In February 1861 he told a Cincinnati audience: "In regard to the Germans and foreigners . . . . It is not my nature when I see a people borne down by the weight of their shackles—the oppression of tyranny—to make their life more bitter by heaping upon them great burdens; but rather would I do all in my power to raise the yoke, than to add anything that would crush them."

Lincoln's sympathies for the lowly and the underprivileged extended to people of all creeds and colors. He was especially interested in the welfare of the Negro. "I want every man to have the chance—and I believe the black man is entitled to it— in which he *can* better his condition," he declared in March 1860. True, he was slow in coming around to a policy of emancipation, but this did not mean that he was tolerant of human bondage. In a letter of August 24, 1855, to his Kentucky friend, Joshua F. Speed, he wrote: "I confess I hate to see the poor [slave] creatures hunted down and caught and carried back to their stripes and unrewarded toils; but I bite my lip and keep quiet." He reminded Speed: "In 1841 you and I had together a tedious low-water trip on a Steam Boat from Louisville to St. Louis. . . . There were, on board, ten or a dozen slaves shackled together with irons. That sight was a continual torment to me." In the debates with Douglas he chided his opponent for professing to regard right to property in fellow human beings as the same as that pertaining to "horses and every other sort of property." In the debate at Galesburg on October 7, 1858, he stated: "I confess myself as belonging to that class in the country who contemplate slavery as a moral, social and political evil . . . and [who] desire a policy that looks . . . hopefully to the time when as a wrong it may come to an end."

The end that he hoped for was assured by the Emancipation Proclamation, the Thirteenth Amendment, and the triumph of Federal arms. Once he committed himself to the adoption of emancipation as a war measure and objective, Lincoln worked diligently toward helping the colored people along the road to freedom and the full opportunity for advancement that he believed the inherent right of every human being. He actively pushed the recruiting and training of Negro soldiers. He manifested great interest in their progress in arms. And he insisted that they be treated as soldiers by both their white comrades and their foes. When the report reached him that colored troops had been massacred at Ft. Pillow, he ordered an investigation and promised: "If [it is proved that] there has been the massacre

of three hundred there, or even the tenth part of three hundred
... the retribution shall surely come." The President also followed with deep interest the work of private and government
agencies who undertook to promote the physical and spiritual
welfare of the families of colored soldiers and the other Negroes
who were involved in the tortuous transition from slavery to
freedom. The Negroes sensed Lincoln's solicitude. Those who
were still in bondage secretly uttered many and fervent prayers
for his well-being and the success of the cause which he led. And
when a few days before his death he appeared on the streets of
Richmond, hordes of colored people rapturously hailed him as
the bringer of the "day of Jubelo."

Lincoln's interest in the plain people and the attitude of the
Northern masses toward him during the crisis of the Civil War
is vividly and abundantly recorded in the letters and diaries of
the common soldiers who wore the blue.

In July 1862, while McClellan's army lay at Harrison's Landing licking its wounds after the unsuccessful thrust at Richmond, President Lincoln made one of his fact-finding visits to
the field. Shortly afterward Sergeant Felix Brannigan, an Irish-
born member of a New York regiment, wrote his homefolk:

Old Abe was here a few days ago and saw for himself the state of
things. He, we are all convinced, is the soldier's friend, and the man
above all men in the right place. We feel that he takes an interest in
us, that he has done what not one of ten thousand in a similar position would have brains enough to think of doing, i.e., to take nobody's word or reports got up for effect. He came and saw for himself.
Talk of McClellan's popularity among the soldiers—It will never
measure 1/100th part of Honest Abe's. Such cheers as greeted him
never tickled the ears of Napoleon in his palmiest days.

Sergeant Brannigan's estimate of Lincoln's popularity among
the rank and file was not exaggerated. It is not meant to imply
that acclaim was unanimous, for the President had bitter dis-
paragers, but these were notably few. Indeed, it is doubtful if
any war President in American history ever elicited as pervasive
and as enthusiastic admiration among the fighting forces as did
the rail splitter from Illinois. The warmth with which he was
regarded is suggested by the nicknames applied to him. Rela-

tively few soldiers spoke of him as "President Lincoln," "Mr. Lincoln," or "the President." But thousands referred to him as "Old Abe," "Father Abraham," or "Honest Abe"; and a popular song in camp was entitled "We Are Coming, Father Abraham." But far and away the most widely used nickname for the President was the intimate and affectionate "Old Abe." This term appears in letters and diaries several times as frequently as any other.

Of the various factors contributing to Lincoln's popularity among the rank and file, none was more important than the active interest which he manifested in the soldier's individual welfare. Scores of references appear in soldiers' letters to reviews by the President, and these camp visits were frequently cited as evidence of his concern for the men who carried musket and carbine. Private A. Davenport of the 5th New York Regiment informed his homefolk in the summer of 1862:

> President Lincoln Reviewed the whole Army in a flying visit . . . the men were all glad to see him & like him & have full confidence in him to a man. They . . . feel he is not to be fooled & that he wants to see with his own eyes how matters are. I heard him asking questions of our generals myself, he wants all the details and he is right.

But the thing which probably did most to impress Lincoln's kindly interest on the soldiers was his frequent interposition to soften the harsh discipline of the Union Army. Study of Lincoln indorsements on court-martial proceedings plainly shows the President's softening influence in cases calling for the death penalty. It is fairly well known that in no instance did a Union soldier forfeit his life for sleeping on post. Less publicized but equally true is the fact that Lincoln consistently alleviated the death sentence in cases where responsible commanders or the Judge Advocate General suggested clemency; and that on his own initiative he frequently ordered lesser punishments where courts had prescribed death for purely military offenses, such as insubordination, mutiny, and desertion. The only cases in which he habitually approved death sentences were those involving offenses not strictly military and which civil courts usually classified as capital, such as arson and rape.

Reports of the President's numerous acts of clemency were

widely circulated in the army, and lifted him greatly in the
esteem of the rank and file.

Another factor promoting Lincoln's popularity with ordinary
soldiers was his reputation for plainness and lack of pretension.
Billy Yanks probably did not know about Lincoln asking his
wife shortly after he took his seat in Congress not to prefix
"Honorable" to his name in addressing letters to him, but numerous stories pointing up the quality which lay back of this
request made the rounds of the camps; and while accuracy no
doubt took a severe beating as they passed from mouth to mouth,
their influence was probably enhanced rather than lessened by
the coloring of imagination.

Soldiers liked the simplicity of the President's dress and the
plainness of manner which marked his appearance among them.
They also appreciated his reputed fondness for unrefined stories,
of the sort which brought chortles when seasoned campaigners
held forth about the campfire. His alleged enjoyment of a chew
of tobacco also tended to bring him down to the level of the
common soldier. A veteran of a New York artillery unit, recalling an early review of his regiment by Lincoln and Seward,
stated:

While the presidential party was looking at the parade, Mr. Lincoln threw out a chew of tobacco onto the parade-ground. One of
the boys of — Company saw it, and when the parade was dismissed
he went and picked up the old chew and, wrapping it carefully in
a paper, prepared to save the same as a souvenir, but the boys teased
him so unmercifully, and put other chews with the president's, that
the poor man threw away the whole outfit.

Another factor contributing greatly to Lincoln's esteem by the
soldiers was their undeviating and apparently almost unanimous
belief in his integrity. The concept of "Honest Abe" may have
had its beginning as a mere shibboleth, but in the crucible of
war it seems to have acquired a status akin to religious faith. It
became a conviction, based more on emotion than on evidence,
but for that very reason sacred and beyond question.

This faith in the President's incorruptibility is all the more
impressive in view of the low opinion which the soldiers, cursed
as they were by such unhappy consequences of shady politics as

shoddy clothing, ineffective weapons, wormy rations, leaky tents, and inferior generals, had of politicians in general. Soldier opinion at low ebb of Washington leadership is well exemplified by Private Charles E. Goddard of Minnesota, who wrote in the dark days following Burnside's repulse at Fredericksburg:

> There is so many vilians in Washington that rap the cloak of patriotism around them and go in hand over hand robbing the helpless soldier of what are his dues. It matters not to them how long the war lasts. They are growing rich. . . . I realy think if we wer to go as straight to Washington as we could and burn the city and some of those vilians with it, we would be doing more good than to engage the enemy and whip him.

Pervasive distrust on the one hand of politicians in general and fervid belief on the other in the honesty of the man who in the hustings' rough and tumble had climbed to the top of the political ladder, finds ready explanation in refusal of most soldiers to identify the one with the other. To the overwhelming majority of the rank and file Lincoln was not a politician in the usual sense of the word. Rather, he was a plain, honest citizen, brought forward by a combination of the democratic process and the workings of Divine Providence to save the nation in a time of peril. And with the help of the soldiers and other good people, save the Union he would, and this in spite of hindering acts of scheming politicians. This concept of Lincoln versus the politicos is plainly evident in Sergeant Matthew Marvin's notation in his diary after the President's review of Hooker's army in April 1863: "He looks poorer than when he was at H[arrison's] Landing the boys think they dont use him well in Washington & propose to give him a furlough to recrute."

The feeling of the President's oneness in kind, purpose, and suffering with themselves caused enlisted men to write letters to him detailing their woes, and even to call at the White House to greet him and wish him well.

Lincoln's eloquence in speech and writing, while not as widely appreciated by soldiers as some of his other qualities, deserves mention as a factor in his popularity. In March 1865 a Yank wrote from camp:

I have just read the President's inaugural. I consider it the most remarkable state paper of modern times. Beautiful in its simplicity: grand and majestic in its expressions of lofty faith in the "Great Ruler of Nations;" it resembles more the production of one of Israel's ancient rulers than the Inaugural Address of a modern politician. I gathered strength and courage from its perusal.

Following Lincoln's speech at the White House a few days before his death a New York soldier who had not previously been an admirer of the President wrote his parents:

I will send you *Abraham's* speech which I heard the other night. I presume you have read it but it is worth studying. One might read it *forty times* over and then not have as much an idea of it as to hear him speak it. He speaks *very slow,* and makes every word *very emphatic* and after he is through one who has listened attentively (and everyone does that) could *almost repeat* it word for word. I love to hear him speak.

Some Billy Yanks registered disapproval of Lincoln because of his Emancipation Proclamation, his placing of Negroes in the ranks, or his dealing with high commanders. Early in December 1862 an admirer of General McClellan wrote his homefolk:

I believe ... that the President had as much confidence in his loyalty and ability the day he removed him as he ever had. "Why did he remove him then?" you will ask. On account of the pressure of public opinion. There was a strong feeling among the people that he was not the right man, and they had lost confidence in him.... The President saw the people did not like him, would not enlist, would not come forward with their money, and thought best, though against his better judgment, to yield.

This quality of Lincoln which caused him to be regarded as pure in the midst of iniquity and which enabled him to win the support and even the defense of those who opposed his major policies is difficult to pin down and define. But it was real, and to it must be credited much of his reputation for greatness. Significant of this quality was the observation of a veteran: "I doubt if any other man than Lincoln could have issued [the Emancipation Proclamation] and had it so generally received with good nature as it was coming from him."

Lincoln's standing with the rank and file was put to test in the presidential campaign of 1864. McClellan had a substantial following among soldiers from Democratic areas, but Billy Yanks as a group gave Lincoln a whopping majority. The reason that most of them gave for supporting Lincoln's re-election was the President's record in prosecuting the war, and the importance of keeping him in the saddle until the stream was crossed. "I Voted for him in 1861, and have fought for him three years," wrote a Wisconsin soldier in June 1864, and "I shall vote for him in 1864 and fight for him three years more, that's fair." A Hoosier wrote about the same time: "I want Abrham to handle the rains until this rebellion is crushed and the old Flag waves proudly over this land again. I think to elect any other man than Old Abrham will only prolong the war." "Perhaps another man could have done better," observed a Massachusetts corporal in April, "but I dont believe in turning a foreman off with his job most done." Other soldiers indicated association of Lincoln's re-election with early victory in the field, and this no doubt was a powerful influence in their support of the President.

Announcement of Lincoln's re-election was greeted by hearty rounds of hurrahs in camp. And as many blue-clad supporters of the President had predicted, triumph of the Union cause was not long in coming. But success on the battlefield lost much of its thrill when the assassin's bullet struck down the man whom the rank and file credited most with victory. Reaction to the tragedy was swift and terrific. In Memphis, Tennessee, soldiers left their barracks and paraded the streets looking for some manifestation of satisfaction among the natives, with a view to venting their wrath on such as should dare register approval of the tragedy. In Maryland a citizen who had the bad judgment to indorse Booth's act was knocked down by a Union general, had his head shaved, and was whipped out of camp with rawhide straps. A Federal soldier who received the news of the assassination with the statement, "I'm glad of it. If I had been there, I would have helped do it," was immediately seized by his comrades, tied around the neck with a rope and hustled to a nearby tree. Only the vigorous interposition of officers saved him from hanging.

During the course of the war Lincoln repeatedly manifested his awareness and appreciation of the esteem in which he was held by the rank and file. Reference has already been made to his visits to the camps to make a firsthand check on the condition of the soldiers. Regiments passing through Washington sometimes called at the White House to see "Uncle Abe." If he was at home, the President usually favored his visitors with a short speech. In these informal talks Lincoln was wont to dwell upon the "nature of the struggle in which we are engaged," the preservation and perpetuation of "a free government where every man has a right to be equal with every other man." He also tried to impress upon them the stake which they as ordinary citizens had in the conflict. "This government must be preserved," he said to members of the 148th Ohio Regiment on August 31, 1864. "It is worthy your every effort. Nowhere in the world is presented a government of so much liberty and equality. To the humblest and poorest among us are held out the highest privileges and positions. The present moment finds me in the White House. Yet there is as good a chance for your children as there was for my father's." And he praised the soldiers for their sacrifices and achievements. He told the 189th New York volunteers: "It is said that we have the best Government the world ever knew, and I am glad to meet you the supporters of that Government. To you who render the hardest work in its support, should be given the greatest credit."

Lincoln's course with reference to the plain people stands in marked contrast to that of Jefferson Davis, President of the Southern Confederacy. Davis, like Lincoln, was born in humble circumstances. But early in his life he became the protégé of his older brother Joseph, an affluent Mississippi planter who took over Jefferson Davis's education and obtained for him a cadetship at West Point. After a brief career in the army, Jefferson Davis, with Joseph's help, acquired a plantation and became a leader in Mississippi politics. From the time that he left home in his seventh year to enter school in Kentucky he had very little contact with the plain people. He did not have to depend on their support to achieve political success as did Lincoln. He did not feel close to them, nor did they manifest any feeling of intimacy with him. He did not understand their ways or their thinking. During the war he made no effort comparable to Lincoln's to convince the masses that the cause he represented was the cause of the people and that their support was essential to its success. He remained relatively aloof from the masses. Apparently he did not realize the necessity of winning their minds and their hearts for the Confederacy. In no sense was he a popular leader. It may well be that Lincoln's closer identity with the plain people, his greater awareness of the importance of their role in the conflict, and his greater success in rallying them to the cause that he represented was the most influential factor in the triumph of the North and the preservation of the Union.

LINCOLN AND HUMAN RIGHTS

By Harvey Wish

Dr. Harvey Wish, Professor of History, Western Reserve University, is the author of George Fitzhugh, Propagandist of the Old South *(1943) and* Society and Thought in America *(2 vols., 1950–52). In 1954 he was Fulbright Professor of History at the University of Munich.*

DURING 1808–9 two pioneer families in backwoods Kentucky living about eighty miles apart celebrated the birth of boys destined to be linked in an ironically strange fate. The first child was Jefferson Davis whose family later settled in the rich Mississippi black belt, acquired vast plantations, and became wealthy slaveowners. Davis rose to become President of the Confederate States of America dedicated to Negro slavery. The other was Abraham Lincoln, son of a small farmer who chose to move out of the slave area into southern Indiana and Illinois. Young Lincoln's final destiny was the White House leading the Union forces against the Confederate armies of Davis until all America was cleansed of slavery.

Lincoln, like the average Illinois farm worker, store clerk, and self-made lawyer of his day, probably never had more than ten months of formal schooling; yet he acquired a sensitive prose style that is notable in American literature and an even greater sensitivity to social ills and the universal struggle for human rights. He undoubtedly saw slavery when he took a flatboat down the Mississippi River to New Orleans and, even in his early years as an Illinois state legislator, he worked for its abolition, called for mass schooling as the bulwark of free institutions, and introduced laws to protect the small farmer from high interest rates.

At no time was Lincoln a radical given to violent methods. While he said that labor had superior rights over capital, he always added that capital also deserved protection. But capital must not *own* labor as under slavery. Besides, he believed firmly in the frontier ideal of equality of opportunity and in a fluid society. "There is no permanent class of hired laborers amongst us. Twenty-five years ago I was a hired laborer. The hired laborer of yesterday labors on his own account today and will hire others to labor for him tomorrow." Even in the twentieth century of large industry, this small enterprise ideal influenced Americans because society and opportunity continued to be fluid as in Lincoln's day. He was a younger contemporary of Karl Marx, but the notion of an implacable class struggle was wholly foreign to him as it was to his countrymen.

His early reputation was based on his simple dramatic skill as a trial lawyer gifted with the ability to reach the minds of ordinary men and sympathetic to the feelings of plain farm jurors. His frontier neighbors trusted him. When he spoke before a lecture audience occasionally, his message was for social justice. He denounced frontier mob incidents in Mississippi and in nearby Missouri, asserting that liberty must be "hewn from the solid quarry of pure reason" combining "general intelligence, sound morality, and a reverence for the Constitution and the laws." A law partner later recalled his platform appeal: "Lincoln's gray eyes would flash fire when speaking against slavery or spoke volumes of hope and love when speaking of liberty, justice, and the progress of mankind."

When Britain and France abolished slavery in their colonies, this example influenced many antislavery men like Lincoln. Elected to Congress for the 1847–49 session, he joined his fellow Whig Party members in combating the spread of slavery westward. He thought that the War with Mexico was merely a slaveowners' conspiracy to create more slave states out of the West. Therefore he voted against the war and voted, so he said later, about forty times for the Wilmot Proviso which forbade slavery in any territory acquired from Mexico.

Returning to Illinois, he reopened his law practice and joined the newly organized Republican Party which had proclaimed

Jefferson's doctrine of human equality. It is not the purpose here to relate the significant story of emancipation, but it should be noted that he refused to join the left-wing abolitionists who demanded immediate abolition regardless of violent consequences. Not an academic man, he was perplexed by the "scientific" anthropologists of his day who insisted that Negroes were innately inferior to whites, but he replied that even if this were true, it was no argument for enslavement. The earth, he said, was large enough for *all* races and conflict was not inevitable.

Lincoln observed the mind of the South through its newspapers and books. No one aroused him more than George Fitzhugh, an extremist Virginian lawyer who went far beyond slavery to attack modern liberty altogether. "Slavery, white or black, is right and necessary," Fitzhugh said and drew from the same racialist doctrines of the French diplomat Comte Joseph Arthur de Gobineau which later served modern racists. Free competitive society, he argued, was a recent development that had already failed judging from the factory exploitation of labor in Western Europe and America and the appearance of socialism, another form of coercion. Slavery and liberty, he said, "cannot long co-exist in the Great Republic of Christendom."

This basic attack on human rights which went far beyond a defense of Southern slavery aroused Lincoln to write his most famous political speech, the so-called "House Divided" address delivered in Springfield on June 16, 1858:

"A house divided against itself cannot stand." I believe this government cannot endure, permanently half slave and half free. I do not expect the Union to be dissolved—I do not expect the house to fall—but I do expect it will cease to be divided. It will become all one thing, or all the other. Either the opponents of slavery will arrest the further spread of it, and place it where the public mind shall rest in the belief that it is in course of ultimate extinction; or its advocates will push it forward, till it shall become alike lawful in all the States, old as well as new, North as well as South.

Later in reply to those who charged that he had uttered an incendiary statement, he made it clear that violence and inevitable war over slavery were far from his mind.

Lincoln's House Divided speech meant that he believed that

in a democracy where public opinion was dominant, a single "central idea," as he put it, eventually won out in the competition of ideas. This central idea in our government had always been the *equality of men.* "And although it [public opinion] has always submitted patiently to whatever of inequality there seemed to be as a matter of actual necessity, its constant working has been a steady progress toward the practical equality of all men."

Thus he made clear his belief that the basic incompatibility of freedom and slavery in a land possessing a free public opinion was to be solved by the peaceful advance of free society. Unfortunately, the seceding South, ever fearful of race wars emerging from antislavery pressure, decided that the presidential election of Lincoln was an immediate threat to them and therefore they chose the path of civil war.

During those decades before the war, immigrants arrived in such numbers as to frighten those who feared domination by alien groups. One secret organization, the American Party, worked to reduce the political power of newcomers by greatly extending the time of naturalization. Lincoln attacked those within his party who had joined this group and denounced discrimination against immigrants. As President, too, he appealed to Congress to liberalize its immigration policy. Bar only the enemies of the human race, he asked and praised each national group for its special contributions.

In 1848, when revolutions swept Europe, he led political meetings to express sympathy for the liberal Forty-Eighters. He secured resolutions praising the struggle for liberty of Louis Kossuth and the Hungarian patriots. When the entire world was shocked by the Russian Czarist troops which destroyed Hungarian freedom, Lincoln secured a vehement public protest condemning Russia's act and encouraging resistance. Lincoln felt the current public enthusiasm for Louis Kossuth and the Hungarian struggle at the time that this leader visited America and was hailed by huge demonstrations in the larger cities.

As President, Lincoln found himself face to face with the grim reality of war which he had always condemned as arousing the worst traits of mankind—deception, suspicion, and brutality. But he saw no alternative but resistance to the slave states and despite the nature of civil war, when the enemy is frequently within the gates, he managed to preserve a large measure of peacetime civil liberties.

He never felt hatred for the South—only against slavery itself. His law partner later said, "He was certainly a very poor hater. He never judged men by his like or dislike for them. . . . If a man had maligned him or been guilty of personal ill-treatment, and was the fittest man for the place, he would give him that place just as soon as he would give it to a friend." In wartime, as so many stories show, he felt as much sympathy for the suffering Confederate boy as for his own Union wounded. Once, during his numerous visits to military hospitals, a dying Confederate soldier called for him, evidently thinking to get some diversion at the sight of the man whom Southerners regarded as the homeliest man in the world. Lincoln paused in his rounds, listened patiently to the boy, inquired after his parents, brothers, and sisters, and remained there during the last hours of death. The Confederate was obviously captivated by this humane man.

Lincoln suffered the necessity of sending armies forth to their ordeal, though this hatred of war did not prevent him from becoming a great war President leading his cause to victory. Many stories are told of his intervention to save prisoners from execution by military courts, of his heroic efforts to find time and patience to listen to innumerable mothers, wives, and others pleading for the lives of their dear ones. Once he told his former law partner, "Get out of the way, Swett; tomorrow is butcher day, and I must go through these papers and see if I cannot find some excuse to let these poor fellows off." Secretary of War Stanton was not always happy about the way that Lincoln used the pardoning power, but recent biographers feel that he used careful judgment, not mere sentimentality. But his personal suffering was immense.

Critics complained that the President was too generous in his policy of freeing prisoners willing to take an oath of loyalty (providing their cases showed that they could be trusted). He intervened to protect Negro Union troops whom their former masters refused to treat as prisoners of war when captured. "To sell or enslave any captured person on account of his color, and for no offense against the laws of war, is a relapse into barbarism, and a crime against the civilization of the age," he said. The South yielded on this point.

Once the objectives of war were attained, he was ready to offer a magnanimous peace, permitting the Confederates to return at once to their homes, and discouraging most efforts to punish their leaders. "We would welcome Jefferson Davis' escape from the country," he told a friend. His kindliness is memorably reflected in his speech:

With malice toward none; with charity for all; with firmness in the right as God gives us to see the right, let us strive on to finish the work we are in; to bind up the nation's wounds; to care for him who shall have borne the battle, and for his widow and his orphan— to do all which may achieve a just and lasting peace among ourselves and with all nations.

On January 1, 1863, Lincoln issued the famous Emancipation Proclamation freeing slaves in all rebel areas and thus proved to world opinion that the North was fighting not only for the Union but for human freedom. Middle-class people and workmen felt enthusiastic and issued resolutions of solidarity. In England, overflowing crowds of workmen, many of them thrown out of work because the Civil War had cut off supplies for their factories, nevertheless praised Lincoln and the Union. Manchester workmen declared:

We honor your Free States, as a singularly happy abode for the working millions where industry is honored. . . . The erasure of that foul blot upon civilization and Christianity—chattel slavery—during your presidency will cause the name of Abraham Lincoln to be honored and revered by posterity. . . . Our interests moreover are identified with yours. We are truly one people, though locally separate.

Lincoln replied understandingly:

I know and deeply deplore the sufferings which the workingmen of Manchester and in all Europe are called to endure in this crisis. . . . Under the circumstances, I cannot but regard your decisive utterances upon the question as an instance of sublime Christian heroism which has not been surpassed in any age or in any country.

The import of the struggle for human freedom everywhere was as easily understood in Europe as in America.

This same world context for Lincoln's ideas is clear in the famous Gettysburg address. Lincoln said that "our fathers brought forth upon this continent a new nation, conceived in liberty and dedicated to the proposition that all men are created equal." He also said that the war tested "whether that nation or any nation so conceived and so dedicated, can long endure." He called upon his hearers who were mourning the dead to dedicate themselves to this unfinished task of freedom—"that government of the people, by the people, for the people, shall not perish from the earth." Here was a timeless message that could have been said in 1959 as well as in 1863.

While waging a war for freedom that cost 600,000 lives on both sides, Lincoln and his Congress also advanced the interests of all classes at home. He urged successfully that Congress fulfill its promise to give "land to the landless" which had been delayed by the representatives of the planters in Congress until 1861. "A homestead shall be granted to every poor man who needs and desires it and will cultivate it," he said. Railroads were also given extensive lands to build their tracks and stations far ahead of current traffic, out in the wilderness, uniting the Atlantic and Pacific coasts. Immigrants were welcomed, offered exemption from military service, though many gladly served in the war for freedom. Lincoln also supported the important Morrill Land Grant College Act which promoted education in scientific agriculture, industrial subjects, and the liberal arts by offering to subsidize them through vast gifts of public land. This meant the famous "cow colleges" which eventually evolved in so many instances into first-rate state universities offering schooling at a tuition cost so low that nearly all could afford it.

Lincoln has been described as a wise, informal "diplomat in carpet slippers." Not all of his energies were expended abroad in winning support for the Union. He pursued conciliatory policies in faraway China and Japan which had only recently entered the comity of modern nations.

One singularly wise step was the appointment of the highly civilized Anson Burlingame as envoy extraordinary and minister plenipotentiary to China, then in danger of disintegration. So successful was Burlingame in fulfilling the anticolonial and anti-imperialistic policy of the Lincoln administration that the Chinese took the unusual step after Lincoln's death of making Burlingame their own envoy to the United States! Lincoln's championship of human rights had circled the globe.

LINCOLN, THE EMANCIPATOR

By Kenneth A. Bernard

Dr. Kenneth A. Bernard, Professor of History, Boston University, is Curator of Lincoln Collections, Boston University, and Secretary of the Lincoln Group of Boston. He has written on Lincoln and his times in the Abraham Lincoln Quarterly *and other magazines.*

ABRAHAM LINCOLN was born in a slave state, Kentucky, and while he could not in later years remember much concerning his boyhood there, he did state in an autobiographical sketch in 1860 that his father, a man of modest circumstances, had moved from Kentucky across the Ohio River into the free state of Indiana "partly on account of slavery."

As a youth in Indiana and a young man in Illinois, Lincoln had, however, not only read and heard about slavery, but had seen something of it. He had made two trips down the Mississippi River to New Orleans by flatboat, and had thus had opportunity to observe it where, public opinion maintained, it was at its worst.

When, as a member of the Legislature of the State of Illinois, Abraham Lincoln introduced a protest into that body that "slavery is founded on both injustice and bad policy" he was making his first known public pronouncement on an age-old institution which had been brought from the Old World to the English colonies in America over two hundred years before.

Since that time slavery had become a part of the very fabric of American society; it was accepted in half the states and was recognized by the Constitution itself, and it was inextricably bound up with the race question inasmuch as the slaves were Negroes.

The immense complexity of the whole question was already becoming apparent to the twenty-eight-year-old legislator when he entered his protest in 1837, for his protest included not only a condemnation of slavery but also of abolitionist doctrines—abolitionist doctrines which ignored the complexities and were oblivious to the results of such a drastic step. Immediate emancipation tended, Lincoln maintained, to increase rather than lessen the evils of the institution.

But, withal, the slavery question was not primary in Lincoln's thoughts or actions until several years after this protest. As a lawyer, Lincoln was occasionally involved in legal cases concerning slaves. As a Congressman in the United States House of Representatives (1847–1849), he had voted "at least forty times" in favor of the principle of the nonextension of slavery into new territories; and on his visits to Kentucky and in his travels elsewhere he had additional opportunity to see slavery firsthand.

Although he did not actively oppose it, slavery bothered him whenever he came in contact with it, and the depth of his real concern is revealed in a letter written to Joshua F. Speed, one of his closest friends in his own state of Kentucky:

I confess I hate to see the poor creatures hunted down, and caught, and carried back to their stripes, and unrewarded toils; but I bite my lip and keep quiet. In 1841 you and I had together a tedious low-water trip on a Steam Boat from Louisville to St. Louis. You may remember, as I well do, that . . . there were, on board, ten or a dozen slaves, shackled together with irons. That sight was a continual torment to me; and I see something like it every time I touch the Ohio, or any other slave border. It is . . . a thing which has, and continually exercises, the power of making me miserable.

Actually, when this letter was written (August 24, 1855), Lincoln was no longer biting his lip and keeping quiet. He had been aroused and he had spoken. The thing that had aroused him and stirred him to speak was the enactment by the Congress of the United States of a law which turned out to be momentous for the country, for it aroused hundreds of others as it did Abraham Lincoln. This was the famous Kansas-Nebraska Act of 1854 which opened to slavery a large portion of the Louisiana Territory purchased from Napoleon in 1803.

On the evening of October 16, 1854, Lincoln spoke against the Kansas-Nebraska Act before a large audience in the town of Peoria, Illinois. The speech was a landmark in his whole career, and it revealed a new Lincoln. He spoke with great earnestness, for the first time facing directly and discussing more fully than he had ever done before, the question of slavery. No speech of Lincoln's before this had shown such depth of thought, such vigor of expression, or seriousness of purpose.

From this time on until he became President of the United States in 1861, Abraham Lincoln spoke many times on the subject of slavery (in his famous contest with Stephen A. Douglas in 1858 for a seat in the United States Senate he and Douglas spoke more than one hundred times). His position, which he emphasized again and again, was essentially this: Slavery was morally wrong and it was contrary to our highest ideals as expressed in the Declaration of Independence. But slavery, already here when the country was formed, was of necessity recognized in the Constitution. Slaveholders therefore had certain constitutional rights to their property in slaves, and the Congress had no right to interfere with slavery in the states *where it already existed.* But Congress had the right and the duty *to prevent the spread of slavery into new territories,* and by not allowing it to spread but by confining it within limits, we could look forward to *its ultimate extinction.*

This was Lincoln's main point of emphasis—the prevention of the spread of an evil thing and its ultimate extinction.

But *how* was it to be extinguished? How was emancipation to be achieved? Lincoln was not, in these years, clear in his own mind about this. He thought that colonization in Liberia might be a solution theoretically, but unworkable practically; he thought that perhaps gradual emancipation might be the best solution, and yet he saw no hope that slaveholders would consider voluntarily giving up their slaves. "The problem is too mighty for me. May God, in His mercy, superintend the solution." So he wrote in 1855.

In all his thinking on the question, Lincoln was acutely aware of the many problems that would arise if the Negroes were emancipated suddenly and thrust into American society as free men, for he well knew that many people in the North as well as in the South were not ready to accept or practice racial equality. Lincoln himself, while he did not believe in complete racial equality as it is understood today, insisted that all men regardless of color should have equal opportunity. Equality of opportunity was the right of all men, he said, and should be denied to none. As he expressed it numerous times: ". . . in the right to put into his mouth the bread that his own hands have earned, he [the Negro] is the equal of every other man, white or black." And he pointed the way by saying that ". . . in relation to the principle that all men are created equal, let it be as nearly reached as we can."

When civil war engulfed the United States less than two months after Lincoln became President, the fundamental issue at stake was the preservation of the Union and the vindication of the principle of democratic self-government. It was a people's contest; if the Union was broken, this nation "conceived in Liberty, and dedicated to the proposition that all men are created equal" would fail and democracy everywhere would be the loser. The paramount issue Lincoln thus made clear at Gettysburg on November 19, 1863, in words that have since become immortal—this war was being fought that "government of the people, by the people, for the people, shall not perish from the earth."

But the Civil War was also concerned with the question of slavery, for, after all, slavery was a fundamental cause of the dissension which had brought on the war. As the sentiment for emancipation increased in the North, President Lincoln gave it much thought, for he, too, wished all men to be free. It was on his mind day and night, and more so than any other problem, he said.

He hoped for a gradual form of emancipation—he recommended compensation by the Federal government for slaveholders in states that would adopt such a plan, he appealed to the leaders of the loyal slave states to act in this direction, and he urged an amendment to the Constitution providing for it. He even considered the possibility of colonization and took preliminary steps to have such a project investigated and to interest prominent Negro leaders in it.

There was, however, little favorable response to these proposals; instead there was the continuing demand for direct and
immediate action. In the early summer of 1862, the President
decided to act—when the right time came. The right time came
in September of that year, after the Southern army had been
forced back into Virginia following a bloody battle at Antietam,
in Maryland. On September 22, Lincoln issued a preliminary
Emancipation Proclamation, which was followed by a final
Proclamation on January 1, 1863.

This momentous step, affecting nearly four million Negroes
held in bondage, Lincoln took by virtue of his position as Commander-in-Chief of the Army and Navy. Only as a war measure,
designed to weaken the enemy and aid the cause of the Union,
would such a step be warranted, for the American Constitution
gave the President *no authority* to act otherwise.

The Proclamation was in accord with his own sentiment, yet
Lincoln, with his scrupulous regard for the propriety of his actions as President, wanted to make it clear that he had *no right*
to make his personal feelings the basis of official action. He said
(on April 4, 1864) in a letter to A. G. Hodges:

I am naturally anti-slavery. If slavery is not wrong, nothing is
wrong. I can not remember when I did not so think, and feel. And
yet I have never understood that the Presidency conferred upon me
an unrestricted right to act officially upon this judgment and feeling.

Although it did not free all slaves at once, for it applied only
in areas still in rebellion, the Emancipation Proclamation was
a high point of the Civil War. Lincoln considered it the central
act of his administration and the great event of the nineteenth
century. It became a landmark in human progress—it was the
beginning of the end of slavery in the United States, it changed
the whole nature of the war and made it, at least in large part,
a crusade for human freedom and as such gave hope and encouragement to those interested in freedom everywhere, and it
made Abraham Lincoln the Great Emancipator. As a result of
the Proclamation thousands of Negroes had become free men
when the war was ended.

But the work of freedom was not completed by the Proclamation. The next logical step was to write this freedom into the

Constitution where it would thus be recorded for all time. Lincoln favored so amending the Constitution as "a fitting, and necessary conclusion to the final success of the Union cause," and in his Annual Message to Congress in December, 1864, he urged the passage of the necessary amendment. When in January, 1865, the amendment did receive the necessary votes in Congress, he considered it a great moral victory, but he urged that the work be consummated by the approval of the required three-fourths of the states.

Ratification of the amendment by the states began immediately, with the President's own state, Illinois, in the lead, a fact to which he alluded with some satisfaction.

December 18, 1865. The war had been over many months, but this was a day of special rejoicing for all those who had worked and fought for emancipation and freedom, for on that day the Thirteenth Amendment was officially proclaimed a part of the Constitution—"Neither slavery nor involuntary servitude, except as a punishment for crime . . . shall exist within the United States . . ."

Abraham Lincoln was not present when this event took place, for his life had been cut short by an assassin's bullet eight months before. Had he been alive, he, too, would have rejoiced and been glad.

LINCOLN, THE LAWYER

By William H. Townsend

William H. Townsend is a member of the Kentucky and Lexington Bar Associations and of the Abraham Lincoln Association. Among his books are: Abraham Lincoln, Defendant *(1923);* Lincoln the Litigant *(1925);* Lincoln and His Wife's Hometown *(1929) and* Lincoln's Rebel Niece *(1945). He completed and revised the late Dr. William E. Barton's* President Lincoln *(1932).*

BORN in a log cabin with a dirt floor in the wilderness of Kentucky, reared to manhood in the backwoods of Indiana, Lincoln's formal schooling totaled less than one year. He was old enough to cast his first vote when he arrived at New Salem. There, he clerked in a store and worked as a farm laborer. Soberly he pondered his future—thought about learning the blacksmith trade, but saw no future in it—considered being a lawyer, but his lack of education made success in this field unlikely.

However, he still had the law in the back of his mind when, as some say, he found in a barrel of old rubbish a battered copy of Blackstone's *Commentaries* and, thereafter, he carried this bulky volume with him wherever he went. On one occasion at the end of a hard day's work for farmer Russell B. Godbey, Lincoln, in his short sleeves and patched pants rolled halfway to his knees, stretched out on the woodpile and opened Blackstone. His employer, passing by, inquired:

"What are you reading, Abe?"

"I am not reading," replied Lincoln, "I am studying law."

"Good Lord Almighty," exclaimed the astonished Godbey, as he walked on.

It was about this time that Lincoln came in contact with John T. Stuart, an able lawyer of Springfield, who offered to lend him books, and he now began the study of law with unfaltering energy and purpose. Usually he was able to catch a ride to Stuart's office in Springfield, but, failing in this, he walked the entire twenty miles and back, reading earnestly as he trudged along the dusty road.

In the spring of 1837, at the age of twenty-eight, Abraham Lincoln obtained a license to practice law. Packing his meager belongings in an old pair of saddlebags, he borrowed a horse and jogged up to Springfield—a town to be forever associated with his name. Stopping at a large general store, the tall stranger went in and inquired the price of a mattress, blankets, sheets and a pillow for a single bed. The proprietor, Josua F. Speed, made a quick calculation which totaled $17.00.

"It is, no doubt, cheap enough," said his customer sadly, "but cheap as it is, I am unable to pay it. If you can credit me until Christmas, I will pay you then, if I am able, but if I fail as a lawyer, I do not know that I can ever pay you."

Seeing the young stranger so much pained at contracting so small a debt, Speed invited him to share, without cost, his double bed upstairs, and thus began an abiding friendship.

After a period of four years as a junior partner of John T. Stuart, and three and one-half years with Stephen T. Logan, Lincoln, in 1844, formed his own firm with William H. Herndon, a young man who had studied law in the office of Logan & Lincoln, a partnership which would last until dissolved many years later by the bullet of an assassin.

More than half of the senior partner's time was spent "riding the circuit," where he quickly rose to leadership at the bar, while Herndon kept the Springfield office open and took care of local business. The Eighth Judicial Circuit of Illinois was comprised of fourteen sparsely settled counties and in winter the mud was deep, the rivers and creeks swollen and treacherous. But it was a merry and carefree company that forded these streams and galloped across the wide, rolling prairie in fair weather and foul. Some of the lawyers visited only a few of the most accessible county seats in the district, while others made nearly all of them. Only two men, however, David Davis, judge of the court, and Abraham Lincoln rode the entire circuit. Davis because he had to, Lincoln because he loved it.

Always scrupulously clean and closely shaven, but clad in a wrinkled homespun suit, his tall, "stovepipe" hat sometimes looking as if a calf had gone over it with its wet tongue, carrying an old saddlebag filled with books, papers and a change of linen, and a huge, faded, green cotton umbrella, Lincoln was the plainest personality and the best-liked "circuit rider" in all the fourteen counties.

Sitting at the trial table, Lincoln was not an imposing figure. Slouched in a chair, his long legs crossed, hands sometimes crammed in trouser pockets, he seemed no taller than the average man. His coarse, thick, rebellious hair fell carelessly over the massive, deep-lined forehead. His rugged, weather-beaten face with its angular jaws and firm upturned chin looked careworn and haggard. His gray eyes, which lay in deep caverns beneath heavy, overhanging brows, were dull, dreamy, brooding.

However, when he rose and began to speak, the jury and courtroom audience were startled at the phenomenal change in his appearance. His height of 6 feet 4 inches was majestic; his voice, ordinarily rather high-pitched, became resonant and well modulated; the dark eyes now flashed and twinkled; the droll, captivating smile which expanded his furrowed cheeks revealed a mouth full of white regular teeth and wreathed his whole countenance in animation.

Sparing in the use of gestures, Lincoln stood squarely on his feet, his hands clasped behind his back, or one hand clutching a lapel of his coat and the other hanging easily at his side. His gaunt, loosely knit frame had great vertical elasticity and, when deeply moved, he would stretch himself beyond his already impressive height, throw his long, sinewy arms high above his head —pause for an instant in this attitude—and then sweep his huge fists through the air with a crashing emphasis no one ever forgot.

Lincoln was probably at his best in the cross-examination of witnesses. He knew his facts and the rules of evidence. He moved cautiously. He never asked unnecessary questions. He was direct and courteous. Without seeming effort, he sought to establish, whenever possible, an easy, relaxed—even friendly—relationship with the witness. In almost every instance, he saw the logical conclusion of an answer long before it dawned upon the person making it and was thus able to lead him without appearing to do so. His professional associates marveled at the way men openly hostile to Lincoln gradually melted under his magnetism. One who tried many cases against him said: "Mr. Lincoln instinctively saw the kernel of every case at the outset, never lost sight of it and never let it escape the jury."

However, his remarkable success as a trial lawyer has tended to obscure the fact that, as the records show, his power of analysis, irresistible logic and strong grasp of important and intricate subjects won a large majority of his cases before the Supreme Court of Illinois, and two of the three cases he had in the Supreme Court of the United States.

Lincoln enjoyed the confidence of the high and low, rich and poor. The fact that he represented many of the largest and wealthiest corporations in the state, including the Illinois Central and the Rock Island railroads, the Bank of Illinois, and the North American Insurance Company, did not lessen his popularity in any degree with the masses of the people.

"No lawyer was more unassuming," said another lawyer who also rode the circuit. He arrogated to himself no superiority over anyone, not even the most obscure member of the profession. He was remarkably gentle with young lawyers. The result was, as time went on, he became the much-beloved senior member of the bar.

"Resolve to be honest in all events," was Lincoln's advice to law students. "If, in your judgment you can not be an honest lawyer, resolve to be honest without being a lawyer. Discourage litigation. Persuade your neighbors to compromise whenever you can. Point out to them how the nominal winner is often a real loser—in fees, expenses and waste of time. As a peace maker, the lawyer has a superior opportunity of being a good man."

Lincoln had an unfailing good humor and never indulged in personalities, then quite common in trials of that day, unless in self-defense. However, he was known to possess a withering sarcasm which, though rarely employed, never failed to drive an adversary to cover. During the selection of a jury on a certain case, a lawyer objected to a juror because of his acquaintance with Lincoln, who represented the other side. Such an objection was then considered a personal reflection and Judge Davis promptly overruled it. When Lincoln's turn came to examine the jury, he also began to inquire whether any of them knew opposing counsel. "Now, Mr. Lincoln," the Court said severely, "You know my ruling on that. The mere fact that a juror knows your opponent does not disqualify him." "No, Your Honor," responded Lincoln dryly, "but I'm afraid some of these gentlemen may *not* know him, which would place me at a disadvantage."

The close of Lincoln's legal career found him at the very top of the Illinois bar. By industry and his own peculiar genius, he had slowly, steadily forged to the front of a most unusual body of men whose names and achievements are written large upon the pages of the nation's history. This little circuit-riding group produced five Congressmen, three Governors, four United States Senators, two Major Generals, one Cabinet Member, one Justice of the Supreme Court and one Chief Executive of the Republic.

February 10, 1861, was Abraham Lincoln's last day in Springfield. He had been elected President of the United States. The Southern states were seceding. Civil War was imminent. Strangely enough, a seemingly whimsical destiny had placed in the big, untried hands of a country lawyer the distracting problems of a disintegrating union. It was late afternoon when he came into the small second-floor office on the west side of the Springfield public square, where the faithful junior partner waited. Going over to the opposite side of the room, he threw himself down on the rickety lounge. For a few minutes he lay with his face to the ceiling, without speaking. These four walls held recollections of poverty, disappointment, bitter struggle and ultimate success, never to be erased from his memory. Then, suddenly, Lincoln began to talk of the early days of his practice, recalling the humorous features of various lawsuits on the circuit and his reminiscences ran on happily until dusk crept through the dingy little windows, reminding him that it was time to go home.

As he gathered a bundle of books and papers under his arm, he spoke wistfully of the old sign *Lincoln & Herndon* that swung on rusty hinges over the doorway at the foot of the steps. "Let it hang there undisturbed," he said softly, "give our clients to understand that the election of a President makes no change in the firm of Lincoln & Herndon. If I live, I'm coming back sometime and then we'll go right on practicing law as if nothing had happened."

He lingered for a moment as if to take a last look at the old quarters, then walked reluctantly through the door into the hallway and down the narrow stairs.

LINCOLN AS POLITICIAN

By David Donald

Dr. David Donald, Professor of History, Columbia University, and a member of the Institute for Advanced Studies,
Princeton, has written four books on Lincoln: Lincoln's
Herndon (*1948*), Divided We Fought (*1952*), Inside Lincoln's War Cabinet: The Diaries of Salmon P. Chase (*1954*),
and Lincoln Reconsidered; Essays on the Civil War Era
(*1956*).

WHEN President-elect Abraham Lincoln reached Washington in February 1861, cultivated Easterners were shocked
by his appearance. Everything about him bespoke the Western
provincial. He had an ambling Western style of walking and
used awkward, untrained gestures. His clothing was ill-fitting,
and he committed the social *faux pas* of wearing black kid gloves
to the opera. He spoke with a coarse Western accent, and he told
homely anecdotes from his apparently inexhaustible store of
Western folk tales.

When first introduced to Lincoln, Charles Sumner, the elegant, Harvard-trained Senator from Massachusetts, was "greatly
amazed and puzzled by what he saw and heard." Though he
"noticed, now and then, flashes of thought and bursts of illuminating expression" in Lincoln's conversation, he found the
President-elect woefully lacking in dignity, social poise, and
breadth of culture, and he "could not get rid of his misgivings
as to how this seemingly untutored child of nature would master
the tremendous task before him." Charles Francis Adams, of the
famous Massachusetts family, shared Sumner's doubts about this

"tall, illfavored man, with little grace of manner or polish of appearance," and concluded that both Lincoln and his wife were "evidently wanting in all the arts to grace their position."

Though Adams and Sumner may have been correct in their appraisal of Lincoln's personal appearance, they quite obviously misjudged the new President in other respects. Misled by his Western mannerisms, they failed to observe that "this seemingly untutored child of nature" was master of at least one of the "arts" requisite for success as an American President—the fine art of politics. Recognizing early in his career that "the man who is of neither party is not, and cannot be, of any consequence" in American life, Lincoln brought to the White House a realistic understanding that the most statesmanlike policies enunciated by a President are of no consequence unless they are backed up by effective political support. Even in the oppressive crisis of the Civil War, he understood that the American President must be not merely titular head of state, commander-in-chief of the armed forces, and chief administrative officer of the government, but also the head of his political party, an astute manager of the political machinery.

Lincoln's realism about the President's role as politician derived from his long experience in Illinois public life. For more than twenty-six years before he became President, politics was his passion. For four successive terms he served as Whig member of the Illinois House of Representatives (1837–41), during part of which he was his party's floor leader; for one term (1847–49) he was a member of the United States House of Representatives in Washington; during most of the other years before the 1860 election he was campaigning either for himself or for his party. His active participation in the rough-and-tumble game of Western politics gave him an intimate acquaintance with what his partner delicately called the "details of how we get along," and in very large measure his success in Washington stemmed from the lessons he had learned during his Illinois apprenticeship.

In part these lessons were negative. Through painful experience he became convinced that in politics personalities do not pay. With a quick wit and a lively style, Lincoln early fell into the habit of making fun of his political opponents, and for a time he was apparently greatly pleased with the applause these tactics won him.

But in 1842 he made a great mistake in satirizing the rather dandified Democratic state auditor of Illinois, James Shields. Shields, Lincoln joked, seemed to think he was irresistible to the ladies; his very features appeared to speak audibly and distinctly: "Dear girls, *it is distressing,* but I cannot marry you all. Too well I know how much you suffer; but do, *do* remember, it is not my fault that I am *so* handsome and *so* interesting." The hot-tempered Irish auditor promptly challenged Lincoln to a duel, and only at the last minute was bloodshed averted.

The whole affair caused Lincoln the keenest embarrassment, and years later the merest mention of it made him unhappy. Never again did he permit himself to become involved in a personal altercation. Despite all the pressures upon him in the White House, no political opponent was ever able to prick him into personal recriminations. "No man resolved to make the most of himself can spare the time for personal contention," he had learned. "Better give your path to a dog, than be bitten by him in contesting for the right. Even killing the dog would not cure the bite."

From a dozen political campaigns in Illinois Lincoln had also learned the danger of being doctrinaire. Long before he became President he observed that attachment to inflexible solutions and ideological labels could only lead to political impotence. In 1844, for example, he energetically supported Henry Clay for President, believing that the Kentuckian, though himself a slaveholder, would not permit the further expansion of slavery. Simon-pure abolitionists took the opposing view—how could a real antislavery man vote for a slaveholder?—and they wasted their votes on the doctrinally pure but politically hopeless third-party candidate. Their vote helped elect James K. Polk and to bring on the Mexican War.

To Lincoln the abolitionists' way of thinking seemed "wonderful." To their contention that "We are not to do *evil* that *good* may come," he countered with another, more apt Biblical injunction: "By the *fruit* the tree is to be known."

As President, Lincoln had many occasions to remember his

own advice. At the end of the Civil War, facing the crucial problem of restoring the subjugated Southern states to the Union, he recognized the danger of becoming "inflexibly committed to any single plan of reconstruction." He had his own program for the speedy, secure re-establishment of the Union, but he knew that doctrinaire insistence upon it might result only in the defeat of the very objective he sought to promote.

Lincoln's Illinois experience also warned him of the perils of a direct appeal to the people. The American President is frequently tempted—and often urged—to take his case straight to the voter in an attempt to override opposition to his policies in Congress. It was a tactic Lincoln never employed. He had every faith in the democratic process; he believed that the American experiment in self-government was "the last, best hope of earth"; he saw as the central idea of the great struggle in which the nation was engaged the task "of proving that popular government is not an absurdity." But with his trust in the people, Lincoln also had come to understand that a hasty appeal for support might find the electorate temporarily ill-informed or the political machinery through which they must speak poorly organized.

Lincoln himself, it must be remembered, had never been a spectacular vote-getter in Illinois. He was never chosen to major office by the people of his state; state legislator and one-term member of Congress he was, but never governor and never senator. His vigorous debates with Stephen A. Douglas in 1858 gained him a majority of the popular vote, but, because of the inequitable arrangement of the electoral system, he did not win the election. In the campaign of 1860 only a minority of the American people voted for Lincoln.

Understandably, then, Lincoln was reluctant to risk the prestige of the presidency upon an appeal to the people which, in those days before the advent of mass media of communication, could only bring limited success and which, if unsuccessful, might permanently impair his executive leadership.

Not merely Lincoln's service in the Illinois legislature but his term in the United States House of Representatives stood him in good stead as wartime President. Experience taught him that, in the American form of government, there is a certain inevitable amount of tension between the Congress and the President. From observing the fierce animosity which grew up between President John Tyler and Henry Clay, who led the Whig party in the Senate, and the deadlock which existed between President Zachary Taylor and his Congressional party leaders during the 1850 crisis, Lincoln knew that such tension, if exacerbated, could render his administration impotent. He resolved not to permit incidents to arise between the executive and legislative branches of the government and especially not to allow himself to become alienated from the Congressional spokesmen of his own party.

When Senator Sumner, for example, rose publicly to denounce the Administration's plan for reconstructing Louisiana as a "mere seven months' abortion, begotten by the bayonet, in criminal conjunction with the spirit of caste, and born before its time, rickety, unformed, unfinished," Lincoln did not take offense but wisely ignored this strong language. "I think I understand Mr. Sumner," he said, "and I think he would be all the more resolute in his persistence . . . if he supposed I were at all watching his course. . . ."

Remembering his own experience as a Congressman and exercising his sense of humor, Lincoln was able to endure abuse from members of his own party under which a newcomer to politics might well have flinched. When Republicans openly announced that the President was "as stubborn as a mule," a man "at heart with Slavery," "a Damed [sic] old traitor," "as near lunacy as any one not a pronounced Bedlamite," Lincoln could recall that he himself had once been an expert in vituperation. In 1848, for instance, he had denounced Democratic President Polk as "a bewildered, confounded, and miserably perplexed man," who, having deliberately precipitated the Mexican War, must feel "the blood of this war, like the blood of Abel . . . crying to Heaven against him." It takes a veteran politician to remember that politicians like to talk—and that most of their talk is for buncombe.

Along with these negative lessons, Lincoln's career in Illinois politics had taught him the importance, in a decentralized, democratic government like ours, of special favors and patronage as the surest way of binding local political bosses to the person and principles of the President. From his years in the Illinois legislature Lincoln recognized that local interests are often as important to a representative as his party's public platforms.

Lincoln himself, during his first session in the legislature, had spent most of his time sponsoring bills to authorize his friend Samuel Musick to build a toll bridge across Salt Creek and to name three other friends "to view, mark and permanently locate a road from Springfield to Miller's Ferry." His repeated re-election to the legislature had been chiefly due to his success in removing the state capital from southern Illinois to Springfield. As the only Whig Congressman from Illinois in 1849, he learned the great importance of having the incoming Whig President, Zachary Taylor, distribute the Federal patronage to his active and loyal party supporters, and, having himself made an unsuccessful attempt to become Commissioner of the General Land Office after failing to be re-elected to Congress, he knew firsthand the immense value office seekers placed upon the government favors they were seeking.

Consequently Lincoln brought to the White House an extraordinarily frank and realistic use of the power and the positions at his disposal. The importunities of office seekers naturally tired him, and he chafed occasionally at the burden thrust upon him. Nevertheless he recognized the importance of taking time, even at the height of the secession crisis, to decide between rival candidates for the Chicago post office and to appoint the naval officer for the port of Boston.

For the favors he distributed Lincoln demanded—and he received—the support of the politicians. Virtually every major measure advocated by his administration was enacted into law, and Lincoln himself became the first President in a quarter of a century to achieve re-election. Since patronage was the necessary grease for the party machinery upon which he depended, Lincoln was pleased that it was used efficiently. As Chief Executive he proudly claimed that his had "distributed to its party friends as nearly all the civil patronage as any administration ever did."

All these lessons from Lincoln's Illinois apprenticeship

amounted to a single rule: To be successful, an American President must be not merely a statesman but also a politician. If it is something of a shock to picture the Great Emancipator as the Great Politician, one must remember the observation of that astute British historian, Mr. Denis W. Brogan, that "the United States was made by politicians."

LINCOLN—LIBERAL OR CONSERVATIVE?

By Donald W. Riddle

Dr. Donald W. Riddle is Professor of History and Head of the Division of Social Sciences, University of Illinois. He has written two books on Lincoln: Lincoln Runs for Congress *(1948) and* Congressman Abraham Lincoln *(1957).*

WHEN Lincoln was born, government under the American Constitution was twenty years old. When he first voted, political parties were emerging. Party lines were indistinct, and candidates were not classified as liberal or conservative. One must discover what Lincoln became.

His environment was a factor of deep influence. He was a child of the frontier, where conditions were fluid. He was born in poverty but he accumulated property. There was no permanent social status; he began without educational or cultural advantages and attained gentility. There were optional ways of making a living—as a farmer, an artisan, or a professional man. Lincoln's choice put him on the path to political distinction, usefulness, and fame.

Taken by his parents from Kentucky to Indiana and to Illinois, Lincoln found himself, when he came of age, in the Sangamo region settled by Kentuckians, where rich soil promised prosperity. He was among people of aristocratic manners and attitudes, of whom several had already become political leaders. He determined to become one of their kind. The young rail splitter, flatboatman, and storekeeper became a lawyer; a professional man, not a laborer. Assiduously cultivating knowledge of law, mathematics, writing, and reading, he also cultivated people of education and refinement and of social status and wealth.

Lincoln undertook a political career together with his legal practice. He was elected to the state legislature four times and to Congress once; he also canvassed as a presidential elector for his political party.

His choice of party was important. In the year he was born Jefferson was President, and the party which Jefferson had formed was dominant. Indeed that party in subsequent elections completely defeated the rival Federalist party, so that when Jefferson died there was but one party in existence. Thus when Lincoln entered politics voters adhered to *men,* not to parties. But the advent of Andrew Jackson upon the political scene ushered in a second era of parties, so that by 1834 distinction between Democrats and Whigs was sharp. Lincoln became a Whig.

Lincoln's party was conservative. It looked to the interests of wealth and property. It favored a National Bank and a high protective tariff. With its commitment to property interests members of the Whig party accepted slavery; three-fourths of the slaves in America were owned by Whigs. While all social and economic classes were represented in the party, its leaders were merchants, capitalists, and professional men. The Jacksonian Democrats, not without justice, asserted that the Whigs were a party of aristocrats. Lincoln represented such Whigs in the legislature and Congress. He sought their support. His marriage related him to prosperous, conservative Whig families.

In the state legislature and in Congress Lincoln generally followed the conservative principles of his party. His manifest ability led to success as a politician. Although his party was always a minority in Illinois, its strength was concentrated in his home district, so that he was successful in running for office.

A decisive change came with his election to Congress. Previously Lincoln's experience had been on the municipal, county, district, and state level; now it was national. But on the higher level Lincoln closely followed party leaders. Congressman Lincoln was usually an orthodox, conservative Whig.

Yet he voiced liberal principles worthy of Jefferson, most frequently when liberty was concerned. For example, after his return from Congress in 1849 he was active in organizing public sentiment in support of Kossuth and the revolutionary party in Hungary, and urging the diplomatic recognition of the revolutionary Hungarian government.

Lincoln's record as Congressman was so unpopular that he was forced to retire from politics until he could live down his failure. But he did not abandon his goal: He aspired to election to the United States Senate. He was a Whig candidate for Senator in 1855, but by that time the Whig party was dying. Lincoln joined the new Republican party, recently organized in 1854. As that party's candidate for Senator and for President all that was liberal in Lincoln was brought out, expressed, and made effective.

It was his commitment to liberty which led Lincoln to liberalism. He saw that there was only one issue upon which he could run for office: slavery. He made it his issue, and over this issue he broke with the Whigs. He had never held the usually accepted Whig attitude toward slavery. He believed that the rights of property were fundamental, but he had never accepted the idea that property in slaves was a right. With a host of others he saw that slavery was morally wrong, and it was apparent that it had ceased to exist where it was economically unprofitable. He therefore labored to prevent its spread to the newly acquired territories and thus put it on its way to ultimate extinction. But slavery became a political issue, and its fate would be determined by politics. Lincoln dealt with slavery politically, and under him as President it was abolished.

Lincoln's liberalism in regard to liberty was fundamental. Experience had taught him that only in an environment of political, social, and economic freedom any person might, if his rights were secured, move where he chose, work at what he chose, attain that status which his abilities enabled him to win, and accumulate and save property. It was all-important that the essential rights be secured. At this point Lincoln found the liberal Jeffersonian philosophy to be congenial.

Here one may note the two principal American political documents: the Declaration of Independence and the Constitution.

The former is a classic articulation of liberalism. The latter is conservative. It is noteworthy that from the time he ran for the Senate in 1858 Lincoln appealed time and time again to the Declaration, emphasizing the famous passage on unalienable rights. This was the basis of his opposition to slavery.

But it was not the plight of slaves only which led Lincoln to liberalism. He labored to secure the rights of all classes of people. To illustrate, during his career there was a strong antiforeign movement in American life. It was particularly prevalent among the Whigs. But Lincoln never accepted it, and when nativism became an issue he disavowed every kind of discrimination against foreigners. Many Whig politicians joined "American" or "Know-nothing" lodges, as the nativist organizations were called; Lincoln refused to do so. Repeatedly he opposed nativism, demanding for the foreign-born the same rights and opportunities possessed by the native-born. In his final debate with Douglas he insisted that immigrants should have rights and freedom so that

Hans and Baptiste and Patrick, and all other men from all the world, may find new homes and better their condition in life.

Indeed Lincoln's emphasis upon *rights* had the broadest possible base. It is noteworthy that as early as 1836 he considered that women should be permitted to vote.

He also reflected upon the role of the laborer. Speaking in Wisconsin in 1859 he presented a point which he restated in superior form later. He said that labor is the source from which human wants are mainly supplied. But some suppose that labor is available only as an adjunct of capital, so that nobody labors unless somebody hires him to work. Some think that labor may be owned instead of hired; these believe that a hired laborer is in a fixed condition, a condition as bad as that of a slave.

This, Lincoln remarked, was the "mud-sill" theory of labor. He repudiated that theory. He pointed out that a few men own capital and hire labor to avoid laboring themselves, but the majority are neither hirers nor hired; they are men who work for themselves. Many of these become independent; some of them continue to work for themselves; some hire others to work for them. This is free labor, which in a situation of freedom enables that rise in status which Lincoln sought for everybody.

Lincoln envisaged a social mobility in a free country in which fundamental rights are guaranteed to all.

It is unnecessary to relate the story of Lincoln's success, culminating in election as President. Nor is it necessary to chronicle his leadership in saving the Union, abolishing slavery, and getting the Jeffersonian unalienable rights written into the Constitution as the Thirteenth Amendment. It is relevant to note that despite occasional conservatism and arbitrary exercise of executive power, liberalism prevailed.

Sometimes the liberal purpose was explicit. In his 1861 Annual Message the war situation led to his superb statement of the relation of capital and labor:

Labor is prior to, and independent of, capital. Capital is only the fruit of labor, and could never have existed if labor had not first existed. Labor is the superior of capital, and deserves much the higher consideration. . . . The prudent, penniless beginner . . . labors for wages . . . saves a surplus with which to buy tools or land . . . then labors on his own account another while, and at length hires a new beginner to help him. This is the just, and generous, and prosperous system, which opens the way to all—gives hope to all . . . and improvement of condition to all. No men living are more worthy to be trusted than those who toil up from poverty. . . . Let them beware of surrendering a political power which they already possess.

Lincoln correctly saw the Civil War as a people's contest, a struggle to maintain government of the people, by the people, and for the people, a conflict to maintain human rights. The liberal Lincoln found the way to victory. "In giving freedom to the slave," he said, "we assure freedom to the free. . . . We shall nobly save or meanly lose the last, best hope of earth."

Lincoln was not consistent in liberalism any more than he had been a consistent conservative. He did upon occasion assume arbitrary power. But as he never abandoned the view that this was a struggle to maintain people's rights he spurned the concept of dictatorship. He saw to it that elections were held. Democratic processes were preserved.

Thus the balance ultimately leaned to the liberal side of the scale. He was no doctrinaire liberal, nor did he seek to secure all the rights of all the people. Yet in the outcome he became the symbol of liberty.

The result was an increase of democracy, an enlargement of the scope of human rights.

Lincoln was moderate, not radical, in his plans for postwar reconstruction. In this, also, he stopped short of presenting an ideal goal. What he did look toward was binding up the nation's wounds, and a rededication, "with malice toward none and with charity for all, to cherish a just and lasting peace among ourselves and with all nations."

He did not live to accomplish this high purpose, but his life was one in which the interplay of conservatism and liberalism led to the secure establishment, increase, and extension of liberty, justice, and right.

LINCOLN'S VIEWS ON GOVERNMENT

By Ralph G. Lindstrom

*Ralph G. Lindstrom, a lawyer, living in Los Angeles, has
written two books on Abraham Lincoln:* Lincoln and Prevention of War *(1953) and* Lincoln Finds God *(1958). He is
President of the Lincoln Sesquicentennial Association of
California.*

T O Abraham Lincoln the American Declaration of Independence set forth the basis of government for free people, the
world over. He said:

> The assertion that "all men are created equal" was of no practical
> use in effecting our separation from Great Britain; and it was placed
> in the Declaration, not for that, but for future use. Its authors meant
> it to be, thank God, it is now proving itself, a stumbling block to
> those who in after times might seek to turn a free people back into
> the hateful paths of despotism. . . .
>
> They meant to set up a standard maxim for free society, which
> should be familiar to all, and revered by all, constantly looked to,
> constantly labored for . . . constantly spreading and deepening its
> influence, and augmenting the happiness and value of life to all
> people of all colors everywhere.

Thus no man should enslave any other, no group should domi-
nate any other group, no nation should make a satellite of another nation.

Lincoln lived, he gave his life, to preserve this concept of
government; government created to foster and protect genuine
equality among men, equality of opportunity, the equal and un-

fettered start in life, without regard to race, creed, color or nationality; free enterprise and individual initiative, in the business of making a life no less than in making a living.

His thinking embraced all men, everywhere. Of the work of the authors of that great Declaration he said:

This was their majestic interpretation of the *economy of the universe*. This was their lofty, and wise, and noble understanding of the justice of the Creator to His creatures. Yes, . . . to all His creatures, to *the whole great family of man*. . . . In their enlightened belief, nothing stamped with the Divine image and likeness was sent into the world to be trodden on, and degraded, and imbruted by its fellows.

Lincoln thought in terms of sovereignty of the individual man in his personal affairs, sovereignty of each group of people as a unit of government, for their internal affairs. So he said:

No matter in what shape it [the excuse for depriving any people of their liberty] comes, whether from the mouth of a king who seeks to bestride the people of his own nation and live by the fruit of their labor, or from one race [or group] of men as an apology for enslaving another race [or group], it is the same tyrannical principle. [*Parenthetical matter added.*]

When the workingmen of Manchester sent Lincoln a message of support of his purpose in the Civil War, he answered with gratitude for their "re-inspiring assurance . . . of the ultimate and *universal* triumph of justice, humanity, and freedom." He thought so much in terms of universal good that he came to talk of "man's vast future."

Thus as he journed to Washington to be inaugurated, he said to the New Jersey Senate:

I am exceedingly anxious that that thing which they [the revolutionary fathers] fought for; that something even more than national independence; that something that held out a great promise *to all the people of the world to all time to come;* . . . shall be perpetuated in accordance with the original idea for which that struggle was made.

He pleaded that each generation of Americans "readopt the Declaration of Independence, and with it the practices and policy, which harmonize with it. . . . Let all Americans—let all lovers of liberty everywhere join in the great and good work." Why? So "that the succeeding millions of free happy people, *the world over,* shall rise up and call us blessed, to the latest generation."

To Lincoln democracy was not merely a political phrase. It was no mere slogan. It was a way of life. So he said:

As I would not be a *slave,* so I would not be a *master*. This expresses my idea of democracy. Whatever differs from this, to the extent of the difference, is not democracy.

Yes, he meant government to assure the opportunity to progress to *all* men; to leave men free to achieve and improve their status. He said:

We propose to give *all* a chance; and we expected the weak to grow stronger, the ignorant, wiser, and all better, and happier, together.

Such is our task, our "duty to posterity, and love for our species in general. . . ."

To Lincoln, even free enterprise was the way to advance the general good through the individual good. Sometimes he soliloquized in writing. Fragments later found in his files show how deeply he thought about man's welfare. Once he asked himself: What was "the primary cause" of America's prosperity? Was it the combination of the American "Constitution and the Union"? These were documents of basic importance; but he went even deeper to see and say that

there is something back of these, entwining itself more closely about the human heart. That something is the principle of "liberty to all" —the principle that clears the path for all—gives hope to all—and by consequence, enterprise and industry to all.

Here is no demagogic promise of ease to one class at the expense of another class. Here is no ascendancy by class or color. To every man, everywhere, there must be the promise and assurance of good, in the degree of his "enterprise and industry."

National and universal prosperity will be attained and retained so far, and only so far, as we extend and keep open, clear paths of equal opportunity to achieve. So he went on:

No oppressed people will fight, and endure, as our fathers did, without the promise of something better than a mere change of masters.

There must be no bestridden nor bestriding class. We must never surrender freedom of initiative for promised prosperity through a totalitarian state. He warned those "who toil up from poverty" to "beware of surrendering a political power . . . which, if surrendered, will surely be used to close the doors of advancement . . . and to fix new disabilities and burdens upon them, till all liberty shall be lost."

What did Lincoln think governments should do, and should *not* do? He wrote another soliloquy to say:

The legitimate object of government is to do for a community of people what they need to have done, but cannot at all do, or cannot so well do, for themselves—in their separate and individual capacities. . . . In all that the people can individually do as well for themselves, government ought not to interfere.

This is just another way of saying that people will be free, that individual initiative will thrive, to the extent that people are courageous, energetic, and stand upon their own feet. If they seek government interference *for* their business, there will be government interference *with* and *against* their business.

Why did Lincoln accept Civil War in America? Because it was "a struggle for maintaining in the world, that form and substance of government, whose leading object is to elevate the condition of men—to lift artificial weights from all shoulders . . . to afford an unfettered start, and a fair chance in the race of life." This he said in his first Message to Congress.

No man should be fixed in inferior status. Lincoln rejected the view "that whoever is once a hired laborer is fatally fixed in that condition for life." "This," he said, "is the 'mud-sill' theory." The mud sill of pioneer log cabins was the bottom log, permanently enbedded in the mud, and forever held down by all the logs above it in the building, which rested upon it, and held it down. No man, no race, no people anywhere, should be held down. Men must be free to rise as high as their own efforts and initiative can take them.

Well Lincoln knew that America had not yet fully or nearly attained that ideal of full equality of opportunity; but he knew that government based upon and practicing the civic truths of the great Declaration will finally liberate all men from the tyranny which would fix any man in debased or unfavored status.

At Gettysburg he dedicated more than a cemetery. He rededicated his people and their government, in fact all liberty-loving people everywhere, to a forever "new birth of freedom, that government of the people, by the people, and for the people, should not perish *from the earth.*"

Two phrases crept into Lincoln's thinking and speaking: "The Great Family of Man" and "Man's Vast Future."

This man had a civic prescience. Probably he had no notion whatever of nuclear energy and intercontinental ballistic missiles. Possibly he did not foresee the shrinkage of our planet, in time and space, to the size of a fist. But he knew the horrors of war psychosis which could deform men's feelings into the nature of a fist.

While in the following Lincoln was writing to Missourians about hysterical factionalism between groups of Union men in that state, he seems to be speaking in apocalyptic analysis of hate psychosis in any age, in any place, or on the world scene:

The whole [case] can be explained on a more charitable, and, as I think, a more rational hypothesis. We are in a civil war. . . .

Yet, all being for the Union, by reason of . . . differences, each will prefer a different way of sustaining the Union. At once sincerity is questioned, and motives are assailed. Actual war coming, blood grows hot, and blood is spilled. Thought is forced from old channels into confusion. Deception breeds and thrives. Confidence dies, and universal suspicion reigns. Each man feels an impulse to kill his neighbor, lest he be first killed by him. Revenge and retaliation follow. And all this, as before said, may be among honest men only. But this is not all. Every foul bird comes abroad, and every dirty reptile rises

up. These add crime to confusion. Strong measures, deemed indispensable but harsh at best, such men make worse by maladministra-
tion. Murders for old grudges, and murders for pelf, proceed under
any cloak that will best cover for the occasion. These causes amply
account for what has occurred in Missouri, without ascribing it to
the weakness, or wickedness of any general.

No entire volume on the mental hygiene required to correct war
psychosis could put it more completely.

At long last the American Bar Association is studying the
possibility of world peace under law. Lincoln's whole concept of
preserving our Federal Union, our federal system of apportioned
law power, as "the last best hope of earth," rested on the conviction that the absence of effective law power on any question
or in any area is the presence of anarchy.

He thought through, and he fought through, the Civil War to
prove that man has an alternative to the dilemma of a) central-
ized, over-all, far-removed government for local affairs and b)
only local law vainly seeking to govern in over-all affairs. He
proved there was an alternative, within the area of the United
States, to a) tyranny or b) anarchy at the national level. He did
not invent it. He did not even discover it. He found it in our
federal system; then he preserved the federal system.

Abraham Lincoln was never confused on questions under our
federal system as a result of either too much or too superficial
reading. Too many people suffer from unassimilated ideas super-
ficially read. Remember the few but sound books and documents
of Lincoln's Indiana youth. In his civic thinking he ever com-
panioned with the great Declaration and our Constitution, and
basic discussions of them. Never did he lightly orate as to either.
He studied federal fundamentals. He never was a fadist. He
understood federal fundamentals. He applied them.

But we cannot separate our Federal Union Government from
our Declaration of Independence. The Declaration stated the
principle; the Constitution implemented it. So Lincoln pleaded
at Peoria:

Let us re-adopt the Declaration of Independence, and with it the
practices, and policy, which harmonize with it. Let north and south
—let all Americans—let all lovers of liberty everywhere join in the

great and good work. If we do this, we shall not only have saved the Union; but we shall have so saved it as to make it, and to keep it, forever worthy of the saving. We shall have so saved it, that the succeeding *millions of free happy people, the world over, shall rise up and call us blessed, to the latest generation.*

Whether it be to preserve a state as supreme within itself and within a nation, or a nation as supreme within itself and within a United Nations, see how self-government, from individual man, and individual governments, and individual nations under law solely for world affairs, is envisioned by Lincoln's answer to Douglas:

Now in relation to his inference that I am in favor of a general consolidation of all the local institutions of the various states ... I have said, very many times, in Judge Douglas' hearing, that no man believed more than I in the principle of self-government; that it lies at the bottom of all my ideas about just government, from beginning to end.

... I believe each individual is naturally entitled to do as he pleases with himself and the fruit of his labors, so far as it in no wise interferes with any other man's rights—that each community, as a state, has a right to do exactly as it pleases with all the concerns within that state that interfere with the rights of no other state, and that the general government, upon principle, has no right to interfere with anything other than that general class of things that does concern the whole.

Of course we need to safeguard against the zealot-faddist who seeks precipitate reform through action at some over-all level, where the jurisdiction has wisely and adroitly been left at a local level because a) it *is* a local question and b) requires local vision and acceptance for accomplishment. Thus when Salmon Portland Chase urged Lincoln to apply the Emancipation Proclamation to areas not in rebellion (while the Proclamation rested on military necessity to put down rebellion), Lincoln wrote Chase a letter-lesson in straight-thinking civics:

The original proclamation has no constitutional or legal justification, except as a military measure. The exemptions were made because the military necessity did not apply to the exempted local-

ities. . . . If I take the step must I not do so, without the arguments
of military necessity, and so, without the argument, except the one
that I think the measure politically expedient, and morally right?
Would I not thus give up all footing upon constitution or law?
Would I not thus be in the boundless field of absolutism? . . . *Could
it fail to be perceived that without any further stretch I might . . .
even change any law in any state?*

In Lincoln's files is a communication from John C. Hamilton
quoting his father, Alexander Hamilton, at age seventeen in
what could only have been the product of intuitively perceptive
civics:

All men have one common original, they participate in one common nature, and consequently have one common right. No reason
can be assigned why one man should exercise any power or pre-
eminence over his fellow creatures more than another, unless they
have voluntarily vested him with it. I consider civil liberty, in a
genuine unadulterated sense, as the greatest of terrestrial blessings.
I am convinced, that the WHOLE HUMAN RACE is entitled to it.
. . . It is not a thing in its own nature precarious and dependent on
human will and caprice, but it is conformable to the constitution of
man, as well as necessary to the well being of Society.

The "well being of Society" in a world so constricted that
what happens anywhere affects the welfare of men everywhere,
is now the prescription for survival. With the potential of race
suicide, man's choice is, indeed, a "vast future"—or oblivion.

LINCOLN AND DEMOCRACY

By T. V. Smith

Dr. T. V. Smith, Professor Emeritus of Poetry, Politics and Philosophy, Maxwell Graduate School of Citizenship and Public Affairs, Syracuse University, is the author of some twenty books, including Lincoln: Living Legend *and* Abraham Lincoln and the Spiritual Life.

I. Democracy Described

IN a world where the very meaning of democracy is made ambiguous by diverse usages, it is best to indicate our understanding of the term before we utilize it to appraise and to praise Abraham Lincoln. Our description must be ample to do justice to complexity. *Democracy is an ideology; it is a way of life; it is a form of government.*

As an ideology, democracy is such emphasis upon the ideal of equality as prevents liberty from turning into license (which it is wont to do) and prevents fraternity from becoming fanaticism (which it is most prone to do). As a way of life, it is ability to stomach if not to love cultural variety. And as a form of government, democracy is organization to facilitate compromise, despite deep differences among participants as to what in particular cases is just and right. *Democracy is, in short, a pluralistic way of thought and a tolerant way of action.*

Abraham Lincoln is America's best exemplification in the flesh of both this way of thought and this method of collective action. Before we turn to these points, however, let us observe that Lincoln's democracy was a profound feeling before it was either thought or action. Lincoln was not only a democrat; he was a "democratical" sort of man. He spontaneously accorded the other man the rights he claimed for himself. "As I would not be a slave," said he, "so I would not be a master." This attitude is no deduction from dogma but a simple extension of feeling that lay deep in his frame. His feeling was furthered by the biographical fact that Lincoln had none of the external trappings for any of the elites to which he belonged. He was a natural aristocrat without the desire to exclude anybody from any rank to which nature had assigned him. America, like Whitman the poet, had come "more and more to rely upon his idiomatic western genius, careless of court dress or court decorum." Lincoln had the ready friendliness of a man lonesome from too much solitude. Whitman's question, addressed as it was to the social cosmos, would have appeared to Lincoln the rhetorical query it was to Whitman: *If you meet me and I meet you, why should we not speak to one another?*

II. Lincoln's Conduct Was Democratic

Lincoln was a democrat in action because he believed that no basis for common action exists save by achieved agreement. No man is wise enough, not even Abraham Lincoln, to dictate public policy, not even out of his private conscience. Since good men do as a matter of observation differ, and differ profoundly, and differ permanently, the "engineering of consent" becomes the only way of getting men together for common action. This spells the odious thing to idealists called "compromise."

It was the "Dred Scott decision" of the American Supreme Court which awakened Lincoln from his civic slumber. This decision set aside, or Lincoln thought it did, a national compromise which had long kept the tenuous peace over slavery and for which no substitute compromise was in sight. Lincoln puts this matter more feelingly than any other man of his time. His words are these:

The Missouri Compromise ought to be restored. For the sake of the Union it ought to be restored ... the spirit of national compromise—that spirit which has thrice saved the Union. ... We thereby restore the national faith, the national confidence. We thereby re-instate the spirit of concession . . . which has never failed us in past perils, and which may be safely trusted for all the future.

In a democracy, action must rest on agreement; and between men equally honest and equally intelligent, there is no basis for agreement save compromise. Lincoln speaks of compromise not to damn it but to praise it as a method, the method, of reaching agreement between equally patriotic men. And of the Southern-ers, Lincoln said: "They are just what we would be in their situation." This commitment to compromise means, however, that in a democratic culture—is it really different in any culture? —action lags behind thought in ideality.

III. *Lincoln's Thought Was Democratic*

So saying, we must now make explicit what is already implicit in the relation of action to thought. Thought is better—both freer and more ideal—than is action, and it must remain so. As touching thought, Lincoln said: "If slavery is not wrong, nothing is wrong. I cannot remember when I did not so think and feel." As to action, however: "Yet I have never understood that the Presidency conferred upon me an unrestricted right to act offi-cially upon this judgment and feeling." It will be remembered in this connection that Lincoln did not justify his Proclamation of Emancipation upon moral grounds, but upon the grounds (and with the timing) of political expediency and military ad-vantage. His principle in the matter is made clear by another declaration of his: "Wrong as we think slavery is, we can yet afford to let it alone where it is, because that much is due to the necessity arising from its actual presence in the nation."

There is a scrupulosity of thought, imperative upon an honest soul; but there is leeway of action; and the two are not one and the same. Some things right can be wrong to perpetrate, and some things wrong can be right to do. Each must be recognized in its own time and place and be properly adjudged.

Democracy requires complete freedom for private conscience, but for a price which is often overlooked; and the price is that public agreement must be publicly arrived at, not dictated by the private conscience in question. Privacy remains sacrosanct only so long as it does not pretend to be public. It is a fearful price to pay, but not too grievous. Common action must rest on common thought, and the only way to attain common thought is by the leeway of give-and-take. Consent comes only by concession. Whoever insists upon short-cutting this laborious discipline is not a democrat but a fanatic. Think what you will, and treasure it as you may, but *do* only what can be agreed upon (at the least by a majority). "I aver," says Lincoln, "that to this day I have done no official act in mere deference to my abstract judgment and feeling on slavery."

Lincoln is a perfect example of democracy because he illustrates in the crucial matter of slavery both the necessity of compromise and the immunity of conscience from compromise. He illustrates, too, that when these two realms meet, heroism requires either total sacrifice of one party or partial sacrifice of both parties—or it implies a creative ambivalence which has not yet clearly emerged in our analysis. Lincoln appropriated this creative principle, and becomes our supreme symbol of democracy. I speak of something "creative" because we are not reduced to a rigid dualism, with thought forever on the one side, and action on the other. There is fraternization and so a certain resiliency. What is private today may become collective tomorrow, and vice versa. Lincoln was unique in finding a working monism permeating this metaphysical dualism. How he did this concludes our story.

IV. *The Surplusage of Value*

In every meeting of the public and the private there emerges what we may call a surplusage of value, something privately imagined yet collectively unrealizable in full. This is to say that sensitive men are urged by their better natures to demand more, not only of others but of themselves as well, than the situation allows. This is true if for no other reason than the simple one that different natures demand discrepant values in the name of common ideals.

When have all good men been agreed upon goodness, or just men on justice, or holy men on holiness? When others fall short of the demands made by this surplusage, the will to perfection easily turns one to fanaticism, and all is lost because too much is demanded. When one himself falls short before the surplusage of demand, a sense of guilt naturally supervenes. Either way (and it may go both ways at once), the principle of surplus value reduces the total ideality of any conflict situation below the level of comfort—and perhaps of safety. The best becomes enemy of the better; and a value-minimum ensues partly because a value-maximum has been required. Conscience always leans toward despotism.

A good man, that is to say, can become a dependable democrat only when he learns to accept for public action less of ideality than his private insight demands. He must lower his sights for action in order to keep from having to lower his sights for thought. The surplusage of thought over action must be privately contained. This is the more intimate and the harder discipline which democracy requires. Lincoln had "insides" (imaginative amplitude) roomy enough to contain such ideals as for the time and place could not be made fully to inform action by means that were amiable. Let us resort in conclusion to Lincoln's own example of this recondite point: his doctrine and strategy as touching the reconstruction of the defeated South.

Just before his assassination, Lincoln was charged in Congress with trying to pacify the South (the so-called Louisiana Reconstruction Plan) without having faced the question as to whether the Confederacy was in or outside the Union. Had the seceding states withdrawn or only tried to withdraw? It was a question on which honest men might differ, indeed had differed to the point of war. Men might differ on this and still unite on a common course of action.

To the charge in Congress Lincoln admitted that he had not raised the previous question as to the nature of the Union. He went further and declared he would not entertain that question. He went still further and explained why the question should not be put. Such a question, said he, is "practically immaterial." Such a question, said he, is "a pernicious abstraction." Such a question, he said, "could have no other effect than the mischievous one of dividing our friends." Settle the practical question as to how neighbors could again be neighborly and then, he concluded, each might "forever after innocently indulge his own opinion"—as to speculation on the nature of the Union.

It was his clearing the road to action of such sectarian road-blocks that made Lincoln the very voice of Western democracy. If men know that all ideals transcend action, they will not be so quick to persecute each other for divergence in ideals. Lincoln knew this. If men understand in advance that the price of common action is compromise for all concerned, they will not so adamantly stick up in conference for their own interpretation of the ideal. Lincoln knew this. If men understand that the options of action are more narrowed than the amplitude of thought, they will not insist that all of any ideal be embodied in its appropriate action. Lincoln knew this. He knew that for many questions, and for all collective questions, it is more important to get them settled than to get them settled exactly "right."

Lincoln knew, finally, what ideals are *not* good for. And so he could use all ideals that are relevant for all the difference they can make—and could then contain the rest as objects of wonder and as manna for the soul. Only such insight can make common action possible through peaceful compromise and can leave private thought uncommon through individual celebration of its transcendent worth.

LINCOLN, THE DIPLOMAT
AND STATESMAN

By Jay Monaghan

Jay Monaghan, Consultant, Wyles Collection of Lincoln-iana, University of California, Santa Barbara, is a former State Historian of Illinois. He has written a two-volume Bibliography of Lincolniana, 1839–1939 *and other books on Lincoln, among them* Diplomat in Carpet Slippers *(1945)*.

WHEN Abraham Lincoln was elected President of the United States in 1860 people prophesied that he would fail as a diplomat. He had had less than a year's schooling in his whole life and was commonly considered a backwoodsman. Now he must match his wits against highly educated foreign heads of state who were trained for international intrigue.

Yet the future of democracy depended on Lincoln's success, for democracy had broken down in America—the only country of any size where it was practiced. A group of Southern states had seceded from the Union rather than accept the result of an election which threatened slavery. This flouting of majority rule made thoughtful liberals everywhere wonder if it was possible to have a government of the people, by the people, and for the people.

Lincoln said "Yes," but the great powers in Europe were against him. Ruling classes abroad hoped that the American experiment would fail. Popular government—they called it mobocracy—threatened to destroy the vast rural estates of the gentry. It would also doom the great commercial and banking families so important to European society. Moreover, an America divided into two or three nations would cease to be a formidable rival.

The two most powerful countries of Europe—England and France—had still another reason for hoping that the Southern states would become independent. Cotton was indispensable for their mills and they preferred to buy it direct from the planters rather than through trade agreements with the United States. Thus Lincoln's first diplomatic objective was to prevent England and France from interfering in the American war.

Lincoln's first domestic objective was to hold the South in the Union. To do this he declared a blockade of all Southern ports. Any ship going to or from these ports would be subject to capture and confiscation. Thus the South would be starved into submission. This solution caused new difficulties, however. A blockade, according to international law, could be imposed by any nation against an enemy country. But Lincoln dared not call the South "an enemy country." To do so would acknowledge its right to secede. Moreover, as an independent country it could purchase its own warships abroad, perhaps destroy American shipping, and break the blockade.

Another and even more dangerous dilemma resulted from the blockade. It deprived Europe of cotton and caused widespread unemployment there. Instead of holding the South in the Union it might force European intervention. To prevent this, Lincoln decided on his second diplomatic objective. He would appeal directly to mass opinion in Europe. He must convince the enlightened world that the Civil War was more than a domestic squabble. He must prove that it was a test of constitutional government and majority rule. To do this he decided to send a corps of writers and speakers abroad, each to work independently of the American foreign ministers.

As representative of the press Lincoln sent that master of diplomatic suavity, Thurlow Weed, editor of the powerful *Albany Journal*. Meanwhile in London, Henry Adams, son of the American minister, grandson of President John Quincy Adams, and great-grandson of President John Adams, wrote constantly for both English and French newspapers. To carry the message of democracy to churchgoers Lincoln sent Episcopalian Archbishop John J. Hughes to England and Roman

Catholic Bishop Charles P. McIlwaine to France. These prelates understood human rights and human welfare. Moreover, their words would carry weight. Lincoln also dispatched to Europe America's popular Congregational preacher, Henry Ward Beecher. His sister, Harriet Beecher Stowe, was author of *Uncle Tom's Cabin,* which had deeply stirred antislavery interest abroad. Appealing to humble folk, Lincoln sent New England's "learned blacksmith," Elihu Burritt, who had devoted his life to a campaign for penny postage and cheap newspapers for the purpose of educating poor people. Lincoln also delegated escaped slaves—including the ex-coachman of Jefferson Davis, President of the Southern Confederacy—to address English audiences. Let these Negroes demonstrate their intellectual capacity and the injustice of slavery.

Then, lest his representatives might give the impression that democracy leveled society to a universal mediocrity, Lincoln asked August Belmont, the New York agent of the great European banking house of Rothschild, to go to Europe. Here was a man of millions who rose to his financial eminence in the free society of a republic. To demonstrate further the opportunity of every man in free America, Lincoln sent William H. Aspinwall, merchant-prince who bought shipping lines and built railroads as casually as other men bought new hats. Aspinwall had started life as an apprentice in a shipping firm, so "mobocracy" held no fears for him. Lincoln also dispatched that other transport magnate, John M. Forbes, a self-made man of great wealth. Ralph Waldo Emerson said of Forbes: "Wherever he moved he was the benefactor. It is of course that he should ride well, shoot well, sail well, keep house well, administer affairs well; but he was the best talker in any company." Let Europeans note, Lincoln thought, that the athletic pastimes enjoyed more exclusively by squire and baron in Europe were available to all in democratic America.

The most spectacular of Lincoln's good-will ambassadors was Robert J. Walker, ex-Secretary of the Treasury under President Polk, and ex-Senator from Tennessee. When the South seceded Walker allied himself with the North. He had never belonged to Lincoln's political party—better the reason to select him and thus demonstrate American political tolerance. Robert J. Walker

knew international finances as well as August Belmont, and he
also knew the South. When the Confederacy offered to small
English investors a cotton loan which, in case the South won the
war, would pay all holders like a winning lottery ticket, Walker
chartered a balloon, inflated it on the Surrey side of the Thames
and floated over London, dropping hundreds of leaflets exposing
the Confederate scheme and extolling Northern democracy.

All these speakers and writers were careful never to criticize
the government of the people they addressed. Thus Henry Ward
Beecher told a Manchester audience that the seed corn of America's liberalism had come from Britain, "and if, on a larger
sphere, and under circumstances of unobstruction, we have
reared mightier sheaves, every sheaf contains the grain that has
made old England rich for a hundred years." Even the Czar of
Russia was complimented for recently emancipating his serfs.

Thus every American speaker's job was to convince Europeans
that a victory for the North was a victory for themselves—for
democracy in which every man had equal rights and equal opportunities. Lincoln had begun life as a laborer and he believed
in a fluid society where every man might hope to rise just as
he had.

For almost two years the war dragged on indecisively. Mill-
workers in France and England reached the verge of starvation.
The suffering was appalling. In Lancashire, England, the mills
reduced their work schedule to half time, later to two days a
week. Finally they closed entirely. In town after town, 50 per
cent of the assessed taxes were not paid on account of pauperism.
Hundreds of hunger-pinched people stood around the newspaper offices, staring at the bulletins, waiting for word that the
American war had ended, that the North had won. Workers
deserted their families, their villages, to wander south begging
food. A report from Burnley, Lancashire, stated that in forty
laborers' cottages on one street, only a half loaf of bread could
be found. A fever, attributed to malnutrition, swept across the
slums in industrial areas. Once a "starvation meeting" resolved
to end its misery in a canal. Police prohibited "starvation meetings" henceforth. Hungry men looked into one another's hollow
eyes and asked again and again about the American war, but
when their rulers suggested intervention in behalf of the slave-

owners in order to get cotton, the laborers showed no interest. Lincoln had won their hearts more completely than he knew.

Then Lincoln played his last diplomatic card in his game against the European autocrats. He had no authority, as President, to emancipate slaves in the South, but he could do so as commander-in-chief of the army. In September, 1862, he took this step, and the effect overseas was electric. In Great Britain liberals, intellectuals, as well as the undernourished workingmen held mass meetings to approve his act. Lincoln's public speakers had sown their ideas concerning American democracy in fertile soil. Poor people in mill towns had become convinced that they were part of Lincoln's crusade for human freedom. They publicly resolved, with bold and unselfish resolutions, that it was an honor to suffer for human freedom. Manchester workmen, as hard hit as any by unemployment, forwarded to Lincoln a hearty letter of congratulation.

The President replied at once with a long and carefully worded message: "I know and deeply deplore the sufferings which the workingmen at Manchester and all Europe, are called to endure in this crisis," he declared. Then, outlining the importance of the American war to the history of democratic government, he concluded: "I cannot but regard your decisive utterances upon the question as an instance of sublime Christian heroism which has not been surpassed in any age or in any country."

Lincoln's letter to the Manchester workingmen immediately became a diplomatic masterpiece. It was printed in English newspapers and distributed in pamphlet form. English school children memorized its best passages. Common people who identified themselves with Lincoln and the principles for which he stood would never march against America in battle.

In France the effect of Lincoln's Emancipation Proclamation is harder to measure. People in regimented countries dared not express their opinions freely. But John Stuart Mill wrote from Avignon that Lincoln's Proclamation won "all *liberal-minded* Frenchmen." The Paris branch of the Evangelical Alliance courageously supported Lincoln. France's powerful Socialist minority did likewise. Guizot, Victor Hugo, even Prince Napoleon, wrote pro-American articles for French newspapers.

With this bulwark of popular approval Lincoln spoke not alone to Americans, but to mankind around the world when he said at Gettysburg: "Our fathers brought forth on this continent a new nation, conceived in liberty, and dedicated to the proposition that all men are created equal. Now we are engaged in a great civil war, testing whether that nation, or any nation so conceived and so dedicated, can long endure."

The wording of this address is important. Lincoln was too realistic a statesman to believe that democracy would necessarily cure all human frailties. Nor did he say that all men were created equal. But he did point out that a government dedicated to the proposition that all men are equal seemed the fairest and most enlightened premise for ruling mankind. This was the basis of democracy and he was determined that it must not fail.

Now, almost a hundred years later, the question may be asked, "Did Lincoln's statesmanship succeed?" Certainly the democracy he championed survived, and after the North's victory every country in Europe followed, to some extent, America's example. Aristocrats in England admitted at once that they must change their government and extend the franchise, for the first time in their history, to a majority of all male citizens. The French Emperor refused to budge and his empire was superseded within six years by the Third Republic.

Perhaps the success of Lincoln's statesmanship can be measured best by the reaction to news of his assassination. In England distraught people flocked by hundreds to mass meetings. Working people in the factory towns of Lancashire trudged to Liverpool where a ship loaded with free cotton stood in port. They got a lorry, draped it with flowers and bunting, then placed a bale of cotton from the ship in the center of the platform. British and American flags were crossed above it, and under them hung the picture of the plain man who appeals to plain people everywhere—Abraham Lincoln. Children filled the rest of the space on the wagon. The throng dragged the lorry from the dock through Exchange Street and Lime Street to St. George Square, where 20,000 persons congregated to hear the Bishop of Manchester preach a sermon on civil liberty. Years later an immigrant to America who had been present declared: "That sermon and the songs of the children still echo in our hearts. I have asked those men again and again, 'Would you do it again? Would you suffer again for liberty's sake?' And I asked myself, 'Would I be willing to sacrifice mother and father at an early age through suffering resultant on that starvation period for this cause?' The answer is with them, as it is with you and me, a great big 'Yes.' "

In other parts of England religious services were conducted to mourn the Emancipator's death. A London *Times* editor stated, "Nothing like it has been witnessed in our generation." The British House of Lords noted the "absence of precedent for such a manifestation." In the Cotton Exchange in Manchester a miniature bale of cotton was placed on exhibition under a glass globe. Behind it gilt letters stated: *Part of the first bale of free cotton. Shipped from West Virginia, U.S., to Liverpool, 1865. Free cotton is King. But what did it cost?*

No one knew better than the English people in 1865 that the Civil War was their own; that a victory for Lincoln's republicanism in America was a victory for democracy abroad. One commentator said: "Abraham Lincoln had come to be the synonym of hope, not only in every slave cabin in the South, where he is canonized already, but in many a shepherd's lodge in Switzerland—in many a woodsman's cabin in the Black Forest —in many a miner's hut in the Harz Mountains—in many a cottage in Italy, for the poor had learned to look upon him as the anointed of God for the redemption of the liberties of mankind."

In Paris a squad of policemen held back excited mourners intent on expressing sympathy at the American Legation. "I had no idea," the Secretary reported, "that Lincoln had such a hold upon the hearts of the young gentlemen of France." The French Academy offered a prize for the best poem on the death of Lincoln. Lodges of the Masonic Order, an organization beyond control of the Emperor's censorship, sent scores of sympathetic resolutions. In Lyons 25,000 workmen subscribed sums as low as ten centimes—large amounts were not acceptable—and employed skilled artisans to weave a United States flag to be presented to Mrs. Lincoln.

In Germany the struggle for liberalism was more protracted, and Lincoln had taken full advantage of it during his own rise to power. A revolution had been suppressed in 1848 and many of the leaders fled to America. Lincoln, while campaigning for the presidency, purchased a newspaper which used German type and with this he explained to the newcomers his own liberal philosophy. After his election, prominent German immigrants were appointed to positions of importance in the Army and diplomatic corps. Notable among these were Carl Schurz and Franz Sigel. The editor of Lincoln's German newspaper, Theodore Canisius, was sent as consul to Vienna. When the war ended and its resulting democratic trend swept eastward across Europe, Bismarck united the German liberals who had remained in the Vaterland with his militarists. This combination carried Germany into a new period of advancement which included municipal democracy and freedom of the press.

The liberal wave rolled on around the world, with Lincoln's name always near the crest. Lincoln biographies, usually available in cheap paper format for poor people, accompanied the overturn of tyranny in Russia, Turkey, and even in far-off Japan. There the new Japanese constitution—although only quasi-democratic—gave Japan a parliamentary government in 1890, and it is significant that the first biography of Lincoln in Japanese characters appeared that same year.

In China, Sun Yat-sen proudly admitted his debt to Lincoln during the long years he planned and worked for the establishment of a Chinese republic. He was deeply impressed by Lincoln's immortal belief in a government of the people, by the people, for the people, and accepted this concept as the basis of his own cherished dream. Liberals in many other countries published books about Lincoln as part of their struggle for human freedom. Writers in thirty languages told downtrodden people about the political ideals of the woodchopper who became President, the common man who saved democracy without veiling the Statue of Liberty.

LINCOLN, THE MILITARY
STRATEGIST

By T. Harry Williams

*Dr. T. Harry Williams, Boyd Professor of History, Louisiana
State University, has written extensively on Lincoln. Among
his books are:* Lincoln and the Radicals *(1941) and* Lincoln
and His Generals *(1952).*

IF a modern poll organization had existed at the beginning of
the American Civil War in 1861 and if it had asked which
President of the rival governments would make the greater war
director, what answer would it have received? Undoubtedly the
average informed observer would have predicted that the head
of the Southern states would outshine his Northern opponent.
Such a judgment seemed justified by the backgrounds of the two
men.

Jefferson Davis, President of the Confederate States, was a
graduate of the United States Military Academy at West Point,
then the only advanced military school in the country. He had
served as a combat officer in the Mexican War, and he had been
a very effective Secretary of War in President Franklin Pierce's
Cabinet. Abraham Lincoln had had no military education and
no military experience, except for a brief and inconsequential
interlude as a militia captain in a small Indian war.

Lincoln always ridiculed his services in the Black Hawk War.
In a speech in Congress he mockingly referred to himself as a
"military hero," and recalled that he had bent a musket acci-
dentally and made some fierce charges on the wild onions and

engaged in many bloody struggles with the mosquitoes. It is possible, however, that his campaign against the Indians gave him a valuable insight into the psychology of the citizen soldier, the kind of men who would compose the armies of the Civil War.

And yet, contrary to all the apparent probabilities, Lincoln turned out to be a great war director and Jefferson Davis a mediocre one. The war records of the two executives demonstrate better than any other example in history the truth of one of Clausewitz's dicta. The great German had said that an acquaintance with military affairs was not the principal qualification for a director of war but that "a remarkable, superior mind and strength of character" were more important. Fortunately for the cause of American nationality, these were qualities that Lincoln possessed in eminent degree.

The American Constitution clearly stated that the President was the commander in chief of the armed forces. Thus Lincoln's authority to direct the Northern war effort was almost unlimited. But if his command position was sharply defined, the command system with which he had to work was loosely and inadequately organized; in fact, in the modern sense it was not a system at all. In the entire military organization there was no agency charged with the function of planning strategy or of integrating strategy with national policy.

The army possessed a body known as the "general staff," but it bore little if any resemblance to a modern staff. The members were the heads of the bureaus in the War Department: the quartermaster general, the chief of ordnance, the adjutant general, and others. This staff held no joint meetings and framed no common plans. Its work was completely technical and administrative, and each bureau head went pretty much his own way with little supervision from above.

Presiding over the staff and the rest of the army organization was the general in chief, the general officer with the senior commission. In 1861 the occupant of this position was Winfield Scott, veteran of the War of 1812 and the Mexican War, who was seventy-five years old and in such bad health that he could hardly walk.

Scott was one of the two officers in the service who before the war had commanded men in numbers large enough to be called an army; the other was John E. Wool, who was two years older than Scott. And the army that Scott had led in the Mexican War numbered only 14,000 men. Small as this force had been, it was the largest aggregation of troops that the younger officers—except a few who had visited Europe—had ever seen. Not one of the junior officers had directed the evolutions of as large a unit as a brigade, and only a handful had administered a regiment.

Most members of the officer corps were able, after the war began, to adjust their thinking to the requirements of the mass armies that came into being. But they had great difficulty in altering their concepts of strategy to meet the realities of modern war. Most American officers were trained in the eighteenth-century tradition of war. War was something that was fought between armies and that did not involve civilian societies; it should be directed by professional soldiers without interference by political officials; and it could be so conducted—by adept maneuver—that victory would result without a showdown battle.

If there had to be a decisive engagement, American soldiers thought it should be fought by the maxims laid down by Henri Jomini, the brilliant Swiss who had served under Napoleon. According to Jomini, or more accurately, according to the American interpretation of him, the largest possible force should be concentrated at one point for one big effort against the enemy.

Most of Lincoln's generals could not understand that many of Jomini's ideas did not apply to their war. In a country as large as the United States and with the North enjoying a distinct numerical superiority, it was possible to mount two or more big offensives simultaneously. And the first Northern generals failed utterly to realize that in a democracy and in a modern war the civilian authorities would insist, and rightly so, on having a voice in the conduct of the conflict.

Almost immediately Lincoln demonstrated that he possessed great natural powers as a strategist. His very first acts were bold and imaginative moves for a man dealing with military questions for the first time. He grasped the importance of naval warfare, and proclaimed a naval blockade of the South. He saw that human and material resources were on his side, and called for the mobilization of over 400,000 men. He understood the advantage that numbers gave the North, and—contrary to Jominian strategy—urged his generals to maintain a constant and relentless pressure on the whole line of the Confederacy until a weak spot was found and a breakthrough could be made. And departing from eighteenth-century concepts, he realized that the principal objective of his armies was to seek contact with the Confederate armies and not to occupy Southern territory.

During the first three years of the war, Lincoln performed many of the functions that in a modern command system would be assigned to the chief of the general staff or to the joint chiefs of staff. He framed policy, devised strategy, and even on occasion directed tactical movements. For this he has been criticized by some writers, who contend that he "interfered" too much with matters outside his proper sphere. But in judging Lincoln's actions, it must be remembered that he operated in the absence of a formal command system. No agency to prepare strategy existed and if Lincoln had not acted no action would have resulted.

Moreover, it was fortunate for the Union cause, in most cases, that he interfered. Many of his alleged interventions were nothing more than attempts to force his generals to fight, to execute the role for which generals and armies supposedly are created. Sometimes Lincoln erred—because he lacked technical military knowledge or because he neglected such mundane problems as supplies and transportation. But the vital point is that even when he was wrong he acted from a sound military basis: to make an offensive strategy more offensive. Conversely, it may be said that Davis's great error was to interfere from a faulty basis: to make a defensive strategy more defensive.

In the beginning months of the war, Lincoln naturally turned to old General Scott for strategic counsel. He soon discovered that Scott lacked the qualities required in a general in chief. All of Scott's experience had been in small wars. Asked by Lincoln to present an over-all plan, Scott came up with a design that called for a naval blockade of the Southern coast and the occupation of the Mississippi River line. The South would be enfolded in a gigantic circle—and with the drawing of the circle Scott would stop. The North could then sit back and wait for the besieged South to yield.

This was the famous "anaconda plan" to squeeze the Confederacy into submission. Although it had obvious merits (the blockade and the Mississippi line became staple items in Northern strategy), it also had basic defects. For one thing, the plan would be a long time in making its possible effects felt. More important, it represented, as Lincoln the civilian saw, the one-weapon or the one-service idea of war. No single strategic procedure was going to win the Civil War.

By November of 1861 Scott had been persuaded to retire. To the post of general in chief Lincoln named George B. McClellan, who was also the field commander of the principal Federal army in the Eastern theater. The young, thirty-five-year-old McClellan demonstrated almost immediately that he did not possess the abilities to plan and direct the movements of a number of armies. At Lincoln's request, he too prepared a strategic design. He proposed that an army of 273,000 men be placed under his command in the Eastern theater. The navy would land this host on the Virginia coast, from whence McClellan would march inland and capture Richmond, the Confederate capital. In a series of similar operations, the army would conquer and occupy the entire Eastern seaboard of the Confederacy.

On almost every count, the plan was defective. It demanded too much of available resources. The government could not have assembled that many men in one theater, or housed and fed them if assembled. Nor did the sea transport exist to take the troops where McClellan wanted to operate. McClellan's scheme, calling for a supreme concentration of effort in one theater, was a complete example of Jominian strategy. Lincoln must have been amazed when he read the document, which he filed safely away without comment.

Outside of this proposal, McClellan indulged in no general strategic planning worthy of the name. When he took the field in the spring of 1862, Lincoln relieved him as general in chief on the grounds that one man could not direct an army engaged in active operations and at the same time plan moves for other armies. The President did not appoint another officer to the position until July.

In the interim Lincoln acted as his own general in chief. There can be little doubt that by this time he had come to have serious misgivings about the professional soldiers. Inclined at first to defer too much to their opinions, he now felt a growing confidence in his own powers to decide military questions, and he was perhaps a little too ready to impose his opinions on the generals.

Nevertheless, in this period Lincoln did not presume to dispense completely with expert advice. Secretary of War Stanton had convened an agency known as the Army Board, consisting of the heads of the bureaus in the War Department. This was only the general staff brought together under a chairman, but the transformation of the bureau chiefs into a collective body was a forward step in command. Lincoln frequently consulted the Board before arriving at an important decision.

Despite his increasing doubts about soldiers, Lincoln seemed to sense that there was something wrong in the existing arrangement. He, a civilian, was doing things that should be done by a military man. Again he decided to fill the post of general in chief. In July, 1862, he named to the position Henry W. Halleck, who had been a departmental commander in the Western theater.

General Halleck seemed to be the ideal man for the job. Before the war he had been known as one of the foremost American students of the art of war, the translator of Jomini into English and an author in his own right. Moreover, he had been a capable departmental administrator. Lincoln intended that Halleck should be a real general in chief, that he should, under the authority of the President, actually plan and direct operations.

At first Halleck acted up to his role—but not for long. His great defect was that he disliked responsibility. He delighted to provide technical knowledge and to advise, but he shrank from making decisions. Gradually he divested himself of his original function and deliberately assumed the part of an adviser and an informed critic.

Halleck's refusal to perform the requirements of his position forced Lincoln to act again as general in chief, but he kept Halleck as titular head of the office. The President had discovered that Halleck could do one valuable service for him—in the area of military communications. Often Lincoln and his generals had had serious misunderstandings because, almost literally, they spoke different languages, Lincoln the words of the lawyer-politician and the generals the jargon of the military. Halleck had lived in both the civil and the military worlds, and he could speak the language of both. Increasingly Lincoln came to entrust the framing of his directives to Halleck.

In those years of lonely responsibility when Lincoln directed the war effort he grew steadily in stature as a strategist. Usually he displayed greater strategic insight than most of his commanders. But he was willing, as he had been earlier, to yield the power to frame and control strategy to any general who could demonstrate that he could do the job—if he could find the general. By 1864 both he and the nation were certain they had found the man—Ulysses S. Grant. And in that year the United States finally achieved a modern command system to fight a modern war.

In the system arrived at in 1864, which was the joint product of Lincoln and Congress, Grant was named general in chief, charged with the function of planning and directing the movements of all Union armies. Grant, because he disliked the political atmosphere of Washington, established his headquarters with the field army in the Eastern theater, but did not technically command that army. In the new arrangement Halleck received a new office, "chief of staff." He was not, however, a chief of staff in today's sense of the term. Primarily he was a channel of communication between Lincoln and Grant and between Grant and the seventeen departmental commanders under Grant. Halleck performed the vital work that in a modern army is done by the secretariat. The perfect office soldier, he had found at last his proper niche.

As a general in chief, Grant justified every belief in his capacities. He possessed in superb degree the ability to think of the war in over-all terms. But his grand plan of operations that ended the war was partly Lincolnian in concept. Grant conformed his strategy to Lincoln's known ideas: Hit the Confederacy from all sides with pulverizing blows and make enemy armies the main objective. The general submitted the broad outlines of his plan to Lincoln, and the President, trusting in Grant, approved the design without seeking to know the details.

The 1864 command system embodied the brilliance of simplicity: a commander in chief to lay down policy and grand strategy, a general in chief to frame specific battle strategy, and a chief of staff to coordinate information. It contained elements that later would be studied by military leaders and students in many nations. Abraham Lincoln, without fully realizing his part, had made a large and permanent contribution to the story of command organization.

LINCOLN, MAN OF PEACE

By William Frank Zornow

Dr. William F. Zornow, Assistant Professor of History, Kansas State College, is the author of Lincoln and the Party Divided *(1954) and of numerous Lincoln studies.*

THE clouds of war hung menacingly when Abraham Lincoln was elected to the presidency in November 1860. His party, the Republican, had announced that it was irrevocably opposed to the further extension of slavery into the unoccupied territories of the West, although it was willing to tolerate it in those states where it already existed.

Many Southerners were concerned over the threat against expansion and were not reassured by the promise against interference. They felt that the economic survival of the South depended upon the expansion of cotton culture to the fertile Western lands, and this was impossible without slave labor. Other Southern leaders were unimpressed by the pledge of noninterference, since they regarded the Republicans as abolitionists who would soon attempt to free all the slaves. The Republican victory to such Southerners was a judgment against the South, which, if permitted to go unchallenged, would soon mean the destruction of the economic and social system upon which their section was based.

South Carolina seceded immediately after the election and called upon her sister Southern states to join her. Under the constitutional system of the day, Lincoln did not take office until March 4, 1861, and by that date six other states had left the Union. During these months every effort was made to find an acceptable compromise, but without success.

Lincoln sought to reassure the South that he would honor his party's pledge. He even was willing to accept a constitutional amendment guaranteeing slavery where it already existed, but he was unwilling to make any concession toward permitting further extension. "The man does not live who is more devoted to peace than I am, none who would do more to preserve it," he told the New Jersey legislature during these critical months, "but it may be necessary to put the foot down firmly." Peace was dear to Lincoln, but it was not to be bought at the expense of surrendering basic principles.

Lincoln was an unknown quantity in March 1861. His career had attracted only a small national audience, and he knew that had the Democrats not split their votes between two candidates, he would not have been elected at all. He had served only one term in the House of Representatives, and in 1858 had tried unsuccessfully to get elected to the Senate from Illinois. However, those who had worked with him in state politics and before the courts where he practiced as an attorney recognized him as a man of remarkable ability. The country soon learned that despite his humble origins and lack of extensive education Lincoln was well endowed with natural qualities of leadership that were to make him one of the greatest of Presidents.

Lincoln realized that his political obscurity made him a difficult factor to assess in 1861. It was for this reason that he continued to reassure the South that he meant no harm. He devoted large portions of his inaugural message to pledges against precipitate action that would jeopardize peace. He intended only to perform his constitutional duties to defend the Union. "There need be no bloodshed or violence," he told the South, "and there shall be none unless it be forced upon the national authority . . . there will be no invasion, no using of force against the people anywhere."

Despite his sincere efforts in behalf of peace, Lincoln was unable to prevent the outbreak of hostilities. He found himself in the position of having to mobilize the North to fight, but this prior task did not divert him from thinking also about peace. He knew that a lasting peace was not just going to happen; it had to be won and planned for no less than war. Such planning involved not only the formulation of definite attainable objectives but considered also the effect of these plans on both the North and the South. Lincoln felt that a well-conceived peace policy might shorten the war by weakening the South's will to resist. For such a policy the keynote was leniency.

Lincoln was not a visionary, but he grounded his peace policies on practical objectives. He had taken an oath as President to uphold and defend the Union, and Lincoln made this the first plank in his peace platform. He never lost sight of his main objective to restore the Union. In 1862 he told the New York editor, Horace Greeley, that whatever he did as President was done for that sole purpose.

Greeley and thousands of other Northerners wished to transform the war to save the Union into one to liberate the slaves, an alteration of objectives that Lincoln at first opposed, although he personally hated slavery. Eventually in 1862 he altered his position and issued an Emancipation Proclamation.

By freeing the slaves Lincoln hoped to deprive the Southerners of a servile labor force that was militarily useful, to placate the strong and rising abolitionist sentiment in the North, and to win the approval of such powers as Britain and France. However, once having proclaimed emancipation, Lincoln admitted that it was inconceivable to return the Negroes to bondage after the war. You could not offer to free the Negroes as a means of winning the war and enslave them again when the fighting stopped. Lincoln added emancipation as a second basic point to his peace program.

In addition to the restoration of the Union and the abolition of slavery, Lincoln called for a third objective—the destruction of the South's military power. Actually this objective is obvious, for the destruction of an enemy army is a prerequisite for the restoration of peace. In Lincoln's case a strong peace movement in the North, which called for a compromise with the South, made it necessary to stress the need for military victory as a preliminary to negotiation. "If they want peace," he told James R. Gilmore, "all they have to do is to lay down their arms." However, Lincoln had little confidence that the South would do so unless defeated in battle.

For this reason he insisted upon total military victory. He had no sympathy for generals like George B. McClellan who wished to fight simultaneously with sword and olive branch. It was not until 1864 that Lincoln found such commanders as Ulysses S. Grant and William T. Sherman who shared his views on total war. They believed that peace could be won by pulverizing the enemy's war machine and systematically destroying his industry and food supplies. Having found his generals, Lincoln gave them a free hand for total victory. To the critics who complained about this type of warfare, Lincoln replied, "I sincerely wish war was an easier and pleasanter business than it is, but it does not admit of holidays."

Nowhere is the Lincoln peace program summarized more succinctly than in his memo to Secretary of State William Seward on January 31, 1865 (the same terms were repeated on the eve of his death, April 13): "1, The restoration of the national authority throughout all the states; 2, No receding by the Executive of the United States on the slavery question . . . ; 3, No cessation of hostilities short of an end of the war and the disbanding of all forces hostile to the government."

Although he had little hope the South would accept his terms, Lincoln did not close the door on negotiations. During 1864 several attempts were made to reach a settlement. One mission went to Richmond to see President Jefferson Davis, while Greeley went to Niagara Falls with the President's terms, "the restoration of the Union and the abandonment of slavery," in Lincoln's famous "To Whom It May Concern" letter.

The most serious effort at negotiation was made in February 1865 when Lincoln and Seward went to Hampton Roads to converse with Confederate leaders Alexander H. Stephens, R. M. T. Hunter, and John A. Campbell. The conference was a failure. Lincoln made it clear that any thought of an armistice was unthinkable unless the South would recognize the restoration of the Union. He did not propose to arrange an armistice when his armies were winning, so that the South would have a respite to redeploy its waning forces.

Although the three-point peace program was Lincoln's blueprint for victory, he did not want a peace that would mean recrimination, hatred, and bitterness between the sections after the war. He wanted nothing of this sort to stand as a psychological roadblock in the way of spiritual and ideological reunion after political reunion had been won on the battlefield.

It was for this reason that Lincoln conceived the idea of offering the South lenient terms. The war had thrown eleven states out of their normal relations with the Washington government; peace should restore that normal relationship as speedily and painlessly as possible. There should be no vindictive measures. As early as 1862 Lincoln announced there would be no Northern men imposed on the South after the war to rule by bayonets.

He made it clear that there would be pardons for all who had taken up arms, that the South would be permitted to administer its domestic affairs without interference, and that there would be no wholesale confiscation of property. He even talked of compensating the owners of the former slaves. Wherever possible, when Northern armies occupied Southern states, Lincoln sought to provide a fair administration.

In a congressional message of December 1863, Lincoln announced his postwar peace plans based on the idea that the South should be restored to its normal relations with Washington as soon as possible. It was provided that whenever 10 per cent of the electorate in each state that had voted in 1860 had taken an oath of allegiance to the United States and accepted emancipation, these people could form a government and receive executive recognition. So eager was Lincoln to bring the rebellious states back into the Union that he was willing to permit a minority to assume the initiative.

The same obvious desire to offer lenient terms was evident during the President's conversations with Grant and Sherman at City Point on March 27–28, 1865. Lincoln made it clear that he wanted the Southerners back at their constructive tasks as rapidly as possible. There were to be no reprisals against Southern leaders for rebelling; even Jefferson Davis was to be left in peace. When the fighting ceased, the Southerners would resume all their rights as American citizens, as if the war had never happened.

It was on the basis of Lincoln's enlightened and liberal proposals that Grant offered terms to Robert E. Lee at Appomattox on April 9, 1865, and on the following day urged the famed Confederate general to make a personal visit to Lincoln. It was

Grant's hope that a *rapprochement* between Lincoln and Lee would rally the responsible and reasonable people of both sections to bury the hatreds of war. Under the terms of this settlement the Southern soldiers were permitted to return home without fear of subsequent prosecution.

On April 18, 1865, Sherman offered even more liberal terms to General Joseph E. Johnston. The settlement, in line with what Lincoln had said at City Point, provided for the peaceful re-establishment of the Southern states with full civil, political, and property rights for their citizens. Regrettably this was not accepted by Congress.

Lincoln's enlightened peace proposals were distributed throughout the South as propaganda, but it has been argued by James G. Randall, the most eminent Lincoln scholar of recent years, that they probably did little toward shortening the war or encouraging dissatisfaction with the Richmond government. However, there can be little doubt that had Lincoln's liberal policies been allowed to go into effect the turmoil of the Reconstruction period together with many sectional problems that persist until the present could have been avoided.

The reason for this tragic failure and consequent continuation of sectional strife for nearly a century was Lincoln's inability to sell his liberal peace policy to his own people. As the war progressed, two trends became evident in the North. The first of these was a spirit of war weariness, which reached its zenith in the Copperhead movement. In 1864 the Democrats tried to defeat Lincoln for re-election by capitalizing on this peace sentiment. They wanted immediate negotiation with the South, and some were willing to accept peace even if it meant disunion. This was the reason that Lincoln was forced to bear down so heavily on the idea that there could be no negotiation unless the South first accepted reunion.

The second trend was one of vindictiveness. While the peace drive centered in the Democratic party, the demand for vindictiveness was largely Republican in inception. Led by such important Congressmen as Thaddeus Stevens, Benjamin F. Wade, Charles Sumner and Zachariah Chandler, the "Radical Republicans" demanded harsh treatment for the South. Lincoln fought this group as vigorously as he opposed the peace men, and the Radicals even tried to prevent Lincoln's re-election in 1864.

After his re-election in November 1864 and before his assassination in April 1865, Lincoln was engaged in winning the war and trying to heal the breach throughout the North caused by the argument over a liberal versus a stern peace. Lincoln insisted upon *moderation* and *justice* rather than excessiveness and mistreatment. In his last speech of April 11, 1865, Lincoln made a pathetic appeal to his fellow Northerners to lay aside their hatreds and concentrate upon the one peace aim which had motivated him from the opening day of the war—to restore the South to "a proper practical relation with the Union."

Within a few days Lincoln was dead and so were his plans for a just and liberal peace. The vindictive politicians who came after him insisted upon creating a long and painful process whereby the South could regain its place in the Union.

LINCOLN AND THE SCIENCES

By Robert V. Bruce

Dr. Robert V. Bruce, Assistant Professor of History, Boston University, was research assistant to Benjamin P. Thomas, author of Abraham Lincoln, A Biography *(1954). He is the author of* Lincoln and the Tools of War *(1956).*

WHEN Abraham Lincoln's two young secretaries called him "the American," as they sometimes did in talking with each other, they touched on a major element of Lincoln's success. Few other Americans have equaled Abraham Lincoln's power to evoke and define the enduring articles of American democratic faith. With his love of homespun yarns, his frontiersman's disregard of caste and ceremony, his tolerance, his lean and sinewy physique, he seemed to embody the national character as well as the national ideal. This was true in a sense not often realized—because of his rural upbringing and small-town rise. Like his countrymen, Lincoln was fascinated by the new age of science and technology.

He had qualities of mind that would have served a scientist or an engineer. As a lawyer, he made good use of a tenacious and accurate memory. He had a deliberate and analytical way of thinking. "I am never easy when I am handling a thought," he said once, "till I have bounded it North, bounded it South, bounded it East, and bounded it West."

Such a mind felt the pull of mathematics. Largely self-educated, he mastered the six books of Euclid after his first term in Congress. Riding the judicial circuit in Illinois, he would pull out his volume of Euclid and study it by candlelight while his colleagues snored in the same hotel room. Euclidean turns of phrase found their way into some of Lincoln's greatest utterances. "The principles of Jefferson," he would say, "are the definitions and axioms of free society." Even in his masterpiece, the Gettysburg Address, he made memorable use of the mathematical term "proposition."

Like his countrymen, Lincoln preferred applied science to pure theory. To be sure, living most of his life in half-tamed wilderness or prairie town, he missed early contact with certain technological advances. The White House was only six years ahead for him when gaslights first flared through the darkness of Springfield's main square. Once, while following the judicial circuit, he went to a little show at a local school and afterward rambled on by the fire about the electrical machine, the magic lantern and other scientific toys he had seen there. His fellow lawyers were not impressed. They had known about those things as schoolboys. "Yes," said Lincoln sadly, "I now have an advantage over you, for the first time in my life seeing those things which are, of course, common to those who had, what I did not, a chance at an education while they were young."

Nevertheless, during the 1850's, the machine age began to take hold in Springfield. Steam engines hissed and pounded in its mills, machine-made clothes piled up on its counters, reapers clattered over its surrounding farms. As he walked along a street one day in 1856, Lincoln paused in fascination to examine a self-raking reaper, the first he had ever seen. His supple mind traced, in imagination, the complex evolutions of sickle, revolving rake and reels; and presently he was explaining it all to the little group of spectators around him. A few months later, he stopped to watch a young telegrapher at work, and he asked questions until he understood the workings of the instrument: the key, the making and breaking of the circuit, the electromagnet. What he could not see in Springfield, he tried to find out from a yearbook of technology and science, the *Annual of Scientific Discovery*. "I have wanted such a book for years," he told his partner, "because I sometimes make experiments and have thoughts about the physical world that I do not know to be true or false. I may, by this book, correct my errors and save time and expense." Thus, by keeping his eyes open to the world around him, by asking shrewd questions and by reading intelligently, Abraham Lincoln learned much more about the new machine age than the world at large gave him credit for knowing.

And he was more than just an interested bystander. In his twenties, he worked for a few months as a surveyor, studying geometry and trigonometry, bounding farms and mapping towns with neat lines and clear, careful script, learning to respect the painstaking accuracy of engineering. Later, when he became a lawyer, patent cases were one of his specialties; and in them, his analytical mind and taste for mechanics served his clients well. From his legal work for railroads came his greatest successes as a lawyer, as well as a further insight into the impact of technology on human life. One case, which involved the question of whether a certain railroad bridge across the Mississippi was a menace to navigation, required Lincoln to apply the principles of fluid mechanics. He won the case, the bridge stood, the trains crossed, and the trade of plains and prairies went to the North instead of the South.

During Lincoln's single term in Congress, he visited the model rooms of the United States Patent Office and stared in amazement at the variety of offspring to which American ingenuity had already given birth: the screw propeller, the turret lathe, the sewing machine, the rotary printing press and hundreds of other devices. A year or two later, he patented an invention of his own for buoying vessels over shoals. On each side of the craft were to be great collapsible chambers which could be expanded by an ingenious system of ropes and pulleys and forced down into the river to buoy up the boat. But Lincoln did little or nothing to promote his invention, and so his little wooden model remains today as the sole physical product of his notion.

As his political career developed, Lincoln did not forget about science and technology. In 1859 he made a speech at a state fair in Wisconsin in which he outlined his ideas about the proper design for a steam plow. In that same year he wrote and delivered a lecture on "Discoveries and Inventions." The lecture was not well received by the public, and this reaction mortified Lincoln. Nevertheless, a few weeks before his death, he mentioned the lecture to a scientist friend of his, Louis Agassiz. "When I get out of this place," Lincoln said wistfully, "I'll finish it up, perhaps, and get a friend of mine to print it somewhere." And despite the failure of his lecture, Lincoln was asked to decide a disputed point by a convention of surveyors who met in Springfield.

As President, Lincoln showed the same zest for mechanical novelties he had manifested at the little show on the Illinois circuit. Inventors flocked to the White House to see him. Hundreds of them wrote letters describing their inventions. Lincoln always received them with sympathy and perception. As President during a war for national survival and for the vindication of democracy, Lincoln necessarily dealt mostly with advances in military technology. He had his own private proving grounds in the form of a vacant lot near the White House, where he would try out the latest ideas in breechloading rifles. At the Navy Yard one day he narrowly escaped death, along with the Secretaries of State and Treasury, when an experimental rocket exploded in its launching stand while they looked on. At the Washington Arsenal and elsewhere, he combined relaxation with the good of the nation by attending many trials of new cannon, armor, explosive mines, gunpowder and other warlike inventions.

On one occasion, he took personal responsibility for a secret project to develop a gunpowder using a chlorate compound in place of potassium nitrate or saltpeter. Until then, Great Britain had controlled the supply of saltpeter, which came mostly from British India; and Lincoln was worried about the possibility of an Anglo-American war. But when technical difficulties cropped up, and Chilean nitrates became available, the project was dropped.

President Lincoln and America's leading scientist of the time, Joseph Henry, became close friends during the Civil War. Lincoln and Henry worked together in evaluating new devices for night signaling. Between them, they also introduced the first successful military air force in American history: the reconnaissance balloons of a Vermont aeronaut named Thaddeus Lowe. Lincoln received the first telegraphic message from Lowe's balloon, and he watched an ascent from the White House grounds. By 1862 Lowe had seven balloons in operation, and his telegraphic reports during the battles of Fair Oaks and Gaines's Mill were of great value to the Union Army.

Lincoln encouraged the building of a submarine by a Frenchman named De Villeroi, who had conducted many submarine experiments at Nantes when Jules Verne was a boy there, and who was probably the inspiration for Captain Nemo in Verne's famous *Twenty Thousand Leagues Under the Sea*. Another friend of Lincoln's was Christopher Spencer of Hartford, Connecticut, inventor of a famous and highly successful repeating rifle, and the probable model for Mark Twain's *Connecticut Yankee in King Arthur's Court*. Lincoln became enthusiastic about the Spencer rifle, tried it out several times in the White House grounds and took the responsibility for introducing it into the Union Army. The Spencer rifle helped to shorten the war.

Lincoln found amusement in some impracticable devices, such as steam centrifugal cannon. But most of the ideas backed by the President were good ones. Lincoln did more than any other official to introduce breechloading rifles into the army. He gave the first government order for machine guns. He backed breechloading and rifled cannon, flame throwers, armored warships and other weapons which might have shortened the terrible Civil War still more, had he not been impeded by stubborn bureaucrats in the ordnance department.

Seeing all these new weapons, Lincoln would have understood the forebodings of young Henry Adams, son of Lincoln's minister to Great Britain. In 1862, Henry Adams wrote his brother in the Union Army: "Man has mounted science, and is run away with. Some day science may have the existence of mankind in its power, and the human race commit suicide by blowing up the world." But chances are that Lincoln would have preferred to hope, as did the magazine *Scientific American* that same year, that "aided by the discoveries of science, we shall reduce the art of war to a fruitless struggle."

Even with a fierce civil war as the central problem of his administration, Lincoln did not lose touch entirely with advances in peaceful technology. In 1862 Lincoln acted on the appeal of Samuel Morse, inventor of the telegraph, to save a fine scientific library captured in South Carolina. Instead of being dispersed by auction, the library was placed by Lincoln in the keeping of Joseph Henry as Secretary of the Smithsonian Institution. (It was not Lincoln's fault that a fire destroyed the library early in 1865.)

President Lincoln came to know men like Cyrus Field, who carried through the project of a transatlantic telegraph cable, and Herman Haupt, a pioneer in the theory of bridge construction. By giving Christopher Sholes an easy and well-paid job as Collector of Customs at Milwaukee, Lincoln made it possible for Sholes to perfect the first successful typewriter. During the war Lincoln also met an American citizen named Laszlo Chandos, who had become a highly esteemed chemist in Russia; and the President once took a boat ride on the Potomac to see the demonstration of a new type of electric arc light invented by an Englishman named John Thomas Way.

A few weeks before Lincoln's tragic death, a reporter for the *Scientific American* interviewed him in the White House. "In the midst of the many cares that press upon the President," reported the interviewer, "he is not indifferent to the claims of our inventors. Himself an inventor and patentee, he readily discerns the intrinsic value of all good inventions, not only to the public service, but also in their application to the industrial arts generally, and he will do all in his power to encourage and to promote the progress of these arts, by sanctioning all wise legislation in behalf of inventors."

Though the first great war of the Machine Age had claimed most of Abraham Lincoln's thoughts and energies for four terrible years, he could still foresee the contributions peaceful technology could make in future years to the realization of his long-cherished dream: "the progressive improvement in the condition of all men everywhere." And in this, as in the cause of human dignity and freedom, we find Lincoln concerned with a problem central to our own troubles and tremendous times.

LINCOLN, MAN OF GOD

By David C. Mearns

Dr. David C. Mearns, Assistant Librarian for the American Collections and Chief of the Manuscript Division, Library of Congress, is the author of numerous works dealing with Lincoln and the Civil War, among them The Lincoln Papers *(1948) and* Lincoln and the Image of America *(1953).*

ABRAHAM LINCOLN'S youngest stepsister, Matilda Johnston More, once recorded his boyhood custom: "When father and mother would go to church," she wrote, "they walked about 1½ miles. When they were gone—Abe would take down the Bible, read a verse—give out a hymn—and we would sing." As he grew older, his Biblical knowledge became so extensive and so exact that his ability to recite chapter after chapter from memory and to correct misquotations from Holy Writ was a constant source of wonder to his friends.

Once, upon being presented with a Bible, Lincoln remarked:

In regard to this Great Book, I have but to say, it is the best gift God has given to man. . . .

But for it we could not know right from wrong. All things most desirable for man's welfare, here and hereafter, are to be found portrayed in it.

But it is alleged that as a youth in New Salem he came under the influence of the writings of Tom Paine and Constantin Volney, with the consequence that his convictions were utterly and permanently destroyed.

This may or may not be so. Yet the understanding of Abraham Lincoln depends on an understanding that maturity came slowly to him; he never stopped growing; in the process, he outgrew many things. His nature was profoundly emotional; his moods altered between ecstasy and despair; there was no accounting for them. He was a changeling.

Only once did Abraham Lincoln give public and personal expression of his convictions. That was in 1846, during his successful campaign for election to the national House of Representatives. His rival, Peter Cartwright, deliberately spread reports of Lincoln's infidelity. Lincoln replied with a handbill addressed to the voters. It read:

> That I am not a member of any Christian Church, is true; but I have never denied the truth of the Scriptures; and I have never spoken with intentional disrespect of religion in general, or of any denomination of Christians in particular. It is true that in early life I was inclined to believe in what I understand is called the "Doctrine of Necessity"—that is, that the human mind is impelled to action, or held in rest by some power, over which the mind itself has no control; and I have sometimes (with one, two or three, but never publicly) tried to maintain this opinion in argument—The habit of arguing thus however, I have entirely left off for more than five years —And I add here, I have always understood this same opinion to be held by several of the Christian denominations. The foregoing is the whole truth, briefly stated, in relation to myself upon this subject.

Lincoln was not, in a theological sense, orthodox. He never was baptized, never joined a church, never made a profession of faith, never affiliated himself with any denomination, never subscribed to any particular liturgy or ritual. At the height of the Southern Insurrection he confessed to a deputation from the Baltimore Synod: "I have often wished that I was a more devout man than I am." His wife, who admitted that he was not, as she put it, "a technical Christian," insisted that "He was a religious man always, as I think."

In Springfield and in Washington he was a pewholder in a Presbyterian church and commendably regular in attendance. Throughout his presidency, he constantly received delegations from religious bodies. On such occasions his statements were eloquently reverent and obviously genuine expressions of his spirit. More, perhaps, than any public man in American history, his personality attracted the clergy of all faiths to himself and to his cause. His acquaintanceship with the clerics of the day was large. They came not to save him from perdition, but to draw renewed inspiration from a truly noble heart.

Dr. Smith Pyne, Rector of St. John's Church, held him in "deep and affectionate regard and respect." He would not have used such phrases in addressing a notorious unbeliever. Once when interceding for an admiral, under a sentence of court-martial, Dr. Pyne wrote to Lincoln: "Let me hope that one more item will be added to the amount of obligation and attachment by which I have long felt myself bound to you both in your official and personal character." There were scores of gentlemen of the cloth who felt just as did Dr. Pyne about the strange tenant of the White House.

In his first inaugural address, Lincoln declared: "Intelligence, patriotism, Christianity, and a firm reliance on Him, who has never yet forsaken this favored land, are still competent to adjust, in the best way, all our present difficulty." But when the issue was joined, his reliance remained firm; he accepted the defense of his cause with fatalistic resignation.

In the fall of 1862, when considering the Proclamation of Emancipation, Lincoln put down on paper this meditation on the Divine Will:

The will of God prevails. In great contests each party claims to act in accordance with the will of God. Both *may* be, and one *must* be wrong. God can not be *for,* and *against* the same thing at the same time. In the present civil war it is quite possible that God's purpose is something different from the purpose of either party—and yet the human instrumentalities, working just as they do, are of the best adaptation to effect His purpose. I am almost ready to say this is probably true—that God wills this contest, and wills that it shall not end yet. By His mere quiet power, on the minds of the now contestants, He could have either saved or destroyed the Union without a human contest. Yet the contest began. And having begun He could give the final victory to either side any day. Yet the contest proceeds.

This fragment was "not written to be seen of men," but, when he was interviewed by a minister of the Society of Friends, a few weeks later, he repeated the musing almost verbatim. Mrs. Lincoln was disposed to think that it was in that year (their son, Willie, had died in its early months) that her husband's religious senses had been most profoundly stirred. It would be progressive. The wife spoke with confidence when she said of him that "he felt religious more than ever before, about the time he went to Gettysburg."

Modern scholarship is inclined to agree that Lincoln's religious yearnings and aspirations were slowly adduced by his own and the nation's tragedy. William E. Barton once put it this way:

> The religion of Abraham Lincoln was part and parcel of his life; and his life was an evolution whose successive stages can be measured with reasonable certainty. Not only did his religious convictions develop and broaden under the stimuli of Lincoln's constantly broadening intellectual and spiritual environment, but they broadened in the growth of his own personality.

Carl Sandburg shares this view, writing:

> A distinct trend toward a deeper religious note, a piety more assured of itself because more definitely derived from inner and private growths of Lincoln himself, this could be seen as the President from year to year fitted himself more deeply and awarely into the mantle and authorities of Chief Magistrate.

But the question persists: What *was* Lincoln's religion? His private secretary, John G. Nicolay, who knew him well, and who, throughout the Administration, lived and worked by his side, a resident of the White House, has left an answer. Nicolay had intended one day to write an essay on "Abraham Lincoln's Faith in God." Among his papers is a note scribbled in pencil; it reads:

> Finally to sum up the whole matter in default of sufficient positive or direct testimony—in default of specific impressions, of church membership, and the strict observance of church rites—yet in [the] presence of the unvarying enunciation of faith and reliance in a supreme ruler, in the practice of justice, of patriotism, of mercy—in the utter oblivion of self—"with malice toward none and charity for all"—the world can utter no other verdict than this—He was a Christian without a creed.

LINCOLN AND THE POETS

By Richard Hanser

Richard Hanser is the author of Meet Mr. Lincoln, *a documentary film portraying Lincoln as seen by his contemporaries, televised by the National Broadcasting Company on February 11, 1959. His studies on Abraham Lincoln and his ideas have been published in many leading magazines.*

THE elegant and learned Senator Charles Sumner, who was Boston-born and Harvard-bred, could find no parallel in all his extensive study of history for the phenomenon that confronted him in Abraham Lincoln. Here was a backwoods politician with a pronounced rustic accent and virtually no schooling who yet composed speeches and letters that clearly marked him as a master of the English tongue. Here, in the White House, was a former country lawyer who still said "git" for "get," and "thar" for "there," but whose state papers, as the Senator noted with barely concealed amazement, "were suffused with a certain poetical color" that made them something new and unique in the annals of government.

The Senator from Massachusetts was by no means alone in being impressed, not to say awed, by the recurrent strain of poetry in Abraham Lincoln. "This was like a sacred poem," said the German-American patriot Carl Schurz of the closing passage of the Second Inaugural Address. The message of sympathy to Mrs. Bixby on the loss of her sons in the Civil War came to be universally recognized as an exquisite little elegy in letter form, and the Gettysburg Address as a major American poem in prose.

With time the poetic element in Lincoln's writings has steadily gained ascendancy in interest and importance over their political content, and today scholars write of his speeches as "applied art" and discuss the "subtle rhythms and cadences" of his style, its "metrical effect" and his "lyrical passages." Of his most memorable lines, as of all great verse, it is now said that "they haunt the memory as much for their sound as their meaning."

Nothing, in short, sets Abraham Lincoln so distinctly apart from other great statesmen of history as this deep and abiding vein of pure poetry that runs all through his speeches, letters and papers. In electing him to office the American people unwittingly did what no other people before them had ever done. At the time of their most crucial testing and trial, when their very survival was at stake, they entrusted their national destiny to the hands of a poet.

There is a certain biographical irony in this. Abraham Lincoln thought himself a failure as a poet. To the end of his life he read the verses of others with profound respect and a wistful sense that the true poetic gift was beyond him. "I would give all I am worth, and go in debt, to be able to write so fine a piece as I think this is," he said of a minor poem which would by now be long forgotten except for his admiration of it. He would have been incredulous at the idea that he himself was a far greater poet than many of the writers whose work sustained and comforted him throughout his life.

There is no way to explain how a poet-statesman of world stature came to be born on the remote American frontier of the early nineteenth century, with nothing discernible in his ancestry or background to account for his coming. "Through one of those freaks of nature that produce a Shakespeare at long intervals," wrote Donn Piatt, an astute contemporary journalist, "a giant had been born to the poor whites of Kentucky." We can, however, roughly sketch the influences that nurtured the poet in him, and trace his more significant and seminal encounters with the poetry of others.

In the primitive settlements where Abraham Lincoln came to maturity—the little cluster of isolated cabins at Gentryville, in Indiana, and the hardly more impressive village of New Salem, in Illinois—"books wasn't as plenty as wildcats." The phrase is from Dennis Hanks, the boyhood companion and cousin who has left us a vivid account of Lincoln's early passion for searching out and devouring anything readable for miles around. Books were scarce, but even in those wild forest clearings, on the outer edges of civilization, the precious power of poetry made itself felt through scattered volumes of Shakespeare, Burns, Byron and, of course, the Bible.

From the constable at Gentryville, Lincoln borrowed *Scott's Lessons in Elocution* which contained selected passages from Shakespeare, and *The Arabian Nights* which he read aloud to his family. There were choice passages of English literature to be found in *The Kentucky Preceptor,* loaned to him by a local farmer named Josiah Crawford who was also wheelwright, doctor and dentist. The catalogue of the books that formed his youth is not long, but it is rich in values and instruction. It included also *Aesop's Fables, Pilgrim's Progress,* a *History of the United States,* Parson Weems' *Life of Washington* and Benjamin Franklin's *Autobiography*.

There were not only books, but men. In New Salem there was Jack Kelso, a feckless village character who passed his time fishing and drinking and avoiding work whenever possible. But Jack Kelso was one of those invaluable personalities who, though making no mark on the world for themselves, leave a lasting imprint on the lives of others. To Abraham Lincoln he opened up the joy of Burns and the wonder of Shakespeare.

Jack Kelso had read much and well, and what he read he savored and remembered. Of a pleasant summer's afternoon he would persuade young Lincoln to lock up the ramshackle store where he was serving as both clerk and postmaster, and come along to the river. In the shade of the willows on the shore, Jack Kelso would fish and drink corn whiskey and recite. Lincoln cared neither for fishing nor drinking, but he listened with inexhaustible fascination to Kelso's impromptu declamations from *Hamlet* and *Macbeth,* and to the melody and merriment of "Highland Mary" and "Tam O'Shanter." It is pleasant to know that a ravine to which the two men used to repair for their sessions of *al fresco* poetry has been christened "Kelso's Hollow" in lasting honor of the man who introduced Abraham Lincoln to two poets whom he was to treasure as long as he lived.

"He delighted in Burns," wrote John Hay, his White House secretary, many years later. Lincoln's modesty toward the poets he loved, and his enduring fondness for Robert Burns in particular, was expressed in a toast he penciled as President at the request of the Burns Club of Washington: "I cannot frame a toast to Burns; I can say nothing worthy of his generous heart and transcending genius; thinking of what he has said I cannot say anything which seems worth saying."

A young man so smitten by the poetry of others is all but certain to try his hand at verses of his own, and Lincoln did. His earliest efforts were doggerel of a comic cast that expressed the joking, fun-loving side of his character. He found the style congenial even as a grown man when he composed the twenty-two verses of "The Bear Hunt," a robust rhyme which, for all its crudities, has something of the flavor of a wilderness folk tale. He experimented more seriously in the melancholy vein of mid-century romanticism which corresponded to a deep and gothic strain in his nature, a fundamental sadness verging often on despair.

On a political speaking trip to Indiana in 1844 he visited the neighborhood of his boyhood where his mother and only sister were buried. "That part of the country is, within itself, as unpoetical as any spot on earth," he wrote his friend Andrew Johnston, a lawyer who also dabbled in verse. "But still, seeing it and its objects and inhabitants aroused feelings in me which were certainly poetry; though whether my expression of those feelings is poetry is quite another question. . . ."

He sent Johnston the resulting poem, which begins "My childhood's home I see again" and includes the verses:

> Near twenty years have passed away
>   Since here I bid farewell
> To woods and fields, and scenes of play,
>   And playmates loved so well.
>
> The friends I left that parting day,
>   How changed, as time has sped!
> Young childhood grown, strong manhood gray,
>   And half of all are dead.

This theme of the corrosion of time, of the decay of youth, of the fleetingness and futility of life with the inescapable grave at its end, was a favorite of his in what he called "my poetizing mood." He found it expressed in a way that moved him profoundly in a poem called "Mortality" which he came to prize above all others. He chanced upon it in an anonymous newspaper clipping and he repeated it from memory with the deepest emotion on innumerable occasions, to himself and to others, throughout his life.

The poem begins:

> Oh, why should the spirit of mortal be proud!
> Like a swift-fleeting meteor, a fast-flying cloud,
> A flash of the lightning, a break of the wave
> He passes from life to his rest in the grave.

The poem continues for thirteen more stanzas, paraphrasing the substance of the third chapter of Job and the first chapter of Ecclesiastes. It touches on the common fate of king and peasant, of the wise and the foolish, and stresses that there is no new thing under the sun. It concludes:

> 'Tis the wink of an eye, 'Tis the draught of a breath
> From the blossom of health to the paleness of death,
> From the gilded saloon to the bier and the shroud—
> Oh why should the spirit of mortal be proud!

This was the poem of which Lincoln said: "I would give all I am worth, and go in debt, to be able to write so fine a piece as I think this is." He quoted it so often that he was sometimes credited in print with being its author. For years he urgently sought to discover the name of the true author who, he said, "has been greatly my benefactor." He continued his search even in the White House in the midst of the Civil War and was at last rewarded. The author was found to be William Knox, a young Scottish poet who died in 1825.

Noah Brooks, the Washington correspondent who was also a warm friend of Lincoln's, recalled that the President was also "strongly impressed" by a poem of similar caliber called "The Weaver." One verse of it stayed in Brooks' mind for years afterward because Lincoln so often murmured it to himself, as in soliloquy:

> A weaver sat at his loom,
> Flinging his shuttle fast,
> And a thread that would wear till the hour of the doom
> Was added with every cast. . . .

This was another of those "waifs," as Brooks called them, which drifted through the newspapers of the time and which Lincoln used to seize on, cut out, and carry with him until he had them by heart. "The Weaver" was by Fanny Forrester, and went on to achieve its predestined place in *Best Loved Poems of the American People*. Among Lincoln's best-loved poetry were several other examples in the same lugubrious strain, including one that began "Tell me, ye winged winds" which he first encountered as he was walking down a street and chanced to overhear an unknown woman singing it. When the words were sent to him (rather romantically by the still-unknown woman), he kept them for years in an envelope on which he wrote: *Poem— I like this.*

It was perhaps a paradox of personality that Abraham Lincoln, himself capable of producing the deep organ tones of his major speeches, should have been so taken by the pensive twittering of such minor bards as Knox and Forrester. Lincoln's literary taste was surer in his admiration for Whitman, the Bible and Shakespeare.

As a rising lawyer and politician, Abraham Lincoln's earlier passion for general reading abated sharply. "The truth about Mr. Lincoln," his law partner William Herndon observed, with some exaggeration, "is that he read less and thought more than any man in his sphere in America." Lincoln himself is quoted as saying that he never finished a novel in his life. But his absorption in poetry remained.

On the circuit of the Eighth Judicial District in Illinois, while riding in his buggy over rutted country roads from courthouse to courthouse and stopping overnight at wretched country inns, the poets were his unfailing companions. He read the *Iliad* and the *Odyssey*, and had the Bible and Shakespeare always with him.

In his Springfield law office, one flight up and to the rear of
a brick building on the public square, discussions of poems and
poets were frequent. A casual visitor once picked up a handsome octavo volume lying on the green baize table and noticed
that it fell open by itself to the well-worn pages of Byron's
Don Juan. It was the "office copy," kept handy for Lincoln's use.
On another occasion a lively argument arose among clerks and
lawyers over the merits of a newly published work called *Leaves
of Grass* by an unknown named Walt Whitman. Lincoln remained silent during the dispute, sunk in one of his periodic
spells of gloom and withdrawal. After a time he reached out
for the book and paged through it. The argument was interrupted when he suddenly began reading aloud, revealing to his
listeners "a charm of new life in Whitman's versification." He
praised the poetry for its "vitality and freshness and unique
form of expression" and said that Whitman "gave promise of
a new school of poetry." He asked that *Leaves of Grass* be left
on the office table, and he frequently picked it up and read aloud
from it.

To the sweep and power of Walt Whitman's democratic trum-
petings Abraham Lincoln, himself a poet of democracy, could
not help responding. The two men never met but Whitman saw
Lincoln many times as President and wrote of him with warmth
and understanding, sensing in him that "vast dreaminess" of
outlook and idea which was so like his own, if so differently
expressed. And the day would come when Walt Whitman composed the four unforgettable poems he called "Memories of
President Lincoln," including one of the greatest ever written
in America, "When Lilacs Last in the Dooryard Bloom'd."

The poetry of the Bible, its language and imagery, were
among Lincoln's earliest literary impressions, and the most lasting. He constantly referred to it in his talks to juries, on the
political platform, in private letters. "There was not a clergyman
to be found so familiar with it as he," wrote one of his contemporary biographers, and the simplicity and grandeur of its style
permeates his greatest speeches and state papers. The key phrase
and basic theme of the speech that first brought him into national prominence—"A House Divided"—he took from the New
Testament. His underlying attitude toward slavery he repeatedly

expressed through the line from Genesis that says, "In the sweat of thy face shalt thou eat bread"—of *thy* face, he insisted over and over, and not in the sweat of other men's faces. In twenty-five speeches from 1839 to 1865, he alluded to the Bible no less than twenty-two times.

From his constant contact with poetry of every sort and quality over the years he caught that marvelous feel for phrase and language which was one of his most telling attributes in the fulfillment of his historic role. He found a satisfaction in the circumstance that the leading American poets of his day responded to this quality in him, besides supporting him politically. It was William Cullen Bryant, celebrated for his *Thanatopsis*, who introduced him to his first great Eastern audience at Cooper Institute in New York. Oliver Wendell Holmes, whose "The Last Leaf" he called "inexpressibly touching," was one of his staunch New England supporters. So was Henry Wadsworth Longfellow whose lines from "The Building of the Ship":

> Thou, too, sail on, O Ship of State!
> Sail on, O Union, strong and great!

moved the President to tears. John Greenleaf Whittier, whose collected verses were in Lincoln's library, wrote an antislavery hymn which was sung in the White House to the tune of Luther's "Ein' feste Burg ist unser Gott."

He never lost his relish for the crudely humorous and the grotesque, and he indulged his taste for them even in the most harrowing days of the Civil War as a means of relief and relaxation. He found endless delight in the odd conceits and comical quirks of the English versifier Thomas Hood, and often roamed the silent White House late at night searching for someone still awake with whom to share a passage that especially pleased him. Once a swarm of impatient applicants were left waiting outside his office door while he read aloud all ninety-six verses of Hood's "The Haunted House" to a spellbound group of friends. But we also know that he read and admired poetry by Edgar Allan Poe, James Russell Lowell, Nathaniel Parker Willis, and the elegies by Thomas Gray and Oliver Goldsmith.

More frequently than all others he read Shakespeare. He could recite from memory long passages of his favorite plays—*Lear,*

Richard III, Henry VIII, Hamlet and especially *Macbeth*—with a power and feeling that astonished those who heard him. "I think nothing equals *Macbeth*," he wrote the actor James Hackett. "It is wonderful." Some of Shakespeare's plays, he said, he had never read, "while others I have gone over perhaps as frequently as any unprofessional reader."

Allusions to Shakespeare, and quotations from the plays constantly colored his private conversation, and he carried with him battered copies of *Hamlet* and *The Merry Wives of Windsor* which he pulled out and read whenever opportunity offered. Shakespearean actors whose work he admired were invited to the White House to read favorite passages for him or discuss problems of interpretation, on which he had acute and unusual ideas of his own.

With Hackett and others he liked to argue that the King's soliloquy in *Hamlet* which begins:

> O my offense is rank, it smells to heaven;
> It hath the primal curse upon it . . .

was much superior to the more usually preferred "To be or not to be." "It always struck me as one of the finest touches of nature in the world," he said. After seeing Edwin Booth (the brother of John Wilkes Booth, the man who one day would kill him) as Shylock, the President observed to a friend: "It was a good performance, but I had a thousand times rather read it at home, if it were not for Booth's playing. A farce, or a comedy, is best *played;* a tragedy is best *read* at home."

He was fascinated by the opening lines of *Richard III*:

> Now is the winter of our discontent, etc.,

and believed that most actors delivered them with false emphasis and in the wrong style. They were, he held, an "utterance of the most intense bitterness and satire" but were usually spoken with a mere theatrical flourish. He once recited these lines for the benefit of Francis Carpenter, an artist, who said that they seemed "like a new creation" in the President's rendition. On another occasion he both startled and enthralled a lone telegrapher in the War Office by declaiming a long scene from

Macbeth "as if there had been a full house." His pronounced gift for reading from dramatic and poetical works made some of his listeners believe that, in other circumstances, he might have been an actor of extraordinary power.

But he was, of course, the protagonist in a tragedy that transcended in scope and stature anything ever put upon the stage. Walt Whitman, indeed, saw Lincoln's whole life as "a tragic play, superior to all else I know—vaster, more fiery and more convulsionary, for this America of ours, than Aeschylus or Shakespeare ever drew for Athens or for England." This note of high poetic tragedy that ran through Lincoln's life was sustained to the very end. With what now seems like an almost mystical vision of coming events, he singled out, six days before his death, the lines from his favorite *Macbeth* that might well have served as his own epitaph.

It was the 9th of April, 1865. The War Between the States had come to an end. Lincoln was returning from his visit to the still-smoking city of Richmond in Virginia. He sat on the sunny deck of the *River Queen* as she steamed serenely back toward Washington, utterly at ease for perhaps the first time in four long and bitter years. It was Palm Sunday, and at Appomattox Court House the Armies of the Confederate States were being surrendered to Gen. Ulysses S. Grant.

Abraham Lincoln sat slouched in his chair, his big hands fondling a "beautiful quarto volume of Shakespeare." From time to time he read aloud to the little party that accompanied him. All present remembered afterward that a certain passage he read not once, but twice, and seemed to linger broodingly over the words. The lines were those in which Macbeth speaks of Duncan's death by assassination:

> Duncan is in his grave;
> After life's fitful fever he sleeps well;
> Treason has done his worst: nor steel, nor poison,
> Malice domestic, foreign levy, nothing
> Can touch him further.

LINCOLN AS A MAN OF LETTERS

By Earl Schenck Miers

Earl Schenck Miers has written extensively on Lincoln and on the Civil War period. Among his numerous books are Gettysburg *(1948)* and The Great Rebellion *(1958). He edited (with Paul M. Angle)* The Living Lincoln *and* Poetry and Prose by Abraham Lincoln.

A BRAHAM LINCOLN possessed a rare ability to express his ideas and ideals. In letters, speeches, memoranda scribbled on scraps of paper, state papers, a few sentimental poems and even a mystery story, Lincoln left a record of himself that, exceeding a million words, would be longer than the Bible, including the Apocrypha, and longer than the complete works of Shakespeare. The discovery of the literate Lincoln is fascinating because it reveals the living Lincoln—this remarkable man who, one hundred and fifty years after his birth, is still so deeply a part of the nation's conscience that he explains why Americans often think and feel and act the way they do.

The key to Lincoln's power, both as a statesman and a man of letters, stems from one source. He never stopped growing in mental or moral stature. From early maturity to death he clung to the same principles and much the same ideas, and in his writings those principles and ideas became living organisms, growing with the man and changing not in substance but in beauty of form. As a result, Lincoln emerged as a man of a fundamental creed that expressed the responsibilities, risks and rewards of the democratic way of life. In whatever he wrote or said, he was always unpretentiously himself—always the self-taught lawyer who examined every proposition first by syllogism, then by how it related to patterns of human behavior, and finally as a man of ethics making a choice between right and wrong.

What were the ideas and the ideals that Lincoln, as a man of letters, bequeathed to humanity as the tenets of a faith in democracy? They are five:

First, he believed in people as the greatest resource of a nation.

Second, he believed in the right of the poor man, through honest toil, to better his lot in life.

Third, he believed in education—that regardless of color of skin or present environment, all people possessed the capacity to live fuller, richer lives if their innate abilities were cultivated.

Fourth, he believed that reverence for the laws should become a "political religion."

Finally, he believed in the liberal tradition; he was always a spokesman for freedom of thought, speech, press, assembly and religion.

The essence of Lincoln, both as a man of action and as a man of letters, is in these five tenets of faith. He was, really, a man of simple definition in an age of troublesome dilemmas, a man who in a stinging letter could fire the headstrong general of an army for usurping civilian authority or who in quiet repose could risk his political future upon the proposition that "the people, under Providence, will set all right."

Lincoln's strength in statement and action was in his clear and moral understanding both of himself and of his age. He never claimed that his ideas were original, nor were they; and his genius rested in perceiving that though he lived in a troubled world his generation had not invented the devil. From the beginning of time, he said, the world had struggled between two principles. One is the common right of humanity. And the other? "No matter in what shape it comes, whether from the mouth of a king who seeks to bestride the people of his own nation and live by the fruit of their labor, or from one race of men as an apology for enslaving another race, it is the same tyrannical principle."

Against such tyranny, in any guise, Lincoln spoke and wrote with passion. No man ever toiled with greater diligence to express in terms that a child could understand the simple moral answer to seemingly unfathomable complexities. He breathed his own life, the beauty of his own character, the splendid vitality of his own good heart into ideas as old as civilization. What might have been stale platitudes on the lips of other men, on Lincoln's lips burst like a sun of understanding. He touched the hearts of all classes and all ages. He articulated what they also knew was the only way in which right triumphed over wrong.

As a man of letters, perhaps more unconsciously than otherwise, Lincoln was influenced by his own group of heroes. He would have been the last to deny that he was moved by the political philosophy of Thomas Jefferson, who believed that "the earth belongs always to the living generation" and who said: "Nothing is unchangeable but the inherent and inalienable rights of man." Lincoln was always a stanch political supporter of Henry Clay, whose speeches were read by Simón Bolívar to armies fighting for freedom in South America.

Nor were Lincoln's literary models of lesser stature. Deeply versed in the fables of Aesop, Lincoln's own writings were filled with homely axioms. He advised a group of young lawyers: "Resolve to be honest at all events; and if in your own judgment you cannot be an honest lawyer, resolve to be honest without being a lawyer." As President, he told his Secretary of War: "On principle I dislike an oath which requires a man to swear he has not done wrong. It rejects the Christian principle of forgiveness on terms of repentance. I think it enough if the man does no wrong hereafter." America a hundred years ago included a large and growing population of persons who had fled from Europe to build new lives under freedom, and they understood the Lincoln who said: "In all that the people can individually do as well for themselves, government ought not to interfere."

Shakespeare had much to offer Lincoln—a sympathy with people of all ranks, a gift for language that communicated in homely, everyday, completely comprehensible images. Who could fail to understand a dramatist who spoke of the "cisterns" of our lust? Perhaps unconsciously, and yet unfailingly, Lincoln reduced his ideas to similar images. Thus for those who argued that labor and education are incompatible, "a blind horse upon a treadmill, is a perfect illustration of what a laborer should be

—all the better for being blind, that he could not tread out of place, or kick understandingly." Thus with the sick, stragglers, deserters and the discharged, an army never equaled its enlisted strength because "it's like trying to shovel fleas across a barnyard; you don't get them all there."

In knowing Lincoln as the man behind his words, one comes finally to the Holy Scriptures as the overpowering influence. He was a strangely mystical man, this Lincoln—who experienced the same dream before every climactic event of the war; who dreamed of himself as dead shortly before his assassination; and who, beholding a double image of himself in a mirror, accepted the explanation that he would live through one term as President but not the second. He could name the passages in both testaments of the Bible where dreams were prophetic. Of the Bible he said: "All things most desirable for man's welfare, here and hereafter, are to be found portrayed in it." Among Lincoln's greatest pronouncements is his Second Inaugural, delivered after almost four years of civil war. It is difficult to find a speech by any modern statesman so intensely religious in feeling; here speaks the Lincoln who believed passionately "that there is a God and that He hates injustice and slavery."

Lincoln, throughout his lifetime, was a prodigious letter writer. Angry letters—to his generals or members of his official family—he usually slept on, then neglected to send, but on those occasions when he did vent his spleen the recipient long remembered it. "I have just read your despatch about sore-tongued and fatigued horses," he once wrote a commanding general. "Will you pardon me for asking what the horses of your army have done since the Battle of Antietam that fatigues anything?" He would never, even in times of war, tolerate military interference with civil rights, telling another general: ". . . the U.S. government must not, as by this order, undertake to run the churches."

All of Lincoln is in his letters—his flashes of temper, his firmness, and also his great patience and tact, his dogged honesty and his enduring sympathy for people. His gift as a man of letters rested in the fact that throughout his life he was consistently himself. A note to a stationmaster said: "The lady bearer of this, says she has freight at the depot, which she cannot get without four dollars. If this be correct, let her have the freight, and I will pay you any amount not exceeding four dollars on presentation of this note." Five days later Lincoln paid the sum. A note told the War Department: "The lady—bearer of this—says she has two sons who want to work. Set them at it, if possible. Wanting to work is so rare a merit, that it should be encouraged." A note told a legal client: "You must think I am a high-priced man. You are too liberal with your money. Fifteen dollars is enough for the job. I send you a receipt for fifteen dollars, and return to you a ten-dollar bill."

Is it stretching a point in evaluating Lincoln's stature as a man of letters to include these everyday communications? Indeed, not! Other American statesmen, notably Thomas Jefferson and Woodrow Wilson, were scholars who wrote with a consciousness of literary style and method, whereas Lincoln, the master of them all, wrote with a consciousness of himself. He felt neither distinguished nor wise; without pose or pretension, he once informed a biographer: "It is a great piece of folly to attempt to make anything out of me or my early life. It can all be condensed into a single sentence, and that sentence you will find in Gray's Elegy: 'The short and simple annals of the poor.' That's my life, and that's all you or anyone else can make out of it."

LINCOLN'S IMAGERY

By Theodore C. Blegen

Dr. Theodore C. Blegen, Dean of the Graduate School, University of Minnesota, and a former President of the Mississippi Valley Historical Association, has written extensively on Lincoln. Among his books are Grass Roots History, The Land Lies Open *and* Norwegian Migration to America *(2 vols.).*

GREAT leadership, in the democratic world, is no trick of style, no device of words, no garment of rhetoric. It is mind and knowledge, character and experience, courage and devotion, oneness with the people, and a vision and imagination that rise above the "torment and the fray" of the passing hour. Man's character, as John Drinkwater says in the epilogue of his play *Abraham Lincoln,* endures and is a "token sent always to man for man's own government."

No single facet of the mind of Lincoln can explain the man and his role in his own day—and his enduring fame. It is the whole man, in the amplitude of his mind and character, who met greatly the crisis of civil war and who lives greatly in the memory of America and the world. But we can help turn the legend of Lincoln into the living reality of the man by looking at the words with which he clothed his thought and conviction. And one of the sustaining sources of his power was his imagery, with its wide range and unmistakable flavor.

While Lincoln was on his speaking trip in Connecticut in 1860, a Norwich minister, J. P. Gulliver, met him and told him that he had been impressed especially by the "illustrations"

Lincoln used in his speech at the town hall the evening before. The illustrations were "romance and pathos and fun and logic all welded together." Gulliver then asked Lincoln to explain his power of "putting things." In his reply Lincoln said, "I am never easy now, when I am handling a thought, till I have bounded it North, and bounded it South, and bounded it East, and bounded it West." Thus even in explaining his method, he resorted to imagery—as, in things great and small, he had done across the years—and doing so, he fittingly ran the very gamut of the compass.

James Russell Lowell made no mistake when he said that the secret of force in writing "lies not so much in the pedigree of nouns and adjectives and verbs, as in having something that you believe in to say, and making the parts of speech vividly conscious of it."

When one studies Abraham Lincoln's mastery of words, there is no difficulty in applying the first part of Lowell's aphorism. Lincoln had something to say that he believed in, and he said it with force. Hundreds of writers have showered his rhetorical power with friendly adjectives in their efforts to explain that force. He respected the meanings of words, and he wrote and spoke with clarity. He knew what he was talking about. He had consummate skill in logical analysis. He was able to put profound thoughts simply. He was sincere and earnest. He had both dignity and humor. He could rise to a lofty eloquence that has not been surpassed in the history of oratory. His language was pungent and he knew the art of timing. He was a master of balance and had an ear for rhythm.

All this and more can be and has been said about his writing, but at the end we are far from unlocking the secrets of his force, and we must consider the implications of the last part of Lowell's phrase. Lincoln patently succeeded in injecting the "parts of speech" with a vivid consciousness of what he had to say, and the question is, how did he do it?

The fundamental answer doubtless lies in the sum total of the man and his experience. Style may be the man, as Buffon has said, but even if this epigram is not wholly true, it is certain that style is not divorced from the man. Nor is the man divorced from his time and place. In Lincoln's case much of the lore of pioneer America was absorbed by the man as he lived his "prairie years"—and by an intelligence that remembered that lore down to its littlest details. It was gathered up, too, by a mind that grew through the prairie years in wisdom and in certain individual qualities that, as Paul M. Angle says, were faithfully mirrored in his words—notably his ruggedness, tenderness, tolerance, and humility.

No study of Lincoln's style can fail to take account of the fact that this was a great man. Great men often leave a tantalizing residuum of mystery even after thousands of books and articles have been written about them, as is unquestionably true of Lincoln. Apparent simplicity may cloak subtlety and complexity. The fibers of great strength and character may be so many and tangled that to identify and untangle them calls for an understanding almost matching that of the subject under analysis, just as a perfect translation of a poem demands a poet as translator.

Granting that the speech and writing of Lincoln reflect the man in the full range of his talents and in the sweep of both his prairie and his presidential years, it remains true that one aspect of his words seems in special degree to have made the "parts of speech vividly conscious" of what he wanted to say. Benjamin P. Thomas puts his finger on it when he says that "the chief charm of Lincoln's writings is in the quaint and homely figures of speech with which they abound." He also refers to Lincoln's "knack of clarifying an idea by a vivid metaphor or simile." The imagery assuredly helps to explain the charm of the Lincolnian style, but it does more. It illuminates Lincoln's power and persuasiveness in the use of words. It catches and reflects his curious interest in and knowledge of the world of everyday things about him. Viewed in its totality, it adds something to one's understanding of the intellectual and cultural resources of a central figure in the history of the modern world.

The homely quality in the style of Lincoln owes not a little to his familiarity with the earthiness of pioneer farming, of soil and implements and animals and produce. Who but the prairie statesman could have said as President, after completing an irksome task, "Well, I have got that job husked out"? Or what chief

executive, discounting his influence in the arena of his war secretary, could have confessed, "I don't amount to pig tracks in
the War Department"?

Lincoln did not scorn the saying that "broken eggs can never
be mended," but he adapted it in less conventional forms. In his
last speech, he said, "Concede that the new government of
Louisiana is only to what it should be as the egg is to the fowl,
we shall sooner have the fowl by hatching the egg than by smash-
ing it." Popular sovereignty, he once pointed out, "is to be
dished up in as many varieties as a French cook can produce
soup from potatoes." Of a speech stripped of trash and unnecessary words, he said that "all the chaff was fanned out of it." As
to himself, nobody, he thought, expected him to be President.
"In my poor, lean, lank face nobody has ever seen that any
cabbages were sprouting out."

Lincoln had a fondness for similes having to do with horses
and oxen. One of his most famous was his modest and brief
acceptance of renomination in 1864, in which he suggested that
the people "have concluded that it is not best to swap horses
while crossing the river, and have further concluded that I am
not so poor a horse that they might not make a botch of it in
trying to swap."

Great as is his interest in horses, he does not forget oxen.
There was a certain wisdom in his thanks that the "good Lord
has given to the vicious ox short horns, for if their physical
courage were equal to their vicious dispositions, some of us in
this neck of the woods would get hurt."

Bears, dogs, other animals, and bees and birds often came to
his mind as he sought telling comparisons. His political opponent, Douglas, was, of course, the victim of his sharpest gibes.
"I might as well preach Christianity to a grizzly bear as to preach
Jefferson and Jackson to him," he wrote in notes for a speech in
1858. When a group of visitors, after criticism of certain officials,
suggested to President Lincoln that he should replace them with
men whose loyalty, like their own, was unquestioned, he instantly replied, "Gentlemen, I see it is the same old, old coon.
Why could you not tell me at once that you wanted an office,
and save your own time as well as mine?" In mock alarm he
taunted Douglas in a Chicago speech by saying that he was "not

a dead lion, nor even a living one—he is the rugged Russian bear!"

In the campaign of 1864 General Grant made a characteristic decision that brought forth one of the most famous of Lincoln's picturesque sayings. "I have seen your despatch expressing unwillingness to break your hold where you are," wrote the President. "Neither am I willing. Hold on with a bulldog grip, and chew and choke as much as possible."

Now and then he spoke of snakes. Among several illustrations, the most vivid is from a speech in which he drew an elaborate picture of rattlesnakes on the prairie and in a bed where children were sleeping. In the latter case he cautioned that in striking at the rattlesnake, one might strike the children "or arouse the reptile to bite the children." And so he drew his moral, declaring that slavery "is the venomous snake in bed with the children." Given a choice between killing the rattlesnake on the prairie or putting it in bed with children, he dismissed the matter by saying, "I think we'd kill it." An impossible task he describes as an attempt "to penetrate the hard shell of a tortoise with a rye straw."

Plants, food, housekeeping, and clothing furnished many ideas to Lincoln for adroit figures that saved him from lengthy expositions of reasoning. "Would you drop the war where it is?" he wrote to a Louisiana man who complained of the war's interference with business. "Or, would you prosecute it in future with elder-stalk squirts, charged with rose water?"

At every great turning point in the career of Lincoln—indeed every national crisis in which he was concerned—his words of appeal and challenge were buttressed with metaphors. From the days of his youth until his final address as President he consistently used imagery to infuse the "parts of speech" with vividness and concreteness. And it is evident that his power grew steadily with his experience and responsibility.

Thus it is no chance circumstance that the addresses he delivered in the critical years just before the Civil War and during his presidency are illuminated by figures that time has woven into the American heritage. These figures, with perhaps a single exception, sprang from Lincoln's mind. They were written by his pen and uttered by his voice. It is part of the glory of Lincoln's words that they were in fact his, not the concoctions of ghost writers.

That part of the great "House Divided" speech at Springfield in 1858 which interested the entire country, according to Carl Sandburg, was its opening paragraph. What Lincoln said, in accepting the senatorial nomination, was "so plain that any two farmers fixing fences on a rainy morning could talk it over in all its ins and outs." And what he said was dramatized in imagery taken over from the Bible: "A house divided against itself cannot stand." Americans have never forgotten the prophetic words with which Lincoln expounded the meaning of the figure: "I believe this government cannot endure, permanently half slave and half free. I do not expect the Union to be dissolved—I do not expect the house to fall—but I do expect it will cease to be divided. It will become all one thing, or all the other." As these words sped across the land in daily and weekly newspapers, the people of the country began to realize that a national leader was emerging on the Illinois prairies. Imagery bore the man to the people. In America's "great variety" of local institutions Lincoln perceived, not "matters of discord," but the making of a house united, not divided.

The house figure fascinated Lincoln, as it did his hearers, and he used it again and again with remorseless pertinacity. In a fragmentary note for a speech he jotted down yet another comment on Douglas: "He shirks the responsibility of pulling the house down, but he digs under it that it may fall of its own weight."

When Lincoln took the oath of office a second time, he kissed the Bible at a passage in Isaiah that contained the words: "Whose arrows are sharp, and all their bows bent, their horses' hoofs shall be counted like flint, their wheels like a whirlwind." In the imagery of Lincoln there were the sharp arrow, the bent bow, the beat of the hoof, the flint, and, if not the wheels of the whirlwind, at any rate the wings of an imagination. The passage was apposite to a mind which, in its unending and flexible imagery, was in command of the "parts of speech," consistently, but with advancing force, making language serve its needs with vividness and precision.

LINCOLN AND MUSIC

By Carl Haverlin

Carl Haverlin, President of Broadcast Music, Inc., is a Trustee of Lincoln Memorial University and a member of the Abraham Lincoln Association, Illinois. He has written a radio series The Abe Lincoln Story *(with Harry Bedford Jones), and is a collector of Lincolniana.*

NO ONE would wish to attempt to increase the stature of Lincoln by claiming for him attributes he did not possess. Indeed it is refreshing to the student of Lincoln's life as it is to the casual reader to find that one who excelled in so many things was so fond of the music that was popular with the average man of his time. We would not, if we could, take this common touch away from him. It is, of course, beyond argument that he found great enjoyment in the ballads and the minstrel songs so carefully sought out and recorded by John Lair. He writes that if "Lincoln could not himself produce music, he had a soul for its appreciation. He was a great lover of music if not a lover of great music."

If we were to presume that the fifty-odd musical selections mentioned by Abraham Lincoln's contemporaries as having been heard or favored by him constituted the full extent of his musical appreciation, we would have to conclude, as does Mr. Lair in *Songs Lincoln Loved,* that "he had no fondness for the classics." For reasons that seem persuasive to me, I for one do not agree with Mr. Lair's limitations of Lincoln's musical tastes.

Lincoln was very modest about all his abilities and his personal appearance, but in matters concerning letters, the arts and music, his modesty became downright self-depreciation. But from a few shreds of evidence, we discover that on occasion, at least, he could exert sound critical judgment. In acknowledging the gift of a statuette in 1864 from John Rogers, its sculptor, Lincoln wrote, "I cannot claim to be a judge in such matters," and goes on to term the group "very pretty and suggestive and, I should think, excellent as a piece of art." Qualified critics, in agreement with Lincoln, point out how easily he might have overelaborated his praise. In his letter to the well-known Shakespearean actor, James H. Hackett, Lincoln is apologetic: "For one of my age, I have seen very little of the drama"—though it is generally agreed that he knew the theatre well and attended whenever he had the opportunity to do so. Those who were close to him testify that he had committed a number of Shakespeare's plays to memory. Despite his real knowledge of the plays, after stating he preferred the King's soliloquy to Hamlet's "To be or not to be," he asks Hackett's pardon for "this small attempt at criticism." Some students of *Hamlet* have agreed with Lincoln's preference.

I have not been able to find any positive evidence that Lincoln disliked the classics. To his friends and contemporaries, like Ward Hill Lamon whose musical abilities were bounded by wholly popular "little ditties," he was considered a lover of their simple repertoire. Since Lincoln seemed to hold William Knox's poem "Immortality" in equal embrace with *Macbeth,* it is irresistible to argue that he would have liked the music of Mozart no less than "Kathleen Mavourneen." B. H. Haggin suggests interestingly enough in his book *Music for the Man Who Enjoys "Hamlet,"* that if one is not as susceptible to a Beethoven sonata as to a play by Shakespeare, it is only because one is not so familiar with the music as with the drama.

This brings us to the fact that Lincoln had little opportunity to learn to love *great* music, for he could have heard none in Kentucky and Indiana. Even in his later years in Illinois, on his occasional out-of-state trips on political missions, and during his years in Washington as a Congressman and as President, the occasions on which he could have heard such music were few and far between.

So that we may place Lincoln's musical tastes in perspective, we must realize that it was not until 1825, when he was sixteen years old, that New York heard its first Italian opera—*The Barber of Seville*; that the New York Philharmonic Society was not founded until 1842 when he was thirty-three; and the country's first formal chamber music organization, the Mendelssohn Quintet, gave its first performance in Boston in 1850, when he was forty-one.

It is as tempting as, of course, it is fruitless to speculate as to what Lincoln's musical tastes would have been had he been born and brought up in New York, Philadelphia, Boston, Cincinnati or New Orleans where operas and concert music were often heard and where the well-to-do in their homes could indulge their trained musical appetites.

We know how zealously Lincoln sought out great books and made them so much his own that they became a living part of his intellectual processes. It can be assumed that the young man who could delight as he did in the majestic poetry of the Bible, Shakespeare and Homer would have had equal appreciation for the music of Mozart, Beethoven and Bach had it been available to him. If, as has been said so well, his reading helped Lincoln to become one of the lords of language, then surely the repeated hearing of their compositions would have helped him to become a master of music.

Indeed the contrast between his known musical and literary favorites not only underscores the fact that the enjoyment of great music is a communal act, while the enjoyment of reading is a solitary one, but it also brings into focus some aspects of life in the frontier while he grew up.

A saying popular with the American pioneers—"Guns and grub are easier packed than tarradiddle and tub"—was used to explain the Spartan furnishings of their homes. These words or something like them must have been spoken by many a man to his wife as she bade a tearful farewell to her "nice" things before moving from the Eastern seaboard to new lands: over the Cumberland Trail to settle Kentucky, Indiana and Illinois, and later to trickle out over the prairies and the deserts across the mountains to the far Pacific.

Left behind with the ottoman, whatnot, pictures, gewgaws and mirrors were the larger instruments of the orchestra, the piano, the melodeon and their printed music. Only the fiddle, flute and the small guitar might have been snugged down among the blankets, kettles and bare necessities of life. Even the banjo would have been missing when the Lincolns first moved into Indiana from Kentucky, for it was not invented until 1831. Those who could play these few instruments had memorized their small repertories of traditional folk songs, the mournful ballads, simple hymns and the ever-popular nonsense songs that we know Lincoln heard over and over again as he grew older.

First editions of most of the forty-odd songs established as Lincoln's favorites are in the archives of Broadcast Music, Inc., in New York. They are all attractive, albeit most of them are curiously sad and melancholy.

John Lair lists in his book no song as being a favorite of Lincoln's for which he has not found some trustworthy source. Among those that are still popular today are "Barbara Allen," "Ben Bolt," "Dixie's Land," "Gentle Annie," "Hail Columbia," "Home, Sweet Home," "The Blue Tail Fly," "Lorena," "Old Dan Tucker," "Rock Me to Sleep, Mother," and "Turkey in the Straw."

From a practical standpoint, however, it is difficult to believe that Lincoln, with his love for the sentimental, would not have been equally as fond of many of the charming songs that appeared during his life, such as "Woodman, Spare That Tree," "Annie Laurie," "The Old Arm Chair," "Long, Long Ago," "Old Folks at Home" and "Old Kentucky Home."

There are many indications that as opportunity offered itself, he made every effort to hear all the music he could. While serving as a member of Congress in 1848, Lincoln attended some of the concerts given by the Marine Band on the Capitol grounds. In a letter to his wife dated July 2 of that year, he mentions that interest in them is "dwindling down to nothing." What sort of music was performed there we have not so far discovered, but it was probably a combination of arrangements of the classics and the popular.

On Lincoln's trip to his inauguration he went to the opera in New York to hear Verdi's *Ballo in Maschera*. Eyewitnesses said he enjoyed the performance and applauded vigorously. A few months later, at a concert in the Navy Yard in Washington, he was to hear Dodsworth's famous band give a rendition of a fantasy on that opera together with the finale of *La Traviata,* the Miserere from *Il Trovatore* and Mendelssohn's "I Would That My Love." Among operas that he heard were Gounod's *Faust* and Boieldieu's *La Dame Blanche.*

Mr. and Mrs. Lincoln made it a habit to invite to the White House many of the famous artists who appeared in Washington. On one such occasion he told Adelina Patti that he had heard her sing as a child prodigy, probably in Chicago. In her reminiscences of that occasion, Patti mentions only one song of her program, "Home, Sweet Home," though it is difficult to believe she did not also offer at least some of her brilliant arias as well.

William H. Townsend once saw a letter written by an officer (he believes it was General Schurz) who wrote of playing the piano for Lincoln at the White House. Lincoln told him how much he was moved by the music.

There are some who believe that Lincoln's own testimony should be accepted as indication of his musicality. They point, for example, to the report made by the well-known singer, Lillie De Hegermann-Lindencrone, of her meeting at the White House. The President told her that "music is not much in my line, but when you sing, you warble yourself into a man's heart.... I think I might become a musician if I heard you often, but so far I know only two tunes." He said that one was "Hail Columbia" and that he remembered that because he had to stand up and remove his hat when it was sung. Asked about the other one, he hedged a bit concerning the title, saying merely—with a smile—that it was the song for which he did not have to stand up. It is my opinion that this conversation should not be taken too literally, but as further indication of Lincoln's self-depreciation.

Many who have studied his writings and his life are in agreement that his tremendous sensitivity alone would inevitably have led him to the fullest appreciation of the music of Bach, Beethoven and Mozart. It is to be hoped that continuing research into the manuscripts and memoirs of Lincoln's contemporaries will lead to further evidence in support of these logical contentions, and reveal even more clearly the man who is the most unforgettable American the world has known.

LINCOLN, HUSBAND AND FATHER

By Richard N. Current

Dr. Richard N. Current, Professor of History and Head of the Department of History and Political Science, The Woman's College of the University of North Carolina, has written a number of books on Lincoln, among them Lincoln the President; Last Full Measure *(with J. G. Randall) for which he received the Bancroft Prize in 1956. His latest book,* The Lincoln Nobody Knows, *appeared in 1958.*

L INCOLN'S home life was a "domestic hell," according to his law partner, William H. Herndon. In Herndon's view, Lincoln never really loved his wife, Mary Todd. His one true love was the backwoods beauty Ann Rutledge, whom he knew and courted when a young man in New Salem, Illinois. After Ann's untimely death he never ceased to grieve for her. He finally took Mary Todd as his wife only because she trapped him into marriage. Indeed, he failed to appear at his own wedding the first time it was scheduled. Once the wedding finally was held, he became a henpecked husband. Often he was saddled with the care of the children she bore him, and he looked after them in an affectionate, overindulgent, and abstracted way. His unhappiness at home helped to account for his eventual rise to fame. To get away from his ill-tempered wife, he devoted himself to the law and to politics far more seriously than he otherwise would have done. Had it not been for Mrs. Lincoln, he might never have set out on the path that led to the presidency, and so the American people owe her a debt of gratitude.

That version of Lincoln's marriage is far from the true one, but it must be mentioned because it appears in countless stories, plays, movies, and radio and television programs, as well as works ostensibly based upon historical fact. It is still widely believed. Yet Herndon, the man responsible for it, though he worked with Lincoln in their Springfield law office for seventeen years, never set foot inside the Lincoln house and never heard Lincoln speak of his feelings toward either Ann Rutledge or Mary Todd. Herndon based his account on his own "intuition" and on the remembered gossip of some of Lincoln's New Salem and Springfield acquaintances.

When, after Lincoln's death, Herndon first told his story of the Ann Rutledge romance, Mrs. Lincoln declared she had never heard of Ann. "My husband was truth itself," the widow protested, "and as he always assured me he had cared for no one but myself . . . I shall . . . remain firm in my conviction that *Ann Rutledge* is a myth—for in all his confidential communications such a romantic name was never breathed." Of course, Ann Rutledge was not entirely a myth, for she actually lived—and died. But Lincoln's affection for her was exaggerated beyond all reality in the recollections of some of those who had known her.

In truth, Lincoln did not desert Mary Todd on her wedding day, though he did break his engagement to her and afterward was reluctant to renew it and go through with the marriage. The reason was not that he doubted his love for her but rather that he feared he could not make her happy. She was nearly ten years younger than he and was in many ways his exact opposite. She was gay, quick-witted, and talkative, sometimes charming, sometimes sharp-tongued. A member of an aristocratic Kentucky family, she was better educated than most young ladies of her time and place. In Springfield, where she lived with a married sister, she had plenty of admirers, and her sister advised her that she could do much better than to marry a man so awkward, ill-bred, and unpromising as Lincoln. Yet the headstrong Mary, in love with him, quickly accepted when he proposed. At the wedding he indicated his devotion to her by placing on her finger a ring on the inside of which were engraved the words: *Love is eternal.*

The married life of the Lincolns lasted about twenty-two and a half years. During the last few of those years Lincoln unquestionably had serious difficulties with his wife. She seemed to lose her sense of values, at least money values, and ran into embarrassing debts. And she staged some painful scenes of wifely jealousy. In 1865, for example, when she with her husband was visiting Grant's army near Richmond, she flew into a rage when she learned that he had ridden side by side with two officers' wives at a military review.

By that time, Mary was no longer quite herself. She had suffered unbearable afflictions in the death of her favorite son, in the ironics of war that made enemies of Kentucky relatives and friends, and in the unfair criticisms of her as mistress of the White House. These experiences aggravated her nervousness, her feelings of insecurity, her lack of self-control. She was beginning to show signs of the insanity which was to engulf her in the lonely years of her widowhood after her husband had been murdered at her side. In that long time of sadness the thing she treasured most was the memory of her love for him and his love for her.

During the first twenty years or so of their marriage, Mr. and Mrs. Lincoln had occasional tiffs. These sometimes were exacerbated by her fits of temper. A Springfield neighbor recalled having once seen Mary with a kitchen knife in her hand chasing her husband down the street. Another neighbor, James Gourley, reported that at times "Mrs. L. got the devil in her," and then Lincoln "would pick up one of his children and walk off, would laugh at her, pay no earthly attention to her when in that wild furious condition." But Gourley sympathized with Mrs. Lincoln. He knew she was lonely by day and terrified by night during Lincoln's long absences on the lawyer's circuit. "She always said that if her husband had stayed at home as he' ought to that she could love him better." Yet Gourley declared that "Mr. and Mrs. Lincoln were good neighbors" and that most of the time they got along very well with one another.

On the whole, the married life of the Lincolns for the first twenty years was pretty much like that of most normal, devoted American couples of the mid-nineteenth century. Abraham and Mary were fond of one another's company and missed each other when apart. There is ample evidence of this in the letters the two exchanged in 1848, while he was a Congressman in Washington and she, with their boys, was visiting relatives in Kentucky. As parents, the Lincolns had a mutual affectionate interest in the doings and the welfare of the children. Touchingly, Mrs. Lincoln reassured their father that they had not forgotten him during their absence from him.

Altogether, four sons were born to the Lincolns: Robert Todd (1843), Edward Baker (1846), William Wallace (1850), and Thomas, known as Tad (1853). "I regret the necessity of saying I have no daughters," Lincoln once wrote. For him, fatherhood brought other and more serious disappointments than the nonappearance of a daughter.

Two of his sons died before him, one in Springfield and the other in the White House. When little Eddie died, in 1850, Lincoln sank into the depths of melancholy, from which he was saved by the necessity of caring for the mother, even more shaken than he. Afterwards Lincoln rented a pew in the First Presbyterian Church and began to attend religious services regularly for the first time in his life. At the death of Willie, in 1862, Lincoln grieved even more deeply—as deeply as the boy's mother, though not so madly. Again and again he shut himself in a room to weep alone. Nights he dreamed happy dreams of Willie, then awakened to the joyless reality of day. Eagerly he listened to the assurances of clergymen who came to tell him and his wife that the boy was not dead, that he still lived, in heaven.

Of the remaining two boys, Lincoln found much companionship in lovable, lisping Tad, who became more precious than ever after Willie's death. Lincoln's concern for Tad (and his belief in dreams) is shown in a telegram he sent Mrs. Lincoln on June 9, 1863. She had gone to Philadelphia and had taken the ten-year-old boy with her. "Think you had better put 'Tad's' pistol away," Lincoln said in the telegram. "I had an ugly dream about him."

Lincoln was always rather remote in spirit from the first-born, Robert Todd, the only one of the children to survive to manhood. Robert Todd Lincoln died in 1926 after a distinguished career as Secretary of War (1881–1885), minister to England (1889–1893), and president of the Pullman Company (1897–1911). Somehow Robert never learned to know and love his father. As a young man of twenty-one, when asked about the

previous life of the newly famous Lincoln, Robert stated: "My
Father's life was of a kind which gave me but little opportunity
to learn the details of his early career. During my childhood and
early youth he was almost constantly away from home, attending
courts or making political speeches." Lincoln, it would seem,
was practically a stranger to this son of his. During all the years
of Robert's adult life he moved in the reflected light of his
father's fame. It has been suggested that Lincoln, dead, had more
influence upon his eldest son than ever while alive.

One can only speculate about the causes of the estrangement
between Lincoln and the boy. Robert may have been affected by
jealousy of his younger brothers. Before the first of them was
born, Robert had been the center of attention for nearly three
years. The coming of a new baby may have been for him, as it
has been for many an erstwhile only child, a traumatic experience. Writing to a friend, several months after the birth of
Robert's brother, Lincoln casually noted that Robert had run
away, had been found and whipped by his mother, and was
expected any minute to run away again. Even when Robert was
at that tender age, Lincoln seemed to have toward him an attitude somewhat different from that of a proud and enthusiastic
father. Referring to the boy as rather short in stature and full of
"mischief" and "animal spirits," Lincoln wrote as if with a touch
of disapproval: "He is quite smart enough. I some times fear he
is one of the little rare-ripe sort, that are smarter at about five
than ever after."

The death of Robert's rival, Eddie, when Robert was seven,
seems to have caused the parents to be excessively lenient with
the next two children. These boys always did about as they
pleased. Herndon recalled that Lincoln sometimes brought one
or both of them in a little wagon downtown with him and allowed them to play in the law office. "The children—spoilt ones
to be sure—would tear up the office, scatter the books, smash up
pens, spill the ink...." So wrote Herndon, who often felt like
wringing their necks.

Herndon considered Lincoln a rather ineffective parent, entirely too weak in discipline. By the standards of the time, to
which Herndon adhered, Lincoln doubtless was insufficiently
strict. By the standards of the twentieth century, with its "per-

missive" attitude toward children, at least in the United States, he was a good enough, easygoing father. Certainly he was fond of both boys and girls, and they of him. In dealing with them he was sympathetic and understanding (though with some qualifications in the case of his son Robert). During his struggles as a rising lawyer and politician, and still more during his terrible responsibilities as wartime President, his family was for him a joy and a comfort that only he could adequately measure.

Undoubtedly there was a close connection between Lincoln's home life and his public career. But it seems a mistake to suppose, as Herndon and others have done, that unhappiness at home sent Lincoln out to achieve success in law and politics. Probably the true relationship between his domestic and his public life was just the reverse. That is, Lincoln to some extent neglected his family in his pursuit of political success, and when at last he won the highest reward in American politics, he brought upon his wife the unendurable strains of wartime living in the White House. Thus his strivings as a public man were more a cause than a result of his difficulties as a husband.

LINCOLN IN SHIRT SLEEVES

By Benjamin Barondess

Benjamin Barondess, a member of the bar of New York State, is Past Vice-President and Director of The Civil War Round Table of New York. Among his books is Three Lincoln Masterpieces (*1955*).

CARL SCHURZ, an 1848 émigré from Germany, who fought in the Civil War as a brigadier general and ultimately rose to a place in the President's cabinet and to office as ambassador to Spain, met Lincoln on a train one day. He has drawn this picture for us:

There he stood, overtopping by several inches all those surrounding him. Although measuring something over 6 feet myself, I had, standing quite near to him, to throw my head backward in order to look into his eyes. Lincoln's face was swarthy, features strong and deeply furrowed, eyes benignant and melancholy. His face was clean shaven and looked even more haggard and careworn than later, when it was framed in whiskers. On his head, Lincoln wore a somewhat battered stove-pipe hat. His neck emerged long and sinewy, from a white collar turned down over a thin black necktie. His lank, ungainly body was clad in a rusty black dress-coat with sleeves that should have been longer; but his arms appeared so long that the sleeves of a "store-coat" could hardly be expected to cover them all the way down to the wrists. His black trousers, too, permitted a full view of his large feet. On his left arm he carried a gray woolen shawl, which evidently served him for an overcoat in chilly weather. His left hand held a cotton umbrella of the bulging kind and also a black satchel that bore the marks of long and hard usage. His right hand he kept free for hand-shaking, of which there was no end until everybody in the car seemed to be satisfied. I had seen in Washington and in the West, several public men of rough appearance; but none whose look seemed quite so uncouth, not to say grotesque, as Lincoln's.

There is another picture of Lincoln drawn by a fellow lawyer named Whitney, which corroborates the fact that Lincoln was a man who cared naught for externals; he was more concerned with the great ends of life: liberty and democracy. Whitney says:

His mobile face ranged, in modes of expression, through a long gamut; it was rare that an artist could catch the expression, and Lincoln's face was of that kind that the expression was of greater consequence than the contour of the features. . . .

He probably had as little taste about dress and attire as anybody that ever was born; he simply wore clothes because it was needful and customary; whether they fitted or looked well was entirely above or beneath his comprehension.

Lincoln was no ordinary man. There has never been another like him. He was and has remained an original.

As for his personal habits, Joshua Speed, who owned a general store in Springfield, and was his closest friend, tells us:

In all his habits of eating, sleeping, reading, conversation and study, he was regularly irregular; that is, he had no stated time for eating, no fixed time for going to bed, none for getting up.

Lincoln was a fitful sleeper and arose early. He would then often walk alone across the White House lawn to find a newsboy and buy the morning newspapers. By 8 A.M., when breakfast was served, he had already been toiling at his desk for an hour. Meals were interruptions to him. Breakfast would consist of an egg and a cup of coffee. Lunch would be similarly Spartan—a raw apple and a glass of milk. Dinner would involve greater consumption of food under Mrs. Lincoln's watchful eye and urging. In fact, she often had guests to dine at the White House, to make certain that he would eat and thereby conserve his strength.

Of his modesty and humility, there were many witnesses. Relatives and close personal friends were not allowed to call him

"Mr. President." Such a formality he reserved for strangers and
for official visitors. To intimates, it was always either "Mr. Lincoln" or just plain "Lincoln." Secretary of the Treasury Salmon
P. Chase and Senator Charles Sumner of Massachusetts both
found him blacking his own boots. In the late evening hours, his
feet encased in worn slippers and his body draped in a faded old
dressing gown, he would relax in the company of close friends.
Nothing of self-importance or grandeur attached to him. The
case for the use of the slippers, an almost daily practice, arose
from the corns with which he was afflicted. The long legs often
were elevated to the desk top, where they rested, allowing him
to recline at ease. In fact, during the Civil War, he could often
be seen at the window of his office in the White House, gazing
through a telescope, one end of which was at his eye and the
other resting on his stockinged feet which were propped on the
window sill, to observe enemy fortifications across the Potomac
River.

The humility of Lincoln began early in life and remained
with him to the end. Thus, when he ran for his first public office,
in 1832, seeking election to the Illinois House of Representatives, and lost ("the only time he was ever defeated by the
people") the opening announcement of his campaign contained
this statement:

I am young, and unknown to many of you. I was born, and have
ever remained, in the most humble walks of life. I have no wealthy
or popular relations to recommend me.

Twenty-seven years later, in 1859, after he had reached years
of maturity and had won the nomination of the Republican
Party for the presidency, he replied to a request for a campaign
autobiography, made by his close friend Jesse W. Fell, in these
modest words:

Herewith is a little sketch, as you requested. There is not much of
it, for the reason, I suppose, that there is not much of me. If anything
be made out of it, I wish it to be modest.

Lincoln almost never smoked tobacco or drank liquor.
Though one of the nation's greatest orators, strangely enough

he did not possess the sonorous tenor or baritone voice that actors who impersonate him employ. On the contrary, his was of a high-pitched, even piercing quality that occasionally rose to a treble; yet withal, it reached to the outermost fringe of the crowd listening to him.

Lincoln had a gift for pithy, epigrammatic expression. To those who refused to trust the common sense of the voters, he is said to have warned: "You can fool some of the people all the time; and all the people some of the time; but you can't fool all the people all the time." As for those who sought to discredit him in the public eye, by accusing him of advocating social and political equality of whites with slaves, Lincoln replied that, though the slave was not his civic or political equal, yet "in the right to eat the bread that he earns with the sweat of his own brow, he is my equal, and the equal of every other white man."

Lincoln had a complex character. He was a man of many moods. He alternated between periods of elation and deepest gloom. "I laugh because I must not cry; that's all," he told friends. He believed in dreams, all of which had a portent of doom about them. He had a penchant for poems and songs which dealt with the futility of life and the inevitability of death. One of them, "Mortality" by William Knox, was a favorite. It began: "O why should the spirit of mortal be proud?"

Herndon, Lincoln's law partner, said of him:

He was a sad-looking man; his melancholy dripped from him as he walked. . . . He was gloomy, abstracted and joyous—rather humorous—by turns; but I do not think he knew what real joy was for many years.

Milton H. Shutes writes:

He seemed to shed tears easier than most men. He wept so uncontrollably at the funeral of his old friend, Squire Green, of New Salem, that he was unable to proceed with the eulogy. He cried over poetry, over beautiful singing and instrumental music, over Sunday School children, mourning homes, the slaughter of soldiers, and even at the sight of their marching.

On the other hand, examples of his wit and humor are legion. In a note to Major Ramsay, October 17, 1861, he wrote:

The lady—bearer of this—says she has two sons who want to work. Set them at it, if possible. Wanting to work is so rare a want that it should be encouraged.

In a message to Secretary of War Simon Cameron, November 13, 1861, he wrote:

Please have the Adjutant General ascertain whether 2nd. Lieutenant of Co. D. 2nd. Infantry—Alexander E. Drake, is not entitled to promotion. His wife thinks he is.

When stricken with variola, a mild form of smallpox, while besieged in the White House by hordes of office seekers, Lincoln told his secretaries, with relief, that he was happy, for "Now I have something I can give everybody." A group of clergymen presented to Lincoln an address in which they called him "a pillar of the church." He replied: "You would have done better to call me a steeple."

It is related that a young man came to Lincoln to thank him for an appointment as American Consul at a South-American port. The nominee was dressed in the height of fashion. It appeared the office was not altogether a joy to the young man. He told the President: "I can't say I'm so very glad of this appointment after all. I hear they have bugs down there that are liable to eat me up inside of a week." Replied Lincoln: "Well, young man, if they do, they'll leave behind them a mighty good suit of clothes."

One of the greatest afflictions the kindhearted Lincoln had to suffer was the persistence with which his generals demanded the death penalty for soldiers who had violated some rule of war. But he went right on pardoning the unhappy victims. To one commander who wanted a deserter shot, Lincoln said: "Can he help it if he has a pair of cowardly legs that run away with the rest of him?"

In his domestic life, Lincoln was a devoted husband and father. True, he annoyed his wife, Mary. He came to table in shirt sleeves; he read a book lying on the floor of the hallway of his home, his head and back propped up on an overturned chair; similarly reclining, he dangled his babies overhead; he answered the doorbell to two haughty ladies, who came to call on Mrs.

Lincoln, likewise in shirt sleeves, and not yet content, announced to them in street parlance that he "would trot the women folks out." To counter the parsimoniousness of his wife, he secretly paid the housemaid one dollar per week extra, as salary. What his wife would have said, had she discovered this, can be imagined, for she had a fiery temper. Yet she practiced economy with cause. Coming as she did from a home of wealth, it must have required the self-control of a Stoic for her to take up married life at the Globe Tavern in Springfield, Illinois, where board and lodging came to four dollars per week.

The four children, all boys, were notoriously spoiled. Lincoln worshiped them. While practicing law at Springfield, he could be seen on winter mornings, walking to market, basket in arm, an old gray shawl around his neck, with little Tad or Willie at his heels, both of them propounding questions which the father was too abstracted to hear. On Sunday mornings when Mary went to church, the neighbors would see Lincoln pulling a little wagon behind him, with his babies in it, reading absorbedly an open book which he held in his hand. Once, a youngster fell out and lay crying in the street, but the father kept on, completely oblivious. There was, however, one who was no sharer of Lincoln's partiality for his children. That was his law partner, Herndon. When Willie or Tad came to the office of the firm, the papers of clients would go flying to the floor, inkwells would be overturned, lawbooks would be stripped of pages, all to the steadily rising anger of Herndon, accentuated by the peals of laughter the children's antics provoked in Lincoln. To Herndon, they were brats, whose necks he was often tempted to wring.

There came a time when Lincoln felt he must take some action which would strengthen the army, weaken its opponents, and also right a great moral wrong. On September 22, 1862, he summoned his cabinet to hear his proposal. But there was something that needed to be overcome, first. The tension he felt had to be eased. He needed it; and his cabinet would also need it. So Lincoln resorted to a characteristic maneuver. He took up a book by Artemus Ward, a noted humorist, and read from it a chapter entitled "High-Handed Outrage at Utica," a hilarious account of an attack by a simpleton on a wax figure, which he had mistaken for a human being, Judas Iscariot.

The story drew laughter from Lincoln as he read aloud, and even from some of the cabinet members. The others were annoyed at what seemed to them an undignified proceeding. But the maneuver succeeded. The tension Lincoln had suffered was gone; the cabinet could hear his proposal to strike at slavery in an atmosphere of relaxation.

The Emancipation Proclamation was issued by Lincoln. A great wrong was righted. Yet the sad man who set in motion the chain of events that brought this about, had to have his laugh first. As the poet Hartley Coleridge said:

> And laughter oft is but an art
> To drown the outcry of the heart.

LINCOLN IN LITERATURE

By Roy P. Basler

Dr. Roy P. Basler, Director of the Reference Department, Library of Congress, is the editor of The Collected Works of Abraham Lincoln (*9 vols., 1953–1955*) *and the author of* The Lincoln Legend (*1935*) *and* Abraham Lincoln: His Speeches and Writings (*1946*).

THE river of Lincoln literature flows undiminished. From 1860, the year of Lincoln's nomination for his first term as President, to the present, there have been few low-water marks, but numerous flood stages, testifying to the emotional, some-times idolatrous, hero-worship of writer and reading public. One must wonder at the personality of the man which is the source of so much narrative, speculation, and interpretation, as well as at the symbolic significance which the Lincoln story has attained as a kind of national epic.

It is difficult now to comprehend the wave of hero-worship which swept over the country after Lincoln's assassination. In reality the tide had already set in before, and his death was but an opening of the floodgates of emotion. The state of the public mind was then, as it has always been, somewhat delirious after a period of war and national stress. Human society must have, it seems, periods of emotional unbalance even during quiet times. So at a period when the nation's emotions were all but out of control, when half a million soldiers were dead in their uniforms and 30,000,000 people were so spent with grief that no man could be quite sane any more, it is not surprising that the entire populace reverted in its mental processes to something common to the childhood of race—the creation of a hero-myth. Drunk with success, the North was ready to apotheosize the leader who had preserved the Union and abolished slavery.

As Lloyd Lewis delineated in his remarkable book *Myths After Lincoln,* Lincoln was suddenly lifted into the sky as the folk-hero, the deliverer, and the martyr who had come to save his people and to die for them. Day by day the impression grew that Lincoln had been the chosen one of God. Those who had known him told everything they had known which was in keeping with the memory of a martyr.

The first biographies of Lincoln, published shortly after his nomination in 1860, were very brief and generally of little permanent significance. The first widely read biography, William M. Thayer's *The Pioneer Boy,* was 90 per cent fiction and extremely laudatory. The first realistic life, a biography (1872) by Lincoln's friend Ward H. Lamon, met with such disfavor that only the first volume was published, and the effort of Lincoln's law partner, William H. Herndon, to record the "real" Lincoln he had known resulted in one of the most controversial books ever published in the United States, *Herndon's Lincoln* (1889).

In spite of the good intentions of many biographers, the early life of Lincoln never received an adequate and understanding treatment until more than fifty years after his death, at the hand of the poet Carl Sandburg. Sandburg realized what others had failed to grasp—that knowledge of the early life of Lincoln is based so largely on the popular opinion, anecdote, and detail of those who knew him, that if any of these should be credited, all or nearly all of them should be woven into a panoramic tapestry of frontier life. Sandburg's biography gave for the first time the story of Lincoln's rise from poverty and obscurity in a manner that comprehended the true epic significance of the subject matter. There have been other biographers and poets who saw, or thought they saw, epic material in the early life of Lincoln. They have failed to grasp or present it, chiefly because they have attempted to make it epical in some classic fashion. Other biographers had seen little except the commonplace and morbid or had sought only for those elements which foreshadowed the statesman, and thus presented either a bald or a gilded account, both incorrect.

Biographers have generally failed to formulate an acceptable conception which embodies both the private and the public Lincoln. Agreement is far more commonly found in the assessments of the public Lincoln. In considering Lincoln's purposes and actions, there are two points of view, however, from which one cannot see the same result; namely, that of the sovereign and sacred individuality of the State which Lincoln supposedly destroyed, and the sovereignty of the Federal Government which he preserved. There are still some who maintain Lincoln's entire political philosophy was wrong. The answer to their argument is, of course, the more generally held contrary opinion.

All criticism of the public Lincoln turns eventually on one question: Was he a mere opportunist? There was certainly a timeliness about all of his important moves. But most of his later critics conclude that Lincoln cannot intelligently be explained as an opportunist, that behind all his gentleness, his slowness, behind his melancholy as well as his humor, there appears a tremendous ambition and an inflexible purpose.

Lincoln's popular reputation and conception have been largely established in other forms of literature than biography and history. A mass of popular narrative has grown up about him in the form of stories supposedly told by Lincoln and anecdotes about him. Poets in every section of the country, even in the South, eulogized the martyr following his death. Probably no European except Napoleon, and of course the great legendary figures like King Arthur, has had more good poems, or more bad ones, written about him. The great Lincoln poems are still those written by his contemporaries, Walt Whitman's "When Lilacs Last in the Dooryard Bloom'd," Herman Melville's "The Martyr," and James Russell Lowell's "Commemoration Ode," but in later years a number of poets have written one of their best about him—notably Edwin Arlington Robinson's "The Master," Edwin Markham's "Lincoln, the Man of the People," John Gould Fletcher's "Lincoln," Vachel Lindsay's "Abraham Lincoln Walks at Midnight," and Carl Sandburg's "The Long Shadow of Lincoln."

Novelists were somewhat slower to find Lincoln than the poets, and he is a central character in no great novel, though a biographical novel such as Irving Stone's *Love Is Eternal* (1954) achieves more than most good novels of any genre.

Few Lincoln dramas have value either as stage plays or as literature, but John Drinkwater's *Abraham Lincoln* (1919) and Robert E. Sherwood's *Abe Lincoln in Illinois* (1939) are exceptionally fine plays, the latter in spite of its incorrect emphasis on Lincoln's lack of ambition and the role of Mary Lincoln as the gadfly stinging him to action. Two plays which have recently appeared also deserve comment: *The Rivalry* by Norman Corwin and *The Last Days of Lincoln* by Mark Van Doren. *The Rivalry* makes very adept use of Lincoln's well-known words, spoken at various periods during his life, but dramatically concentrated in the period of the Lincoln-Douglas debates which are the focus of the play. *The Last Days of Lincoln* achieves a very high literary level indeed, and succeeds movingly in portraying the solemn, weary, and foreboding Lincoln who has already assumed the giant proportions of a mythic hero.

To his contemporaries it seemed indeed a far cry from the prairie Lincoln born in a backwoods log cabin to the President Lincoln who was eulogized in 1865 as his country's martyr. Even some of his friends thought the ugly Illinois lawyer of very mediocre caliber when he was nominated in 1860, but most of them came to praise him five years later as the representative and greatest American. Enemies claimed his authorship for any dirty tale that came along, whispered his illegitimacy and immorality, and hinted that his wife was a Southern spy. After he had assumed the office of President, he was criticized, with some justice, as well as with considerable lack of appreciation for his predicament, for assuming authority arbitrarily and suspending the writ of habeas corpus. His early caution with regard to the institution of slavery called down fire from the abolitionists; one of the most acrid, Wendell Phillips, referred to Lincoln as "a first-rate second-rate man."

Two classes of men were never able to comprehend Lincoln: those who judged entirely by conventional standards of breeding or by superficial sophistication, and those who were poisoned by political hatred or blinded by egotism and worship of their own opinions. An absence of bias and a careful reading of his speeches, however, enabled Lincoln's great literary contemporaries Ralph Waldo Emerson, James Russell Lowell, Charles Eliot Norton, John Lothrop Motley, and others to divine the remarkable genius of Lincoln even before most of his close political associates and friends.

The conception of Lincoln as a man of very ordinary talents who became in five years of stress educated to a point of intellectual greatness cannot hold. It was inevitable that Lincoln should grow and change, but the essential elements of greatness which were generally recognized after his death and canonization were, as evidenced in his speeches and writing, certainly present in Lincoln prior to 1860.

It is largely of two species of material, pure fiction and folklore, that the first accounts of the early life of Lincoln were composed. The cycle of stories which revolve about his father and mother, Thomas Lincoln and Nancy Hanks, passes through many strange and sometimes contradictory phases. Nancy Hanks and the boy Lincoln have become pure legend.

There was no agreement on the physical appearance of Lincoln's mother, even among those who claimed to have known her. Lincoln's purported statement, "All that I am, or hope to be, I owe to my angel mother," has furnished the keynote of the Nancy Hanks legend perpetuated in poetry and works of fiction. His father lived too long to have a sentimental legend. He was apparently just such a man as were the majority of his neighbors, without great ambition, but with a reputation for strength of moral character.

The life of the young Lincoln as it was remembered in after years was inevitably remembered in the spiritual presence of the savior of the nation, the martyr and saint. Most of the episodes picturing "Abe" as a model boy are, although not inconsistent with, still without justification in the adequately documented facts. The honesty of "Honest Abe" had been a byword locally in Illinois for years, but the countless anecdotes of his honesty did not flourish until the campaign of 1860. One of the best-known anecdotes, which tells how he closed up his shop and walked several miles to return an overcharge of a few cents, has not even the usual authority of some old friend. Another cycle of stories concerns the gentleness and sympathy of "Father Abraham," the friend of the bereaved and distracted. There are many authentic episodes in this cycle, but the fact that writers of fiction have not been content to stick to the authentic episodes, and the fact that they have tended to ignore equally authentic episodes in which Lincoln refused his aid or clemency indicate the sentimental exaggeration in this type of fiction.

It would be foolish to assert that Abraham Lincoln was elected because of the popular heroic figure that he came to be within a few days of his nomination, but the importance of the heroic legend which made him forever the symbol of democracy cannot be overestimated. Lincoln inherited to some extent the heroic role established by other frontier Presidents, such as Andrew Jackson and William Henry Harrison. His physical prowess as a young man, wrestler, weight lifter, and rail splitter was part of this frontier legend, and two rails he had split in his youth were brought to the convention at which he was nominated for President. After Lincoln had become universally known as the Emancipator, it was natural that antislavery anecdotes should also be interpolated somewhere in the story of his early life. One such tells of the frontier boy who saw a slave market in New Orleans, where he had gone on a flatboat to sell Illinois produce; he is supposed to have said, "If I ever get a chance to hit that thing [slavery] I'll hit it hard." The true wilderness hero, the wrestling, yarn-spinning youth who enjoyed tales of broad humor, remained somewhat a local legend for many years after the Civil War, while the more sentimental picture of his youth was spread throughout the United States. In the last fifty years, however, perhaps because of the vogue of realism in fiction in general, the portrait of the rough frontier Lincoln in works of fiction has tended to replace the earlier sentimental picture.

The historical basis for the element of romantic love in the Lincoln legend is almost nonexistent, but in the Ann Rutledge romance there is sufficient concentration of fiction to make up for the lack of facts. It was inevitable that this romantic story should arise, perhaps because, if for no other reason, of the apparent lack of the very article in Lincoln himself. The warm and fruitful domestic relationship between Lincoln and his wife, Mary Todd, was well known to be on occasions cross and common.

Thus, what was in reality, if in fact at all, an inconsequential early romance between the twenty-five-year-old Lincoln and a young girl in New Salem, who died of chills and fever, was blown into an episode depicting Ann as Lincoln's only true love, whose death left him forever shrouded in melancholy. All indications are that, although dismissed from serious biography, this legend will never disappear from popular works.

On that Friday night, April 14, 1865, when John Wilkes Booth crept into the President's box at Ford's Theatre and murdered Lincoln, he accomplished what he thought was a just revenge upon the man who had become, to his unbalanced mind, a monster responsible for all the evil and disgrace which had befallen and would befall the beloved South. But he accomplished far more; he gave the world a martyr and saint where it had once had a man. The rail splitter, the flatboatman, the teller of smutty jokes, was forgotten. The popular religious interpretation was that Lincoln's death was to atone, even as Christ's, for the sin of a nation. Although it is known that Lincoln was never a member of any church, there is throughout his works much general evidence of his faith in God, and even of his definite conviction that he was a direct agent of the Lord.

To this extent Lincoln is certainly not miscast in the legend of prophet, saint, and martyr, but the extent to which the legend goes to exaggerate the element of the supernatural is ridiculous. Lincoln had forecast in early speeches such reforms as prohibition, woman's rights, and the end of slavery, but so had numerous other speechmakers whose names are now forgotten. It is true that Lincoln had three dreams or visions foreshadowing his death, not an uncommon psychological phenomenon, but especially apropos in a legend. However one interprets these "mystical" data which are made much of in the legend, it is altogether fitting that the Lincoln Memorial in Washington should be in the form of a temple to a prophet, savior, and martyr, and that the sculptured figure enshrined there should represent a mystical, brooding demigod, for Lincoln was indeed something of a mystic as well as a very practical man.

If all the conspiracy of circumstances and events which cast him at once into the sky should be set aside, and the political interpreters of Lincoln should be found false; still, the words of his Second Inaugural Address inscribed on the memorial walls will be a kind of poetic prophecy and its author somewhat allied with God.

Lincoln's two achievements most often extolled in verse as well as prose within a few months after his assassination were the Emancipation Proclamation and the preservation of the Union. The first of these is still an enduring symbol, a climax episode in the legend of the prophet and martyr. In the United States praise of the emancipator has popularly equaled that of the savior of the Union. Abroad, the emancipator overshadows all conceptions of Lincoln save one, as a symbol representative of individualism and personal democracy.

Although Lincoln was convinced throughout his early life that slavery was morally wrong, he did not feel any of the zeal for its abolition which was inspiring young men in New England. By 1855 he had grown to hate the institution. He repeatedly attempted to influence legislation in behalf of gradual emancipation and compensation for the slaveholders. In connection with these plans, Lincoln proposed colonization for the freed Negroes in other countries.

Many contemporaries criticized the Emancipation Proclamation because it was limited to the states in rebellion and had no effect in the loyal slave states. It could have no effect in the rebellious states until the Union armies were victorious, which seemed a far cry in September 1862 when the Proclamation was first issued. For this reason some said specifically that it was a piece of chicane; yet this act was to become "the central act of Lincoln's administration."

Alexander Stephens, Vice-President of the Confederacy, said that the Union with Lincoln rose in sentiment "to the sublimity of a religious mysticism." Perhaps it did, but one thing Lincoln was practical rather than mystical about; if the Union were destroyed neither he nor anybody could abolish slavery in the foreseeable future.

Lincoln's popular fame was increased in the first instance by a considerable amount of campaign literature which held him up as the veritable democrat and representative American. Lincoln literature has enshrined this symbolism and developed the theme of Lincoln's new and American type of genius, an epitome of the people and a genuine folk hero. But above all, there is the undeniable genius of Lincoln, incontrovertibly evidenced in his writings and his deeds, which must be enshrined as somehow, mystically and uniquely, American.

History and literature are more nearly agreed in the evaluation and interpretation of Lincoln than might be supposed. The bases for estimates of Lincoln are often at variance, but the estimates themselves are in most respects the same in their general terms. Students of Lincoln generally agree that he was the great man of his age.

In spite of Carl Sandburg's monumental *Abraham Lincoln: The Prairie Years* (1926) and *Abraham Lincoln: The War Years* (1939), James G. Randall's scholarly multivolume *Lincoln the President* (1945–55) and Benjamin P. Thomas' excellent one-volume *Abraham Lincoln* (1952), there is as yet no version of Lincoln biography which can be accepted as a final picture of both the private and the public Lincoln; but the Lincoln who lives in the mind of the average American is not greatly dependent upon the interpretation of the biographers, for he has become a symbol and a myth even larger than his reality in life.

The remarkable thing about the mythos is that Lincoln was a worthy man to be made into a symbol of justice, mercy, spiritual and intellectual strength, or a symbol of democracy and freedom. The legend-making propensities of the people of the United States have clothed him in truths that the mere facts of his life could never otherwise have attained. To paraphrase Shelley's differentiation between poetry and history, there is this difference between a history and a legend, that a history is a catalog of detached facts, which have no other connection than time, place, circumstance, and cause, and effect; a legend is the creation of actions according to the unchangeable forms of human nature, as existing in the mind of the creator, which is itself the image of all other minds.

So in the legend of Abraham Lincoln, these very workings of

the poetic mind, whether of the folk or of the creative writer, have made—within a period of recorded history, printing presses, and modern methods of research—a myth which symbolizes the quest of a people for their national identity, for liberty under law, and for a mystical equality of all men in spite of differences. It is impossible to conceive of a time when such a legend will lose its universal appeal. As long as men aspire, the Lincoln story will be a source of encouragement and hope.

LINCOLN'S JOURNEY TO GREATNESS

By Philip Van Doren Stern

Dr. Philip Van Doren Stern is the author of nineteen books, among them The Man Who Killed Lincoln *(1939)*, An End to Valor *(1958) and* Secret Missions of the Civil War *(1959). He also edited* The Life and Writings of Abraham Lincoln *(1940)*.

D URING the fifty-six years of his life Abraham Lincoln never traveled farther west than Council Bluffs, Iowa; he visited New England twice, and twice went down the Mississippi River by flatboat to New Orleans. Except for a year and a half in Washington as Congressman, he spent most of the time before he became President in three states: Kentucky, where he was born; Indiana, where he grew up; and Illinois, where he settled in 1830. The area associated with him in those three states is so compact that it can easily be covered in one day by automobile. Modern highways now go all the way, but in Lincoln's time there were few roads—and even those were bad.

The route Lincoln traveled to greatness begins near Hodgenville, Kentucky, where he was born. There his father had bought a farm of nearly 350 acres of hilly, semiwild land. On it was an unfailing spring in a small limestone cave. On the hill above this, Thomas Lincoln built the simple one-room cabin in which his son was born. A huge oak tree, used even then as a boundary marker, grew nearby. The young child must have noticed its massive bulk towering against the sky. It still flourishes, the only living thing in all that wilderness area associated with the infant Lincoln.

Today the U. S. Department of the Interior has established a national park on the Lincoln birthplace farm. Well-tended lawns replace rough fields, and an imposing granite Doric-columned memorial stands on the hill where Thomas Lincoln's cabin once stood. A broad flight of stone stairs leads up to the memorial which houses a little cabin made of squared logs. Visitors stare at the cabin solemnly, seldom questioning, even in their own minds, whether or not it is the actual building in which Nancy Hanks Lincoln gave birth to her famous son. Actually its authenticity is so doubtful that even the Department of the Interior's pamphlet on the subject says: "The log cabin in the Memorial Building . . . is the traditional birthplace cabin. It is impossible to say with certainty that it is the original birthplace cabin." There is no doubt, however, about the authenticity of the farm. When the Lincolns bought the place it was on the edge of the Barrens, a vast tract of almost treeless land which the Indians had burned over for centuries to provide pasturage for deer and buffalo. The soil was so poor that Thomas Lincoln had a hard time grubbing a living from it. He moved away in 1811, and then, when his title proved to be defective, finally lost his entire investment of $200—a lot of money to a man in his position.

He took his family ten miles northeast to a better farm on Knob Creek, a wild little stream that courses through the stubby limestone hills. His son had been too young to remember anything about the Sinking Spring Farm; Abraham Lincoln's first recollections were about the Knob Creek place where he spent his boyhood. Speaking about it later to a visitor in the White House, he said: "I remember that old home very well. Our farm was composed of three fields. It lay in the valley surrounded by high hills and deep gorges. Sometimes when there was a big rain in the hills the water would come down through the gorges and spread out over the farm. . . . One Saturday afternoon, the other boys planted the corn in what we called the big field; it contained seven acres and I dropped the pumpkin seed. . . . The next Sunday morning there came a big rain in the hills, it did not rain a drop in the valley but the water coming down through the gorges washed ground, corn, pumpkin seed, and all clear off the field."

The farm is privately owned now, but it is open to the public. Near the road stands an ancient cabin which was rebuilt in 1932 from logs taken from a cabin owned by one of the early settlers, Austin Gollaher. Gollaher is remembered only because he used to play with Lincoln as a boy and once saved his life when Lincoln fell into the storm-swollen waters of the creek. The farm has changed very little. There is less water in the creek these days, but it still flows through level alluvial fields past steep limestone bluffs, and just below the bridge across the road is the small tree-sheltered pool where the boy Lincoln once fished and swam and was nearly drowned.

Since the Lincolns lived here for five years, the Knob Creek place is the homesite longest associated with Nancy Hanks. It was the best farm her husband was ever to own, and on it she had more cause to be happy than in any other place. Here she sent her daughter Sarah to a primitive school in the village two miles away. Here the future President, clad only in "a one piece long linsey shirt," tagged along with his sister to attend the same school. Here, too, Nancy gave birth to her third child, a boy she named Thomas. He lived only a short while, and was buried in a neighbor's nearby family plot, where a crude headstone marked with the initials TL was discovered in 1930.

When their son was seven years old the Lincolns moved to Indiana. There they settled in the midst of a great forest where they first lived in a "half-faced camp." This was a roughly built, three-sided shelter with the open face heated by a huge wood fire which had to be kept going day and night. Then Thomas Lincoln constructed a sturdy log cabin. His son, helping him and growing up in the forest, became an expert axman. Because of his skill, he later became famous as the "Rail-Splitter Candidate."

Thomas Lincoln had chosen a poor location for his cabin. The water supply was inadequate, and the ground was so heavily overgrown that life became an endless struggle against brush and trees. But some of Nancy Hanks' relatives joined them, and a tiny community sprang up in the wilderness. Then, in the autumn of 1818, a strange malady known to the pioneers as the "milk sickness" struck them. It is now believed that this was caused by cows eating poisonous white snakeroot and transmitting the toxic juices in their milk. Two of Nancy Hanks' relatives were killed by it, and then she too fell sick and died. Her husband made a rude coffin for her, and her body was hauled through the woods to a tree-covered knoll three quarters of a mile from the cabin. There she was buried in an unmarked grave in the midst of the dark and inhospitable land.

After the death of Nancy Hanks Lincoln, her eleven-year-old daughter Sarah tried to keep house, but she was evidently too young for the task, for about a year later her father returned to Elizabethtown to find himself a wife. He married Sarah Bush Johnston, a widow with three children, and brought them back to Indiana.

The new wife was a kindly and energetic person who put new life into the disrupted household. She mothered Thomas Lincoln's children as well as her own and sent them to school. Lincoln once said that "the aggregate of all his schooling did not amount to one year," but what he did not have a chance to learn in conventional classrooms he got from poring over books. It was in Indiana that he grew to manhood and became the tall, angular figure we think of today.

In 1826 his sister married into one of the local families, the Grigsbys; less than two years later she died in childbirth and was buried near the Pigeon Creek Baptist Church, to which the Lincolns belonged. Shortly after his sister's death in 1828, Lincoln had an opportunity to go by flatboat down the Ohio and Mississippi rivers to New Orleans. It was the first large city he had visited. When he helped to take the flatboat down the Ohio and Mississippi rivers, he and his friends drifted leisurely downstream, passing pleasant river towns that were later to become cities. In New Orleans, Lincoln witnessed a spectacle that has now vanished from the world. As many as 1,500 flatboats could be seen there. River steamers came and went, and ocean-going ships departed frequently for Liverpool or Havre. And in this city of nearly 50,000 people, where more people spoke French than English, and half the population was black, slaves were sold in the public market.

Today New Orleans preserves some of the quaint old-world charm it had when Lincoln visited it more than a century ago. But most of the shipping is gone from the port. Passenger steamers on the Mississippi are hardly ever seen, and only cargo ships and heavy freight barges lie alongside the once-bustling wharves.

The cabin on the Lincoln farm in Indiana had a fireplace made of rough stones. This, and the four wooden ground sills which formed the foundation of the cabin have been reproduced in enduring bronze on the original site. Most of this part of the state has long ago been cleared, so that open farm fields replace the once-endless stretches of virgin forest. But the land Thomas Lincoln owned has been allowed to remain as woodland. The cabin site is in a lonely, tree-shadowed spot; on a slope above it in the silent forest is the grave of Lincoln's mother. Near the public road is a park with a large white stone memorial building decorated with bas-reliefs portraying the life of the Lincoln family as it migrated westward.

Soon after Lincoln returned to Indiana, his family decided to move to Illinois. They went by wagon across the level prairies where there were then no roads. They settled on a farm near Decatur, where they built another cabin and cleared a few fields before winter came on.

That first winter in Illinois was a hard one. Snow started falling at Christmastime, and it kept on until the drifts piled up fifteen feet high. It was unusually cold too, and the housebound Lincolns had to live like hibernating animals until spring came. Then the melting snow flooded the fields and made land travel impossible.

Lincoln had agreed to take another flatboat to New Orleans, so he started down the Sangamon by canoe. On this river journey he first entered the two towns that were to be so important in his life. The first was Springfield, which was then only a small village. When the flatboat got stuck on a newly built mill dam farther down the river, he first set foot in New Salem.

When Lincoln came back from New Orleans in July, he visited his father. The twenty-two-year-old Lincoln then left his parents' home to start out for himself and walked across country to New Salem to begin his career there as a storekeeper. The new enterprise, however, did not do well, and the following spring, when the Black Hawk Indian war broke out, Lincoln gladly enlisted and served for three months, but never saw action. Upon his return to New Salem, he became a candidate for the Illinois State Legislature and was defeated—the only time, he later noted, that he "was ever beaten on a direct vote of the people." He bought an interest in another store, which also soon "winked out"; he became a surveyor, a postmaster, and then, in 1834, he was elected to the legislature. After this he began to study law, and was admitted to the bar in 1837.

New Salem was located on a tree-covered ridge overlooking the river. Here a saw-and-grist mill had been built; log cabins which served as houses, stores, and workshops stood on the crest of the ridge to make a tiny community that was almost entirely self-sustained. The village people practiced the essential handicraft arts and trades which they and their ancestors had developed over many centuries in similar small towns farther east in America and in Europe.

In 1837 Lincoln moved to Springfield. Most of the other townspeople left New Salem about the same time. The village soon decayed, and in ten years the once-thriving community reverted to overgrown wilderness. The place remained deserted until 1918 when the state acquired it. The actual work of restoring the village to the condition it was in Lincoln's time began in 1932. Today the town that played an important part in Abraham Lincoln's career is so perfect a replica of the original village that hundreds of thousands of visitors who come there each year can see just how the young Lincoln and his neighbors lived.

The saw-and-grist mill on the riverbank has been rebuilt; so has a wool-carding factory in the center of the town. Even the complicated circular treadmill by which a slowly moving ox supplied motive power to operate the carding machine has been reconstructed. So have the general stores in which the future President once worked. The cooper shop is the only building that stood there in Lincoln's time, but all the other structures have been reproduced so accurately that New Salem today looks just as it did 150 years ago.

On April 15, 1837, Lincoln rode on a borrowed horse the twenty miles from New Salem to Springfield, where he practiced law. This town had recently been chosen to be the state's capital.

It was hardly more than a village. Work was started on the new State House then, and teams of ten or twelve oxen began dragging great blocks of cut stone to the central square that was to be the focus of Lincoln's career for the next twenty-three years. During those years he saw the prairie village grow into a thriving state capital. New streets were laid out on which new houses were built, and the horse-drawn stagecoach was soon replaced by railroads, while telegraph lines were built to tie once widely separated communities together.

When Lincoln came to Springfield he had no money and so few personal belongings that he carried everything he owned in two saddlebags. He accepted a friend's offer to share a room and bed. His previous twenty-eight years had been spent in isolated wilderness communities, and he was no more prepared for town life than his restless pioneer father. But he was naturally friendly and soon had a wide circle of acquaintances. Five years later when he married Mary Todd he was still so poor that they went to live at the Globe Tavern, paying $4 for room and board.

Lincoln married Mary Todd in 1842. In May 1844 he was able to buy a frame cottage near the center of Springfield, the only home he was ever to own. A second story was added in 1856. The house is still standing just as it was when Lincoln lived in it. It is still a good dwelling, one that any young lawyer would be glad to own today. In the entrance hall a stairway leads to the second floor; on the left is the double parlor in which the Republican notification committee informed Lincoln of his nomination as that party's presidential candidate; on the right is a smaller parlor. Behind the parlors is a small dining room, and beyond that the kitchen. These downstairs rooms are furnished as they were when the Lincolns used them in the seventeen years they spent there. Today Lincoln could walk in and feel that everything is just as it was when he left this comfortable but unpretentious house to journey to Washington as President-elect nearly a hundred years ago.

On a rainy morning in February 1861 he went from this house to the Great Western station to get on the train that was to take him east. There he made his farewell speech to his friends and neighbors. He was never to see Springfield again.

The small brick railroad station still stands on a side street.

It is no longer used for passengers, but a bronze tablet in front of it reproduces the text of the words Lincoln spoke that morning. Around it the small town he knew has grown into a modern city of 100,000 people. The square where Lincoln had several successive law offices has been changed completely by high buildings erected there since, but the old State House—except for an added story—remains much as he knew it. In that building he made some of the speeches which, in turn, made him President.

Some of the courthouses of the old Eighth Judicial Circuit still stand in the small towns around Springfield. In them one can see the actual trial rooms in which Lincoln pleaded for his clients as he and his colleagues helped to shape American jurisprudence while the law of the new nation slowly evolved.

In Washington only a few of the landmarks associated with Lincoln remain, for the semiprovincial little city that was the capital of the United States during his administration has undergone vast changes in recent years. But these landmarks are important ones. The White House, where the Lincoln family lived, underwent extensive renovations in 1948–52, when the sagging interior of the historic old building had to be completely reconstructed inside the original sandstone walls. But the Lincoln bedroom on the second floor, with its extra-large bed used by the very tall President, has been furnished in the style of his day.

And the Capitol of the United States, where Lincoln served as Congressman and as President, is almost exactly as it was in his time. Its vast dome was completed during his administration, and the finishing touches on the exterior of the Senate and House wings were being made at the time of his death. In front of this world-famous building, Lincoln was twice inaugurated, and to it he often came to sign bills or address Congress. And in the rotunda under the great dome, his body lay in state in April 1865, after he had been assassinated in Ford's Theatre. The theatre itself has been made into a museum, showing Lincoln's career from his birthplace to the presidency. Across the street is the little red-brick boardinghouse where the mortally wounded man died. To this unimpressive-looking house the dying man was brought, and here the leaders of the nation gathered in a narrow hall bedroom on that fatal night.

The dead President's body was taken by train to Springfield for burial. From Chicago the train steamed southward through the country Lincoln had known so well. All along the way, day and night, vast throngs lined the tracks to see the heavily draped funeral car pass. The tolling bell of the engine could be heard far across the prairie, and its long plume of black smoke drifted out over the plowed land where tender green corn shoots were springing from the dark, rich soil. When the train arrived in Springfield, the streets were crowded with people who had known Lincoln all their lives.

They buried him on top of a ridge north of the town. There, under the tall shaft of a sculptured monument, his body still lies. At this tomb the Lincoln trail ends. Once only a track through the wilderness, it is now celebrated in marble all the way.

ABRAHAM LINCOLN:
GREAT IMAGE OF AMERICA

By Arnold Gates

Arnold Gates, editor of The Round Table, *official publication of the Civil War Round Table of New York, has written extensively on Lincoln and his times. Among his books are:* Amberglow: Of Abe Lincoln and Ann Rutledge (*1939*) *and* Amberglow: Of Abe Lincoln and Joshua Speed (*1941*).

WITH each passing year since his death on an April Saturday morning in 1865 the memory of Abraham Lincoln increases as a great image of America. Why this is true and what keeps the name and the shadow alive, not only in America but in many lands, has interested practically everyone who has read his well-documented life.

Most Americans have grown to regard Lincoln as a great American who somehow embodies the essence of our democratic way of life without spelling out exactly how this came to be. Accepting the position he holds in the "hearts of his countrymen" as a matter of obvious truth, they readily respond to his name and memory as a symbol. Living, growing and accepting the truth of Lincoln, Americans see nothing incongruous in the behavior of those who live next door to the historic places associated with his life and have never visited them. To Americans, living next door to the hallowed footpaths of greatness, Lincoln is the "good neighbor" who does not suffer through this seeming inattention. A respect for his enduring qualities is so assured and self-evident that many just do not feel it needs the bolstering of constant reaffirmation.

If this was all there was to the place Abraham Lincoln holds, this observation on the man could end right here. But Lincoln was a many-faceted personality and new aspects of his character continue to emerge as students of his life try to fathom his full story. This man of mood and light, the late Benjamin P. Thomas said, "embodied the easy-going, sentimental, kindly spirit of America, which revolts at extreme measures but moves steadily, if haltingly, toward lofty goals." Looking at the same man, but in a physical sense, the distinguished historian James G. Randall was struck by one significant quality in Lincoln's appearance. "The Americanism of the man is revealed with an effect that is almost startling if one looks at the full standing form and then tries to imagine that figure in court costume, with knee-breeches, close fitting stockings, and buckles. The man's appearance was both unique and related to a well known American type, the type that might have been found among people close to the woods or mountains."

Lincoln's very life seemed to have contained the essence of the American Dream. To be born in a crude Kentucky log cabin, to live as simple a life as only the wilderness frontier of the eighteen hundreds offered, to win the regard and support of his fellow men, and to rise slowly by his own abilities and efforts was ever a heart-warming story. In his own day many questioned his ability or fitness to assume the great tasks of a nation during a civil war and his critics were scorching in their estimates of his performance. Lincoln bore all and continued in his unswerving purposes, tapping the great resource of understanding that he had acquired living, mingling and growing with the people of frontier and settlement America. His understanding was great and his capacity to expand in ability with the young nation fitted him for the presidency as few men after George Washington had been prepared.

In a treatise written in 1856 Walt Whitman voiced the thoughts of many when he wrote, "I would be much pleased to see some heroic, shrewd, fully-informed healthy-bodied, middle-aged, beard-faced American blacksmith or boatman come down from the West across the Alleghanies, and walk into the Presidency, dressed in a clean suit of working attire, and with the tan all over his face, breast, and arms. . . ."

After his death a newspaper described Lincoln as "essentially a mixed product of the agricultural, forensic and frontier life of this continent—as indigenous to our soil as the cranberry crop, and as American in his fibre as the granite foundations of our Appalachian range ... taking him for all in all, the very noblest impulses, peculiarities and aspirations of our whole people—what may be called our continental idiosyncrasies—were more collectively and vividly reproduced in his genial and yet unswerving nature than in that of any other public man of whom our chronicles bear record."

Growing up in a frontier community Abraham Lincoln developed an understanding of and a fondness for people. He treated all men and women with equal dignity. While opportunities to acquire social graces were nonexistent in the log cabin environment he spent his youthful days in, his manner was always respectful. It could be said that like Americans in general Lincoln was gregarious. He liked to be with people. Out of his sympathy and understanding—as well as his long and painstaking study of the American Declaration of Independence and Constitution and how they came to be—was born Lincoln's political philosophy.

To Lincoln the "last best hope of earth" was the form of government which had this Declaration as its cornerstone. His very life was dedicated to its proposition which proclaims "all men are created equal" and are "endowed ... with certain unalienable rights" among which are "life, liberty, and the pursuit of happiness." To safeguard these freedoms was, in Lincoln's eyes, a sacred trust which he as President had taken an oath to preserve and further. They were not to be taken lightly or as mere political phrases which could be forgotten after the campaign. The equality of not only Americans but of all men was a principle of his beliefs he never abandoned. To Americans, who have always felt an overriding sympathy for the "underdog," Lincoln's unflinching stand on individual rights and freedom has been a particularly endearing aspect of his image of America.

The image of America prevails regardless of what light is played upon Abraham Lincoln's life. In many ways his early years were the rather common experience of his time: shaping a livelihood in the wilderness of America and trying his skill at any job that came his way. What was uncommon was his purposeful scrabbling for what education was available, reading every book he could get his hands on, and the ceaseless probing of his logical mind. In these shaping years he was a store clerk, postmaster and surveyor in the prairie community of New Salem. Meeting people he talked over their problems, was respected for his plain common sense and honesty, and in time was elected to the Illinois State Legislature. After one rather routine term as a United States Congressman he returned to Springfield and resumed the practice of law. While he made a reputation for himself as a lawyer, accepting all types of cases and patiently riding to the various courts of the Eighth Judicial Circuit, he maintained a close and constant touch with people in all walks of life. The question of permitting slavery into the territories kindled a fire in him and he spoke out against the menace with stalwart vigor.

The famous debates with Stephen A. Douglas over the slavery question, during the senatorial campaign of 1858, paved Lincoln's way to the White House. Once again the image is clear. A man of good will and peace, Abraham Lincoln was suddenly confronted with the grim tasks of a nation at battle. There was no glory in it for him. The presidency, to Lincoln, was essentially the prosecution of a war. Only the fact that Lincoln grew with the task before him made it possible for him to endure its bitter trial. Only a man of unyielding will could have hewed to the hard course it was his destiny to follow. The pleas for change were constant and who can tell but that his nights were not filled with secret doubts and self-incrimination as he ran a finger down the endless columns of casualty lists. Americans can understand his characteristically American resolve to do the job at hand, no matter how personally distasteful it might prove to be.

In his writings on the life of Abraham Lincoln the distinguished historian, James G. Randall, said Lincoln "was like the majority of the people of the nation." This could be enlarged to say that as an image of America to his countrymen and to the peoples around the earth Lincoln appears to be the common, familiar-as-an-old-shoe, average citizen of this nation. His way of doing things, his simple stories to illustrate an idea or drive home a point, his direct and unadorned language to explain his political creed, all contribute toward making that much of Lincoln a warm and understandable public figure. The Lincoln that nobody knows, as one scholar recently has put it, may not be so readily understood, but this "mystery" only adds to his appeal. Whether obvious or mysterious, no one has difficulty understanding a man who indulged his children, gave in to the whims and fancies of his wife, compromised on matters that permitted compromise but stood by his principles and convictions, and could meet problems and irritations with good humor.

Americans can understand their own warm regard for the memory of Lincoln since he so nobly reflected the best hope of all that was good in the democratic way of life. The puzzling element in the Lincoln Story is the interest and regard which his words, life and deeds have engendered among peoples around the world. That of all the national personalities this country has produced, Abraham Lincoln, who never visited another land and could speak no foreign tongue, should appeal to the minds and hearts of many distant lands attests to the universality of his logic. No matter what language his views were translated into, his thoughts always retained the elemental truth of human brotherhood and the dignity of the individual. It was for his words, deeds and indomitable fighting heart that Americans assigned to him the role of their first representative, and men in the four corners of the earth hailed him for much the same reasons. A truth has the first quality of survival. When it is simply and beautifully stated it not only endures but moves men to thinking. That was what Abraham Lincoln, as the spokesman of the United States, did and continues to do with such telling and lasting effect.

Out of a simple, uncomplicated American life came a humaneness, sympathy and tolerance that was to kindle an interest in Abraham Lincoln in some of the remotest regions of the world. After his travels in the wilds of the Caucasus Leo Tolstoi wrote of his experiences:

If one would know the greatness of Lincoln one should listen to the stories which are told about him in other parts of the world. . . .

I have heard various tribes of barbarians discussing the New World, but I heard this only in connection with the name Lincoln. Lincoln as the wonderful hero of America . . .

While traveling in the Caucasus Tolstoi was the guest of a Circassian chief who lived in a remote mountain region. After they had talked awhile the devout Mussulman wanted to hear about the "outside world." But it was not until Tolstoi started to talk about great leaders that the chief showed an interest. At that point he interrupted to call in others to listen. When Tolstoi had finished, the tall, gray-bearded chief said:

"But you have not told us about the greatest general and greatest ruler of the world. We want to know something about him. He was a hero. He spoke with a voice of thunder, he laughed like the sunrise and his deeds were strong as the rock and as sweet as the fragrance of roses. . . . He was so great that he even forgave the crimes of his greatest enemies and shook brotherly hands with those who had plotted against his life. His name was Lincoln and the country in which he lived is called America. . . . Tell us of that man."

Tolstoi told them all he knew of Lincoln.

The next day the chief presented Tolstoi with an Arabian horse and an escort to the nearest town. There he bought a photograph of Lincoln to be sent to the chief. The escort's hand shook as he accepted this gift and his eyes filled with tears. Tolstoi asked him why he looked so sad.

"I am sad," the weather-beaten tribesman answered, "because I feel sorry that he had to die by the hands of a villain. Don't you find, judging from his picture, that his eyes are full of tears and that his lips are sad with secret sorrow?"

To Tolstoi true greatness was based on humanity, truth, justice and pity. All of these, in his opinion, Lincoln possessed and because he did his example was "universal and will last thousands of years." In conclusion, Tolstoi considered Washington and Napoleon as typical of their lands but thought Lincoln "was a humanitarian as broad as the world."

During the Civil War the Marquis Adolphe de Chambrun was with the French embassy in Washington and had an opportunity to visit and observe President Lincoln. In letters to his wife in

France he captured pen portraits of the man and his political philosophy. Lincoln's "arms were strong," he wrote, "and his complexion sunburned . . . his gestures were vigorous and supple, revealing great physical strength and an extraordinary energy for resisting privation and fatigue." As for the man's face, "nothing seemed to lend harmony. . . . Yet his wide and high forehead, his gray-brown eyes sunken under thick eyebrows, and as though encircled by deep and dark wrinkles, his nose straight and pronounced, his lips at the same time thick and delicate, together with the furrows that ran across his cheeks and chin, formed an ensemble which, although strange, was certainly powerful," reflecting "remarkable intelligence, great strength of penetration, tenacity of will, and elevated instincts." This was the man, Chambrun continued, who "well understood that he was the people's agent" and "was well aware of that close union which must exist in a free democracy between the authority representing the nation and the nation itself. . . ."

In a poem titled "The Murder of Abraham Lincoln" Henrik Ibsen, who felt a great sorrow over the assassination, lashed at the show of sympathy displayed by such rulers as the Emperor of France and reminded them of "vows forgotten and words untrue," of "treaties ye tear and despoil" and of "perjured oaths," and thought the expressions of grief were the epitome of hypocrisy when only a few months before they had ridiculed the American President.

In Italy, Giuseppe Garibaldi signed an address to Lincoln, "Emancipator of the Slaves of the American Republic," during the Civil War, saying: "Heir of the aspirations of Christ and of John Brown, you will pass to posterity with the name of the Emancipator; more enviable than any crown or any human treasure." The French historian Henri Martin predicted that Lincoln "will stand out in the traditions of his country and the world as an incarnation of the people and of modern democracy itself."

There were other words of praise from Lord Curzon and Bismarck, and José Marti, Cuban patriot, expressed the feelings of men in many places when he said, "Lincoln's life and his philosophy were universal in their greatness" and that in "loving Lincoln, one could also come to love his country."

That Lincoln is an "image of America" to people around the world is no less true today than it was at the time of his death. Prime Minister Nehru of India keeps a brass mold of the right hand of Lincoln in his study. "It is a beautiful hand, strong and firm and yet gentle," he said, "and I look at it every day, and it gives me strength."

It seems a little unusual that a man of Nehru's intellectual background should admire the mold of a hand used to hard manual labor. The famous French philosopher, Jacques Maritain, recently wrote that the best definition of American democracy was expressed by Lincoln in his first Message to Congress when he said it was the "struggle for maintaining in the world that form and substance of government whose leading object is to elevate the condition of men; to lift artificial weights from all shoulders; to clear the paths of laudable pursuit for all; to afford all an unfettered start and a fair chance in the race of life."

Barbara Ward, the distinguished British authority on world affairs, has expressed very ably the essence of Lincoln's enduring and timeless qualities which so aptly make him a living and vital image of America. As she interprets it, "Lincoln will not dwindle to a historical personage. He is larger than his context and whatever his meaning is in the history of humanity, one generation and even one nation are not enough to decipher him. He is one of the very few of the world's leaders who stay alive."

There is so much of the significant in this observation. Lincoln is the image of his country because he can represent the best qualities of each of its individuals to peoples looking at the nation from across the seas. He is an image of America in the eyes of his own people because they find in his purposes and beliefs the eternal ideals which they mutually believe in. Taking the world-wide view, Lincoln has come to represent a land which contains representatives of every nation within its borders so that peoples in far reaches see something of their very own in the towering image of Abraham Lincoln.

As the doctor pronounced Lincoln dead in the early morning hour of April 15, 1865, Edwin Stanton, the Secretary of War, said, "Now he belongs to the ages." His words were far more prophetic than he or his contemporaries could have realized. Just as he had a great capacity for steady growth in his job, so now does the memory of the man take on new and vigorous dimensions with the passage of years. His influence on the thoughts and ways of many, while perfectly understandable, is also amazing. Considered common and simple by all who quickly read his life story, Abraham Lincoln was at the same time a complex, mysterious and uncommon individual. A man of many paradoxes, his life is still a source of conflicting interpretations, myths and legends. Not an easy man to understand, all men who gaze upon his brooding pictures and read his words or saga feel they *know* and *understand* this apostle of universal brotherhood. Not a full understanding of the man so much as a comprehension of his clear and simple words has wrought this world-wide affinity.

"I wish all men to be free," Lincoln said, and the sincerity of his words stirs the hearts and minds of mankind to the latest generation.

Part 2

LINCOLN AS HIS CONTEMPORARIES SAW HIM

R. B. Rutledge

Lincoln's physical strength has become legendary. R. B. Rutledge, one of his fellow townsmen at New Salem, told this to William H. Herndon in 1866:

Trials of strength were very common among the pioneers. Lifting weights, as heavy timbers piled one upon another, was a favorite pastime, and no workman in the neighborhood could at all cope with Mr. Lincoln in this direction. I have seen him frequently take a barrel of whisky by the chimes and lift it up to his face as if to drink out of the bunghole. This feat he could accomplish with the greatest ease. I never saw him taste or drink a drop of any kind of spirituous liquors.

*   *   *

David Davis

Judge David Davis, who later became a Justice of the United States Supreme Court, in a speech given at Indianapolis, made the following estimate of Lincoln's professional traits and talents:

In all the elements that constitute the great lawyer, he had few equals. He was great both at *nisi prius* and before an appellate tribunal. He seized the strong points of a cause, and presented them with clearness and great compactness. His mind was logical and direct, and he did not indulge in extraneous discussion. Generalities and platitudes had no charms for him. An unfailing vein of humor never deserted him; and he was always able to chain the attention of court and jury, when the cause was the most uninteresting, by the appropriateness of his anecdotes.

His power of comparison was large, and he rarely failed in a legal discussion to use that mode of reasoning. The framework of his mental and moral being was honesty, and a wrong cause was poorly defended by him. The ability which some eminent lawyers possess, of explaining away the bad points of a cause by ingenious sophistry, was denied him. In order to bring into full activity his great powers, it was necessary that he should be convinced of the right and justice of the matter which he advocated. When so convinced, whether the cause was great or small, he was usually successful. He read lawbooks but little, except when the cause in hand made it necessary; yet he was usually self-reliant, depending on his own resources, and rarely consulting his brother lawyers, either on the management of his case or on the legal questions involved.

To his honor be it said, that he never took from a client, even when the cause was gained, more than he thought the service was worth and the client could reasonably afford to pay. The people where he practiced law were not rich, and his charges were always small.

His presence on the circuit was watched for with interest, and never failed to produce joy and hilarity. When casually absent, the spirits of both bar and people were depressed. He was not fond of controversy, and would compromise a lawsuit whenever practicable.

* * *

William H. Herndon

William H. Herndon, Lincoln's law partner from 1844 to 1861, gave the following description of Lincoln at a lecture given at Springfield, Illinois, December 12, 1865.

It is now the time to describe the person of Mr. Lincoln: he was about six feet four inches high, and when he left the city, was fifty-one years old, having good health and no gray hairs or but few on his head; he was thin, wiry, sinewy, raw and big heavy-boned, thin through the breast to the back and narrow across the shoulders, standing he leaned forward; was what may be called stoop-shoul-dered, inclining to the consumptively built, his usual weight being about one hundred and sixty or eighty pounds. . . . His organism and structure were loose and leathery; his body was well shrunk, cadaverous and shriveled, having very dark skin, dry and tough, wrinkled and lying somewhat in flabby folds; dark hair, the man looking woestruck. The whole man, body and mind, worked slowly, creakingly, as if it needed oiling. Physically he was a very powerful man, lifting, as said, with ease four or six hundred pounds. . . . When this man moved and walked along he moved and walked cautiously, but firmly, his long and big bony arms and hands on them, hanging like giant hands on them, swung by his side; he walked with even tread, the inner sides of his feet being parallel; he put his whole foot down flat at once, not landing on his heel; he likewise lifted his foot all at once, not rising from the toe, and hence he had no spring to his walk; he had the economy of full lift of foot though he had no spring to his walk or apparent ease of motion in his tread; he walked undulatory, up and down in motion, catching and pocketing time, weariness all up and down his person preventing them from locating. The very first opinion that a stranger or one who did not observe closely would form of Lincoln's walk and motion was that he was a tricky man, a man of cunning, a dangerous shrewd man, one to watch closely and not to be trusted, but his walk was the manifested walk of caution and firmness. In sitting down on a common chair or bench or ground, he was from the top of his head down to his seat no better than the average man; his legs and arms were, as compared with the average man, abnormally, unnaturally long, though when compared to his own organism, the whole physical man, these organs may have been in harmony with the man. His arms and hands, feet and legs, seemed to me, as compared with the average man, in undue proportion to the balance of his body. It was only when Lincoln rose on his feet that he loomed up above the mass of men. He looked the giant then.

Lincoln's head was long and tall from the base of the brain to and from the eyebrows. His head ran backward, his forehead rising as it ran back at a low angle, like Clay's and unlike Webster's, almost perpendicular. The size of his hat, measured on the hatter's hat block was 7⅛, his head being from ear to ear six and a half inches. Thus measured it was not below the medium or average size. His forehead was narrow but high; his hair was dark, almost black, and lay floating where his fingers put it or the winds left it, piled up and tossed about at random; his cheekbones were high, sharp, and prominent; his eyebrows heavy and prominent; his jaws were long, upcurved, and massive, looked solid, heavy, and strong; his nose was large, long, and blunt, a little awry toward the right eye; his chin was long, sharp and uncurved; his eyebrows cropped out like a huge jutting rock out of the brow of a hill; his face was long, narrow, sallow, and cadaverous, flesh shrunk, shriveled, wrinkled, and dry, having on his face a few hairs here and there; his cheeks were leathery and saffron-colored; his ears were large and ran out nearly at right angles from the sides of his head, caused by heavy hats in which he carried his big cotton or other handkerchief, his bank book, his letters, and his memoranda generally, and partly by nature; . . . his head was well-balanced on his shoulders, his little gray eyes in the right place. There was the lone mole on his right cheek just a little above the right corner of his mouth and Adam's apple on his throat. Beneath this rough and uncouth exterior was a very fine, an exceedingly fine physical organization, a fine and delicate network of nerves being woven through it along which feelings and thoughts traveled and flashed quicker than lightning.

Thus I say stood, walked, looked, felt, thought, willed, and acted this peculiar and singular man; he was odd, angular, homely, but when those little gray eyes and face were lighted up by the inward soul on fires of emotion, defending the liberty of man or proclaiming the truths of the Declaration of Independence, or defending justice and the eternal right, then it was that all those apparently ugly or homely features sprang into organs of beauty, or sank themselves into the sea of his inspiration that on such occasions flooded up his manly face. Sometimes it did appear to me that Lincoln was just fresh from the presence and hands of his Creator.

(From Herndon's "Notes and Monographs")

*

Lincoln's power of memory was extraordinary. Apparently, he could remember with ease what he thought worth while retaining in his mind.

Mr. Lincoln had keen susceptibilities to the hints, insinuations, and suggestions of nature and of man which put him in mind of something known or unknown; hence his power and tenacity of what is called the association of ideas must have been great; his memory was exceedingly retentive, tenacious, and strong; he could write out a speech, as in the Cooper Institute speech, and then repeat it word for word, without any effort on his part. This I know about the "house divided against itself" speech; he wrote that fine effort, an argumentative one, in slips, put those slips in his hat, numbering them, and when he was done with the ideas he gathered up the scraps, put them in the right order, and wrote out his speech, read it to me before it was delivered, and in the evening delivered it just as written without notes or finished speech; his susceptibilities to all suggestions and hints enabled him through his retentive memory at will to call up readily, quickly, and accurately the associated and classified fact, person, or idea.

(From Herndon's "Notes and Monographs")

*

William H. Herndon's description of Lincoln, the speaker, is preserved in his letter to Bartlett, July 19, 1887.

Mr. Lincoln was six feet and four inches high in his sock feet; he was consumptive by build and hence more or less stoop-shouldered. He was very tall, thin, and gaunt. When he rose to speak to the jury or to crowds of people, he stood inclined forward, was awkward, angular, ungainly, odd, and, being a very sensitive man, I think that it added to his awkwardness; he was a diffident man, somewhat, and a sensitive one, and both of these added to his oddity, awkwardness, etc., as it seemed to me. Lincoln had confidence, full and complete confidence in himself, self-thoughtful, self-helping, and self-supporting, relying on no man. Lincoln's voice was, when he first began speaking, shrill, squeaking, piping, unpleasant; his general look, his form, his prose, the color of his flesh, wrinkled and dry, his sensitiveness, and his momentary diffidence, everything seemed to be against him, but he soon recovered. I can see him now, in my mind distinct. On rising to address the jury or the crowd he quite generally placed his hands behind him, the back part of his left hand resting in the palm of his right hand. As he proceeded and grew warmer, he moved his hands to the front of his person, generally interlocking his fingers and running one thumb around the other. Sometimes his hands, for a short while, would hang by his side. In still growing warmer, as he proceeded in his address, he used his hands—especially and generally his right hand—in his gestures; he used his head a great deal in speaking, throwing or jerking or moving it now here and now there, now in this position and now in that, in order to be more emphatic, to drive the idea home. Mr. Lincoln never beat the air, never sawed space with his hands, never acted for stage effect; was cool, careful, earnest, sincere, truthful, fair, self-possessed, not insulting, not dictatorial; was pleasing, good-natured; had great strong naturalness of look, pose, and act; was clear in his ideas, simple in his words, strong, terse, and demonstrative; he spoke and acted to convince individuals and masses; he used in his gestures his right hand, sometimes shooting that long bony forefinger of his to dot an idea or to express a thought, resting his thumb on his middle finger. Bear in mind that he did not gesticulate much and *yet it is true* that every organ of his body was in motion and acted with ease, elegance, and grace, so it all looked *to me*.

As Mr. Lincoln proceeded further along with his oration, if time, place, subject, and occasion admitted of it, he gently and gradually warmed up; his shrill, squeaking, piping voice became harmonious, melodious, musical, if you please, with face somewhat aglow; his form dilated, swelled out, and he rose up a splendid form, erect, straight, and dignified; he stood square on his feet with both legs up and down, toe even with toe—that is, he did not put one foot before another; he kept his feet parallel and close to and not far from each other. When Mr. Lincoln rose up to speak, he rose slowly, steadily, firmly; he never moved much about on the stand or platform when speaking, trusting no desk, table, railing; he ran his eyes slowly over the crowd, giving them time to be at ease and to completely recover himself, *as I suppose*. He frequently took hold with his left hand, his left thumb erect, of the left lapel of his coat, keeping his right hand free to gesture in order to drive home and to clinch an idea. In his greatest inspiration he held both of his hands out above his head at an angle of about fifty degrees, hands open or clenched, according to his feeling and his ideas.

* * *

Harriet Beecher Stowe

When the author of *Uncle Tom's Cabin* and Lincoln met at the White House, Lincoln said: "So you're the little woman who wrote the book that made the great war." Early in 1864 Harriet Beecher Stowe wrote a biographical appraisal of Lincoln, from which the following excerpts are taken:

Lincoln is a strong man, but his strength is of a peculiar kind; it is not aggressive so much as passive, and among passive things, it is like the strength not so much of a stone buttress as of a wire cable. It is strength swaying to every influence, yielding on this side and on that to popular needs, yet tenaciously and inflexibly bound to carry its great end; and probably by no other kind of strength could our national ship have been drawn safely thus far during the tossings and tempests which beset her way.

. . . . .

In times of our trouble Abraham Lincoln has had his turn of being the best abused man of our nation. Like Moses leading his Israel through the wilderness, he has seen the day when every man seemed ready to stone him, and yet, with simple, wiry, steady perseverance, he has held on, conscious of honest intentions, and looking to God for help. All the nation have felt, in the increasing solemnity of his proclamations and papers, how deep an education was being wrought in his mind by this simple faith in God, the ruler of nations, and this humble willingness to learn the awful lessons of providence.

Slow and careful in coming to resolutions, willing to talk with every person who had anything to show on any side of a disputed subject, long in weighing and pondering, attached to constitutional limits and time-honored landmarks, Lincoln certainly was the safest leader a nation could have at a time when the habeas corpus must be suspended, and all the constitutional and minor rights of citizens be thrown into the hands of their military leader. A reckless, bold, theorizing, dashing man of genius might have wrecked our Constitution and ended us in a splendid military despotism.

Among the many accusations which in hours of ill-luck have been thrown out upon Lincoln, it is remarkable that he has never been called self-seeking, or selfish. When we were troubled and sat in darkness, and looked doubtfully towards the presidential chair, it was never that we doubted the good-will of our pilot—only the clearness of his eyesight. But Almighty God has granted to him that clearness of vision which he gives to the true-hearted, and enabled him to set

his honest foot in that promised land of freedom which is to be the
patrimony of all men, black and white—and from henceforth nations
shall rise up to call him blessed.

(From *Littell's Living Age*,
Boston, February 6, 1864)

*   *   *

Gideon Welles

Gideon Welles, Secretary of the Navy throughout Lincoln's
administration, tells in his diary the story of Lincoln's final
hours.

[April 14]
The President had been carried across the street from the theatre
[Ford's Theatre], to the house of a Mr. Peterson. We entered by
ascending a flight of steps above the basement and passing through
a long hall to the rear, where the President lay extended on a bed,
breathing heavily. Several surgeons were present, at least six, I should
think more. Among them I was glad to observe Dr. Hall, who, however, soon left. I inquired of Dr. H., as I entered, the true condition
of the President. He replied the President was dead to all intents,
although he might live three hours or perhaps longer.

The giant sufferer lay extended diagonally across the bed, which
was not long enough for him. He had been stripped of his clothes.
His large arms, which were occasionally exposed, were of a size which
one would scarce have expected from his spare appearance. His slow,
full respiration lifted the clothes with each breath that he took. His
features were calm and striking. I had never seen them appear to
better advantage than for the first hour, perhaps, that I was there.
After that, his right eye began to swell and that part of his face
became discolored.

Senator Sumner was there, I think, when I entered. If not he came
in soon after, as did Speaker Colfax, Mr. Secretary McCulloch, and
the other members of the Cabinet, with the exception of Mr. Seward.
A double guard was stationed at the door and on the sidewalk, to
repress the crowd, which was of course highly excited and anxious.
The room was small and overcrowded. The surgeons and members
of the Cabinet were as many as should have been in the room, but
there were many more, and the hall and other rooms in the front or
main house were full. One of these rooms was occupied by Mrs.

Lincoln and her attendants, with Miss Harris. Mrs. Dixon and Mrs. Kinney came to her about twelve o'clock. About once an hour Mrs. Lincoln would repair to the bedside of her dying husband and with lamentation and tears remain until overcome by emotion.

[April 15.] A door which opened upon a porch or gallery, and also the windows, were kept open for fresh air. The night was dark, cloudy, and damp, and about six it began to rain. I remained in the room until then without sitting or leaving it, when, there being a vacant chair which some one left at the foot of the bed, I occupied it for nearly two hours, listening to the heavy groans, and witnessing the wasting life of the good and great man who was expiring before me.

About 6 A.M. I experienced a feeling of faintness and for the first time after entering the room, a little past eleven, I left it and the house, and took a short walk in the open air. It was a dark and gloomy morning, and rain set in before I returned to the house, some fifteen minutes [later]. Large groups of people were gathered every few rods, all anxious and solicitous. Some one or more from each group stepped forward as I passed, to inquire into the condition of the President, and to ask if there was no hope. Intense grief was on every countenance when I replied that the President could survive but a short time. The colored people especially—and there were at this time more of them, perhaps, than of whites—were overwhelmed with grief.

Returning to the house, I seated myself in the back parlor, where the Attorney-General and others had been engaged in taking evidence concerning the assassination. Stanton, and Speed, and Usher were there, the latter asleep on the bed. There were three or four others also in the room. While I did not feel inclined to sleep, as many did, I was somewhat indisposed. I had been so for several days. The excitement and bad atmosphere from the crowded rooms oppressed me physically.

A little before seven, I went into the room where the dying President was rapidly drawing near the closing moments. His wife soon after made her last visit to him. The death-struggle had begun. Robert, his son, stood with several others at the head of the bed. He bore himself well, but on two occasions gave way to overpowering grief and sobbed aloud, turning his head and leaning on the shoulder of Senator Sumner. The respiration of the President became suspended at intervals, and at last entirely ceased at twenty-two minutes past seven.

*   *   *

Walt Whitman

Lincoln and Whitman never personally met. But Lincoln read *Leaves of Grass* in 1856, soon after it was published, and we are told that the book was in his Springfield law office on a table and that he frequently picked it up and read aloud from it. Whitman saw Lincoln for the first time on February 18, 1860, when the President-elect visited New York. He noticed "his perfect composure and coolness . . . his unusual and uncouth height. . . . He looked with curiosity upon that immense sea of faces, and the sea of faces returned the look with similar curiosity. In both, there was a dash of comedy, almost farce, such as Shakspere puts in his blackest tragedies." Later Whitman's admiration for Lincoln increased, and when he moved to Washington, he often saw Lincoln driving in his barouche through the streets. On March 4, 1865, the day of his second inauguration, Lincoln held a public reception at the White House. Walt Whitman attended it, but did not try to shake the President's hand, as most of the others did. He admired him from a distance. We know that Lincoln had often nodded to the poet in passing him on Pennsylvania Avenue. A. Van Rensselaer reports in a letter that Lincoln once, upon seeing the bearded giant in the broad-brimmed felt, said: "Well, *he* looks like a *man*." Whitman loved Lincoln deeply, as one loves a dear friend. He saw in him a man of the people, a man who "saved the Union of these States." Lincoln was to him "the sweetest, wisest soul of all my days and lands."

In his poetry and his prose Lincoln has an important place.

. . . Though hundreds of portraits have been made [of Lincoln], by painters and photographers, (many to pass on, by copies, to future times,) I have never seen one yet that in my opinion deserv'd to be called a perfectly good likeness; nor do I believe there is really such a one in existence. May I not say too, that, as there is no entirely competent and emblematic likeness of Abraham Lincoln in picture or statue, there is not—perhaps cannot be—any fully appropriate literary statement or summing up of him yet in existence? . . .

One of the best of the late commentators on Shakspere, (Professor Dowden,) makes the height and aggregate of his quality as a poet to be, that he thoroughly blended the ideal with the practical or realistic. If this be so, I should say that what Shakspere did in poetic expression, Abraham Lincoln essentially did in his personal and official life. I should say the invisible foundations and vertebra of his character, more than any man's in history, were mystical, abstract, moral and spiritual—while upon all of them was built, and out of all of them radiated, under the control of the average of circumstances, what the vulgar call horse-sense, and a life often bent by temporary but most urgent materialistic and political reasons.

He seems to have been a man of indomitable firmness (even obstinacy) on rare occasions, involving great points; but he was generally very easy, flexible, tolerant, almost slouchy, respecting minor matters. I note that even those reports and anecdotes intended to level him down, all leave the tinge of favorable impression of him. As to his religious nature, it seems to me to have certainly been of the amplest, deepest-rooted, loftiest kind.

(From *November Boughs*)

*

August 12, 1863—I see the President almost every day, as I happen to live where he passes to or from his lodgings out of town. He never sleeps at the White House during the hot season, but has quarters at a healthy location some three miles north of the city, the Soldiers' home, a United States military establishment. I saw him this morning about 8½ coming in to business, riding on Vermont avenue, near L street. He always has a company of twenty-five or thirty cavalry, with sabres drawn and held upright over their shoulders. They say this guard was against his personal wish, but he let his counselors have their way. The party makes no great show in uniform or horses. Mr. Lincoln on the saddle generally rides a good-sized, easy-going gray horse, is dress'd in plain black, somewhat rusty and dusty, wears a black stiff hat, and looks about as ordinary in attire, &c., as the commonest man. A lieutenant, with yellow straps, rides at his left, and following behind, two by two, come the cavalry men, in their yellow-striped jackets. They are generally going at a slow trot, as that is the pace set them by the one they wait upon. The sabres and accoutrements clank, and the entirely unornamental cortège as it trots toward Lafayette square arouses no sensation, only some curious stranger stops and gazes. I see very plainly Abraham Lincoln's dark brown face, with the deep-cut lines, the eyes, always to me with a deep latent sadness in the expression. We have got so that we exchange bows, and very cordial ones. Sometimes the President goes and comes in an open barouche. The cavalry always accompany him, with drawn sabres. Often I notice as he goes out evenings—and sometimes in the morning, when he returns early—he turns off and halts at the large and handsome residence of the Secretary of War, on K street, and holds conference there. If in his barouche, I can see from my window he does not alight, but sits in his vehicle, and Mr. Stanton comes out to attend him. Sometimes one of his sons, a boy of ten or twelve, accompanies him, riding at his right on a pony. Earlier in the summer I occasionally saw the President and his wife, toward the latter part of the afternoon, out in a barouche, on a pleasure ride through the city. Mrs. Lincoln was dress'd in complete black, with a long crape veil. The equipage is of the plainest kind, only two horses, and they nothing extra. They pass'd me once very close, and I saw the President in the face fully, as they were moving slowly, and his look, though abstracted, happen'd to be directed steadily in my eye. He bow'd and smiled, but far beneath his smile I noticed well the expression I have alluded to. None of the artists or pictures has caught the deep, though subtle and indirect expression of this man's face. There is something else there. One of the great portrait painters of two or three centuries ago is needed.

*

April 16, 1865—I find in my notes of the time, this passage on the death of Abraham Lincoln: He leaves for America's history and biography, so far, not only its most dramatic reminiscence—he leaves, in my opinion, the greatest, best, most characteristic, artistic, moral personality. Not but that he had faults, and show'd them in the Presidency; but honesty, goodness, shrewdness, conscience, and (a new virtue, unknown to other lands, and hardly yet really known here, but the foundation and tie of all, as the future will grandly develop,) UNIONISM, in its truest and amplest sense, form'd the hardpan of his character. These he seal'd with his life. The tragic splendor of his death, purging, illuminating all, throws round his form, his head, an aureole that will remain and will grow brighter through time, while history lives, and love of the country lasts. By many has this Union been help'd; but if one name, one man, must be pick'd out, he, most of all, is the conservator of it, to the future. He was assassinated—but the Union is not assassinated—*ça ira!* One falls, and another falls. The soldier drops, sinks like a wave—but the ranks of the ocean eternally press on. Death does its work, obliterates a hundred, a thousand—President, general, captain, private—but the Nation is immortal.

(From *Specimen Days*)

*

The grand deaths of the race—the dramatic deaths of every nationality—are its most important inheritance-value—in some respects beyond its literature and art— (as the hero is beyond his finest portrait, and the battle itself beyond its choicest song or epic). Is not here indeed the point underlying all tragedy? the famous pieces of the Grecian masters—and all masters? Why, if the old Greeks had had this man, what trilogies of plays—what epics would have been made out of him! How the rhapsodes would have recited him! How quickly that quaint tall form would have enter'd into the region where men vitalize gods, and gods divinify men! But Lincoln, his times, his death—great as any, any age—belong altogether to our own, and are autochthonic. (Sometimes indeed I think our American days, our own stage—the actors we know and have shaken hands, or talk'd with—more fateful than any thing in Eschylus—more heroic than the fighters around Troy—afford kings of men for our Democracy prouder than Agamemnon—models of character cute and hardy as Ulysses—deaths more pitiful than Priam's.)

When, centuries hence, (as it must, in my opinion, be centuries hence before the life of these States, or of Democracy, can be really written and illustrated,) the leading historians and dramatists seek for some personage, some special event, incisive enough to mark with deepest cut, and mnemonize, this turbulent Nineteenth century of ours, (not only these States, but all over the political and social world)—something, perhaps, to close that gorgeous procession of European feudalism, with all its pomp and caste-prejudices, (of whose long train we in America are yet so inextricably the heirs)— something to identify with terrible identification, by far the greatest revolutionary step in the history of the United States, (perhaps the greatest of the world, our century)—the absolute extirpation and erasure of slavery from the States—those historians will seek in vain for any point to serve more thoroughly their purpose, than Abraham Lincoln's death.

Dear to the Muse—thrice dear to Nationality—to the whole human race—precious to this Union—precious to Democracy—unspeakably and forever precious—their first great Martyr Chief.

(From "Death of Lincoln")

*

"When Lilacs Last in the Dooryard Bloom'd," an elegy on Lincoln's death, presents a lament by the poet as he witnessed the funeral procession of the dead President, and makes use of three recurring symbols: a lilac branch, signifying love; "the drooping star in the west," representing Lincoln; and a singing thrush, symbolizing the poet himself. The following is an excerpt from the poem:

> Over the breast of the spring, the land, amid cities,
> Amid lanes and through old woods, where lately the violets peep'd from the ground, spotting the gray debris,
> Amid the grass in the fields each side of the lanes, passing the endless grass,
> Passing the yellow-spear'd wheat, every grain from its shroud in the dark-brown fields uprisen,
> Passing the apple-tree blows of white and pink in the orchards,
> Carrying a corpse to where it shall rest in the grave,
> Night and day journeys a coffin.
> Coffin that passes through lanes and streets,
> Through day and night with the great cloud darkening the land,
> With the pomp of the inloop'd flags with the cities draped in black,
> With the show of the States themselves as of crape-veil'd women standing,
> With processions long and winding and the flambeaus of the night,
> With the countless torches lit, with the silent sea of faces and the unbared heads,
> With the waiting depot, the arriving coffin, and the sombre faces,
> With dirges through the night, with the thousand voices rising strong and solemn,

With all the mournful voices of the dirges pour'd around the coffin,
The dim-lit churches and the shuddering organs—where amid
    these you journey,
With the tolling tolling bells' perpetual clang,
Here, coffin that slowly passes,
I give you my sprig of lilac.

*

The three poems "O Captain! My Captain!"; "Hush'd be the
Camps To-Day"; "This Dust Was Once the Man" were written
shortly after Lincoln's assassination.

O CAPTAIN! MY CAPTAIN!

O Captain! my Captain! our fearful trip is done,
The ship has weather'd every rack, the prize we sought is won,
The port is near, the bells I hear, the people all exulting,
While follow eyes the steady keel, the vessel grim and daring;
      But O heart! heart! heart!
      O the bleeding drops of red,
         Where on the deck my Captain lies,
         Fallen cold and dead.

O Captain! my Captain! rise up and hear the bells;
Rise up—for you the flag is flung—for you the bugle trills,
For you bouquets and ribbon'd wreaths—for the shores
    a-crowding,
For you they call, the swaying mass, their eager faces turning;
      Here Captain! dear father!
      This arm beneath your head!
         It is some dream that on the deck,
         You've fallen cold and dead.

My Captain does not answer, his lips are pale and still,
My father does not feel my arm, he has no pulse nor will,
The ship is anchor'd safe and sound, its voyage closed and done,
From fearful trip the victor ship comes in with object won;
      Exult O shores, and ring O bells!
      But I with mournful tread,
         Walk the deck my Captain lies,
         Fallen cold and dead.

HUSH'D BE THE CAMPS TO-DAY

Hush'd be the camps to-day,
And soldiers let us drape our war-worn weapons,
And each with musing soul retire to celebrate,
Our dear commander's death.

No more for him life's stormy conflicts,
Nor victory, nor defeat—no more time's dark events,
Charging like ceaseless clouds across the sky.

But sing poet in our name,
Sing of the love we bore him—because you, dweller in camps,
    know it truly.

As they invault the coffin there,
Sing—as they close the doors of earth upon him—one verse,
For the heavy hearts of soldiers.

THIS DUST WAS ONCE THE MAN

This dust was once the man,
Gentle, plain, just and resolute, under whose cautious hand,
Against the foulest crime in history known in any land or age,
Was saved the Union of these States.

*   *   *

Ralph Waldo Emerson

Emerson met Lincoln at the White House in 1862. Lincoln
recalled having attended one of Emerson's lectures.

A plain man of the people, an extraordinary fortune attended him.
He offered no shining qualities at the first encounter; he did not
offend by superiority. He had a face and manner which disarmed
suspicion, which inspired confidence, which confirmed good will.
He was a man without vices. He had a strong sense of duty, which
it was very easy for him to obey. Then, he had what farmers call a
long head; was excellent in working out the sum for himself; in
arguing his case and convincing you fairly and firmly. Then, it
turned out that he was a great worker; had prodigious faculty of
performance; worked easily. A good worker is so rare; everybody has

some disabling quality. In a host of young men that start together and promise so many brilliant leaders for the next age, each fails on trial; one by bad health, one by conceit, or by love of pleasure, or lethargy, or an ugly temper—each has some disqualifying fault that throws him out of the career. But this man was sound to the core, cheerful, persistent, all right for labor, and liked nothing so well.

Then, he had a vast good nature, which made him tolerant and accessible to all; fair-minded, leaning to the claim of the petitioner; affable, and not sensible to the affliction which the innumerable visits paid to him when President would have brought to any one else. And how this good nature became a noble humanity, in many a tragic case which the events of the war brought to him, every one will remember; and with what increasing tenderness he dealt when a whole race was thrown on his compassion. The poor negro said of him, on an impressive occasion, "Massa Linkum am eberywhere."

Then his broad good humor, running easily into jocular talk, in which he delighted and in which he excelled, was a rich gift to this wise man. It enabled him to keep his secret; to meet every kind of man and every rank in society; to take off the edge of the severest decisions; to mask his own purpose and sound his companion; and to catch with true instinct the temper of every company he addressed. And, more than all, it is to a man of severe labor, in anxious and exhausting crises, the natural restorative, good as sleep, and is the protection of the overdriven brain against rancor and insanity.

He is the author of a multitude of good sayings, so disguised as pleasantries that it is certain they had no reputation at first but as jests; and only later, by the very acceptance and adoption they find in the mouths of millions, turn out to be the wisdom of the hour. I am sure if this man had ruled in a period of less facility of printing he would have become mythological in a very few years, like Aesop of Pilpay, or one of the Seven Wise Masters, by his fables and proverbs. But the weight and penetration of many passages in his letters, messages and speeches, hidden now by the very closeness of their application to the moment, are destined hereafter to wide fame. What pregnant definitions; what unerring common sense; what foresight; and, on great occasion, what lofty, and more than national, what humane tone! His brief speech at Gettysburg will not easily be surpassed by words on any recorded occasion. This, and one other American speech, that of John Brown to the court that tried him, and a part of Kossuth's speech at Birmingham, can only be compared with each other, and with no fourth.

His occupying the chair of state was a triumph of the good sense of mankind, and of the public conscience. This middle-class country had got a middle-class president, at last. Yes, in manners and sympathies, but not in powers, for his powers were superior. This man grew according to his need. His mind mastered the problem of the day; and as the problem grew, so did his comprehension of it. Rarely was a man so fitted to the event. In the midst of fears and jealousies, in the Babel of counsels and parties, this man wrought incessantly with all his might and all his honesty, laboring to find what the people wanted, and how to obtain that. It cannot be said there is any exaggeration of his worth. If ever a man was fairly tested, he was. There was no lack of resistance, nor of slander, nor of ridicule. The times have allowed no state secrets; the nation has been in such ferment, such multitudes had to be trusted, that no secret could be kept. Every door was ajar, and we know all that befell.

Then, what an occasion was the whirlwind of the war. Here was place for no holiday magistrate, no fair-weather sailor; the new pilot was hurried to the helm in a tornado. In four years—four years of battle-days—his endurance, his fertility of resources, his magnanimity, were sorely tried and never found wanting. There, by his courage, his justice, his even temper, his fertile counsel, his humanity, he stood a heroic figure in the centre of a heroic epoch. He is the true history of the American people of his time. Step by step he walked before them; slow with their slowness, quickening his march by theirs, the true representative of this continent; an entirely public man; father of his country, the pulse of twenty millions throbbing in his heart, the thought of their minds articulated by his tongue.

(From a speech made at Concord on April 19,
1865, at the funeral services for Lincoln)

*   *   *

William Cullen Bryant

One of the leading poets of his day, W. C. Bryant wrote the following ode which was read at a great meeting in Union Square, New York, on the day Lincoln's body had lain in state at the City Hall.

> O slow to smite and swift to spare,
>   Gentle and merciful and just!
> Who, in the fear of God, did'st hear,
>   The sword of power—a nation's trust:
>
> In sorrow by thy bier we stand,
>   Amid the awe that hushes all,
> And speak the anguish of a land
>   That shook with horror at thy fall.
>
> The task is done—the bonds are free;
>   We bear thee to an honored grave,
> Whose noblest monument shall be
>   The broken fetters of the slave.
>
> Pure was thy life; its bloody close
>   Hath placed thee with the sons of light,
> Among the noble host of those
>   Who perished in the cause of right.

*   *   *

Herman Melville

The author of *Moby Dick* has memorialized Lincoln in several poems, among them "The Martyr."

THE MARTYR

Indicative of the Passion of the People on the 15th Day of April, 1865

> Good Friday was the day
>   Of the prodigy and crime
> When they killed him in his pity,
>   When they killed him in his prime
> Of clemency and calm—
>   When with yearning he was filled
>   To redeem the evil-willed,
> And, though conqueror, be kind;
>   But they killed him in his kindness,

In their madness and their blindness,
And they killed him from behind.

There is sobbing of the strong,
    And a pall upon the land;
But the People in their weeping
    Bare the iron hand;
Beware the People weeping
    When they bare the iron hand.

He lieth in his blood—
    The father in his face;
They have killed him, the Forgiver—
    The Avenger takes his place,
The Avenger wisely stern,
    Who in righteousness shall do
    What the heavens call him to,
And the parricides remand;
    For they killed him in his kindness,
    In their madness and their blindness,
And his blood is on their hand.

There is sobbing of the strong,
    And a pall upon the land;
But the People in their weeping
    Bare the iron hand:
Beware the People weeping
    When they bare the iron hand.

(From *Battle Pieces and
Aspects of the War,* 1866)

*   *   *

James Russell Lowell

He knew to bide his time,
And can his fame abide,
Still patient in his simple faith sublime,
Till the wise years decide.
Great captains, with their guns and drums,
Disturb our judgment for the hour,

But at last silence comes;
These all are gone, and standing like a tower,
Our children shall behold his fame,
The kindly-earnest, brave, foreseeing man,
Sagacious, patient, dreading praise, not blame,
New birth of our new soil, the first American.

(From his "Commemorative Ode")

LINCOLN SPEAKS

From a Communication to the People of
Sangamo County. March 9, 1832.*

Every man is said to have his peculiar ambition. Whether it be
true or not, I can say for one that I have no other so great as that of
being truly esteemed of my fellow men, by rendering myself worthy
of their esteem. How far I shall succeed in gratifying this ambition,
is yet to be developed. I am young and unknown to many of you.
I was born and have ever remained in the most humble walks of life.
I have no wealthy or popular relations to recommend me. My case
is thrown exclusively upon the independent voters of this county,
and if elected they will have conferred a favor upon me for which
I shall be unremitting in my labors to compensate. But if the good
people in their wisdom shall see fit to keep me in the background,
I have been too familiar with disappointments to be very much
chagrined.

*　　*　　*

From Address before the Young Men's Lyceum of
Springfield, Illinois. January 27, 1838.

Let every American, every lover of liberty, every well wisher to his
posterity, swear by the blood of the Revolution, never to violate in
the least particular the laws of the country; and never to tolerate
their violation by others. As the patriots of seventy-six did to the
support of the Declaration of Independence, so to the support of the
Constitution and Laws, let every American pledge his life, his property, and his sacred honor, let every man remember that to violate

* *Sangamo Journal,* March 15, 1832. Nicolay and Hay, the editors of *The Complete Works of Abraham Lincoln,* 1930, state that this communication was distributed as a handbill. If so no copies seem to have survived. (*The Collected
Works of Abraham Lincoln,* edited by Roy P. Basler, 1953)

the law is to trample on the blood of his father, and to tear the charter of his own and his children's liberty. Let reverence for the laws be breathed by every American mother to the lisping babe that prattles on her lap. Let it be taught in schools, in seminaries; and in colleges. Let it be written in primers, spelling-books, and in almanacs. Let it be preached from the pulpit, proclaimed in legislative halls, and enforced in courts of justice. And, in short, let it become the political religion of the nation.

* * *

From Address before the Washington Temperance Society, Springfield, Illinois. February 22, 1842.

When the conduct of men is designed to be influenced, persuasion, kind, unassuming persuasion, should ever be adopted. It is an old and a true maxim, that a "drop of honey catches more flies than a gallon of gall." So with men. If you would win a man to your cause, first convince him that you are his sincere friend. Therein is a drop of honey that catches his heart, which, say what he will, is the great highroad to his reason, and which, when once gained, you will find but little trouble in convincing his judgment of the justice of your cause, if indeed that cause really be a just one. On the contrary, assume to dictate to his judgment, or to command his action, or to mark him as one to be shunned and despised, and he will retreat within himself, close all the avenues to his head and his heart; and though your cause be naked truth itself, transformed to the heaviest lance, harder than steel, and sharper than steel can be made, and though you throw it with more than Herculean force and precision, you shall no more be able to pierce him, than to penetrate the hard shell of a tortoise with a rye straw. Such is man, and so must he be understood by those who would lead him, even to his own best interest.

* * *

A Fragment on Slavery. July 1, 1854 (?)

If A. can prove, however conclusively, that he may, of right, enslave B.—why may not B. snatch the same argument, and prove equally, that he may enslave A?—You say A. is white and B. is black. It is *color*, then; the lighter having the right to enslave the darker? Take care. By this rule you are to be slave to the first man you meet with a fairer skin than your own.

You do not mean *color* exactly? You mean the whites are *intellectually* the superiors of the blacks, and therefore have the right to enslave them? Take care again. By this rule you are to be slave to the first man you meet with an intellect superior to your own.

But, say you, it is a question of *interest;* and, if you make it your *interest,* you have the right to enslave another. Very well. And if he can make it his interest, he has the right to enslave you.

* * *

A Fragment on Government. July 1, 1854 (?)

The legitimate object of government, is to do for a community of people, whatever they need to have done, but cannot do, *at all,* or cannot, *so well do,* for themselves—in their separate, and individual capacities.

In all that the people can individually do as well for themselves, government ought not to interfere.

The desirable things which the individuals of a people cannot do, or cannot well do, for themselves, fall into two classes: those which have relation to *wrongs,* and those which have not. Each of. these branch off into an infinite variety of subdivisions.

The first—that in relation to wrongs—embraces all crimes, misdemeanors, and nonperformance of contracts. The other embraces all which, in its nature, and without wrong, requires combined action, as public roads and highways, public schools, charities, pauperism, orphanage, estates of the deceased, and the machinery of government itself.

From this it appears that if all men were just, there still would be *some,* though not *so much,* need of government.

* * *

From a Speech at Peoria, Illinois. Oct. 16, 1854.

The doctrine of self-government is right—absolutely and eternally right—but it has no just application, as here attempted. Or perhaps I should rather say that whether it has such just application depends whether a negro is *not* or *is* a man. If he is *not* a man, why in that case, he who *is* a man may, as a matter of self-government, do just as he pleases with him. But if the negro *is* a man, is it not to that extent, a total destruction of self-government, to say that he too shall not govern *himself*? When the white man governs himself that is self-government; but when he governs himself, and also governs *another* man, that is *more* than self-government—that is despotism. If the negro is a *man* why then my ancient faith teaches me that "all men are created equal"; and that there can be no moral right in connection with one man's making a slave of another.

* * *

From "A House Divided," Speech at Springfield, Illinois. June 16, 1858.

We are now far into the fifth year since a policy was initiated with the avowed object, and confident promise, of putting an end to slavery agitation. Under the operation of that policy, that agitation has not only, not ceased, but has constantly augmented. In my opinion, it will not cease, until a crisis shall have been reached, and passed. "A house divided against itself cannot stand." I believe this government cannot endure, permanently half slave and half free. I do not expect the Union to be dissolved—I do not expect the house to fall—but I do expect it will cease to be divided. It will become all one thing, or all the other. Either the opponents of slavery will arrest the further spread of it, and place it where the public mind shall rest in the belief that it is in course of ultimate extinction; or its advocates will push it forward, till it shall become alike lawful in all the States, old as well as new—North as well as South.

* * *

Farewell Address at Springfield, Illinois. February 11, 1861.

My friends—No one, not in my situation, can appreciate my feeling of sadness at this parting. To this place, and the kindness of these people, I owe every thing. Here I have lived a quarter of a century, and have passed from a young to an old man. Here my children have been born, and one is buried. I now leave, not knowing when, or whether ever, I may return, with a task before me greater than that which rested upon Washington. Without the assistance of that Divine Being, who ever attended him, I cannot succeed. With that assistance I cannot fail. Trusting in Him, who can go with me, and remain with you, and be everywhere for good, let us confidently hope that all will yet be well. To His care commending you, as I hope in your prayers you will commend me, I bid you an affectionate farewell.

* * *

From Speech in Independence Hall, Philadelphia. February 22, 1861.

I have never had a feeling politically that did not spring from the sentiments embodied in the Declaration of Independence.

I have often pondered over the dangers which were incurred by the men who assembled here and framed and adopted that Declaration of Independence—I have pondered over the toils that were endured by the officers and soldiers of the army, who achieved that Independence. I have often inquired of myself, what great principle or idea it was that kept this Confederacy so long together. It was not the mere matter of the separation of the colonies from the mother land; but that sentiment in the Declaration of Independence which gave liberty, not alone to the people of this country, but hope to the world for all future time. It was that which gave promise that in due time the weights would be lifted from the shoulders of all men, and that all should have an equal chance. This is the sentiment embodied in that Declaration of Independence.

* * *

From First Inaugural Address. March 4, 1861.

I hold, that in contemplation of universal law, and of the Constitution, the Union of these states is perpetual. Perpetuity is implied, if not expressed, in the fundamental law of all national governments. It is safe to assert that no government proper, ever had a provision in its organic law for its own termination. Continue to execute all the express provisions of our national Constitution, and the Union will endure forever—it being impossible to destroy it, except by some action not provided for in the instrument itself.

Again, if the United States be not a government proper, but an association of states in the nature of contract merely, can it, as a contract, be peaceably unmade, by less than all the parties who made it? One party to a contract may violate it—break it so to speak; but does it require all to lawfully rescind it?

Descending from these general principles, we find the proposition that, in legal contemplation, the Union is perpetual, confirmed by the history of the Union itself. The Union is much older than the Constitution. It was formed in fact, by the Articles of Association in 1774. It was matured and continued by the Declaration of Independence in 1776. It was further matured and the faith of all the thirteen states expressedly plighted and engaged that it should be perpetual, by the Articles of Confederation in 1778. And finally, in 1787, one of the declared objects for ordaining and establishing the Constitution, was *"to form a more perfect union."*

But if destruction of the Union, by one, or by a part only, of the states, be lawfully possible, the Union is *less* perfect than before the Constitution, having lost the vital element of perpetuity.

It follows from these views that no state, upon its own mere motion, can lawfully get out of the Union—that *resolves* and *ordinances* to that effect are legally void; and that acts of violence, within any state or states, against the authority of the United States, are insurrectionary or revolutionary, according to circumstances.

I therefore consider that, in view of the Constitution and the laws, the Union is unbroken; and, to the extent of my ability, I shall take care, as the Constitution itself expressly enjoins upon me, that the laws of the Union be faithfully executed in all the states. Doing this I deem to be only a simple duty on my part; and I shall perform it, so far as practicable, unless my rightful masters, the American people, shall withhold the requisite means, or in some authoritative manner direct the contrary. I trust this will not be regarded as a menace, but only as the declared purpose of the Union that it *will* constitutionally defend, and maintain itself.

In doing this there needs to be no bloodshed or violence; and there shall be none, unless it be forced upon the national authority. The power confided to me, will be used to hold, occupy, and possess the property, and places belonging to the government, and to collect the duties and imposts; but beyond what may be necessary for these objects, there will be no invasion—no using of force against, or among the people anywhere. Where hostility to the United States, in any interior locality, shall be so great and so universal, as to prevent competent resident citizens from holding the federal offices, there will be no attempt to force obnoxious strangers among the people for that object. While the strict legal right may exist in the government to enforce the exercise of these offices, the attempt to do so would be so irritating, and so nearly impracticable with all, that I deem it better to forego, for the time, the uses of such offices. . . .

One section of our country believes slavery is *right*, and ought to be extended, while the other believes it is *wrong* and ought not to be extended. This is the only substantial dispute. The fugitive slave clause of the Constitution, and the law for the suppression of the foreign slave trade, are each as well enforced, perhaps, as any law can ever be in a community where the moral sense of the people imperfectly supports the law itself. The great body of the people abide by the dry legal obligation in both cases, and a few break over in each. This, I think, cannot be perfectly cured; and it would be worse in both cases *after* the separation of the sections, than before. The foreign slave trade, now imperfectly suppressed, would be ultimately revived without restriction, in one section; while fugitive slaves, now only partially surrendered, would not be surrendered at all, by the other.

Physically speaking, we cannot separate. We cannot remove our respective sections from each other, nor build an impassable wall between them. A husband and wife may be divorced, and go out of the presence, and beyond the reach of each other; but the different parts of our country cannot do this. They cannot but remain face to face; and intercourse, either amicable or hostile, must continue between them. Is it possible then to make that intercourse more advantageous, or more satisfactory, *after* separation than *before*? Can aliens make treaties easier than friends can make laws? Can treaties be more faithfully enforced between aliens, than laws can among friends? Suppose you go to war, you cannot fight always; and when, after much loss on both sides, and no gain on either, you cease fighting, the identical old questions, as to terms of intercourse, are again upon you.

This country, with its institutions, belongs to the people who inhabit it. Whenever they shall grow weary of the existing government, they can exercise their *constitutional* right of amending it, or their *revolutionary* right to dismember, or overthrow it. I cannot be ignorant of the fact that many worthy, and patriotic citizens are desirous of having the national Constitution amended. While I make no recommendation of amendments, I fully recognize the rightful authority of the people over the whole subject, to be exercised in either of the modes prescribed in the instrument itself; and I should, under existing circumstances, favor, rather than oppose, a fair opportunity being offered the people to act upon it. . . .

Why should there not be a patient confidence in the ultimate justice of the people? Is there any better or equal hope, in the world? In our present differences, is either party without faith of being in the right? If the Almighty Ruler of nations, with His eternal truth and justice, be on your side of the North, or on yours of the South, that truth, and that justice, will surely prevail, by the judgment of this great tribunal, the American people.

*   *   *

From First Message to the United States Congress, at the Special Session. July 4, 1861.

This is essentially a People's contest. On the side of the Union, it is a struggle for maintaining in the world, that form, and substance of government, whose leading object is, to elevate the condition of men—to lift artificial weights from all shoulders—to clear the paths of laudable pursuit for all—to afford all, an unfettered start, and a fair chance, in the race of life. . . .

Our popular government has often been called an experiment. Two points in it, our people have already settled—the successful establishing, and the successful administering of it. One still remains —its successful maintenance against a formidable internal attempt to overthrow it. It is now for them to demonstrate to the world, that those who can fairly carry an election, can also suppress a rebellion— that ballots are the rightful, and peaceful, successors of bullets; and that when ballots have fairly, and constitutionally, decided, there can be no successful appeal, back to bullets; that there can be no successful appeal, except to ballots themselves, at succeeding elections. Such will be a great lesson of peace; teaching men that what they cannot take by an election, neither can they take by a war—teaching all, the folly of being the beginners of a war.

*   *   *

From Message to Congress at Its Regular Session. December 3, 1861.

Labor is prior to, and independent of, capital. Capital is only the fruit of labor, and could never have existed if labor had not first existed. Labor is the superior of capital, and deserves much the higher consideration. Capital has its rights, which are as worthy of protection as any other rights. Nor is it denied that there is, and probably always will be, a relation between labor and capital, producing mutual benefits. The error is in assuming that the whole labor of community exists within that relation. A few men own capital, and that few avoid labor themselves, and, with their capital, hire or buy another few to labor for them. A large majority belong to neither class—neither work for others, nor have others working for them. . . . Men with their families—wives, sons, and daughters—work for themselves, on their farms, in their houses, and in their shops, taking the whole product to themselves, and asking no favors of capital on the one hand, nor of hired laborers or slaves on the other. It is not forgotten that a considerable number of persons mingle their own labor with capital—that is, they labor with their own hands, and also buy or hire others to labor for them; but this is only a mixed, and not a distinct class. No principle stated is disturbed by the existence of this mixed class.

Again: as has already been said, there is not, of necessity, any such thing as the free hired laborer being fixed to that condition for life. Many independent men, everywhere in these States, a few years back in their lives, were hired laborers. The prudent, penniless beginner in the world, labors for wages awhile, saves a surplus with which to buy tools or land for himself; then labors on his own account another while, and at length hires another new beginner to help him. This is the just, and generous, and prosperous system, which opens the way to all—gives hope to all, and consequent energy, and progress, and improvement of condition to all.

No men living are more worthy to be trusted than those who toil up from poverty—none less inclined to take, or touch, aught which they have not honestly earned. Let them beware of surrendering a political power which they already possess, and which, if surrendered, will surely be used to close the door of advancement against such as they, and to fix new disabilities and burdens upon them, till all of liberty shall be lost.

* * *

Meditation on the Divine Will.
September 2, 1862 (?)

The will of God prevails. In great contests each party claims to act in accordance with the will of God. Both *may* be, and one *must* be wrong. God can not be *for*, and *against* the same thing at the same time. In the present civil war it is quite possible that God's purpose is something different from the purpose of either party—and yet the human instrumentalities, working just as they do, are of the best adaptation to effect His purpose. I am almost ready to say this is probably true—that God wills this contest, and wills that it shall not end yet. By His mere quiet power, on the minds of the now contestants, He could have either *saved* or *destroyed* the Union without a human contest. Yet the contest began. And having begun He could give the final victory to either side any day. Yet the contest proceeds.

* * *

From Reply to Emancipation Memorial Presented by
Chicago Christians of All Denominations.
September 13, 1862.

The subject presented in the memorial is one upon which I have thought much for weeks past, and I may even say for months. I am approached with the most opposite opinions and advice, and that by religious men, who are equally certain that they represent the Divine will. I am sure that either the one or the other class is mistaken in that belief, and perhaps in some respects both. I hope it will not be irreverent for me to say that if it is probable that God would reveal His will to others, on a point so connected with my duty, it might be supposed that He would reveal it directly to me; for, unless I am more deceived in myself than I often am, it is my earnest desire to know the will of Providence in this matter. And if I can learn what it is, I will do it! These are not, however, the days of miracles, and I suppose it will be granted that I am not to expect a direct revelation. I must study the plain, physical facts of the case, ascertain what is possible, and learn what appears to be wise and right.

* * *

From Annual Message to Congress. December 1, 1862.

We cannot escape history. We of this Congress and this administration, will be remembered in spite of ourselves. No personal significance, or insignificance, can spare one or another of us. The fiery trial through which we pass, will light us down, in honor or dishonor, to the latest generation. We *say* we are for the Union. The world will not forget that we say this. We know how to save the Union. The world knows we do know how to save it. We—even we here—hold the power, and bear the responsibility. In giving freedom to the slave, we assure freedom to the free—honorable alike in what we give, and what we preserve. We shall nobly save, or meanly lose, the last, best hope of earth. Other means may succeed; this could not fail. The way is plain, peaceful, generous, just—a way which, if followed, the world will forever applaud, and God must forever bless.

* * *

Address Delivered at the Dedication of the Cemetery at Gettysburg. November 19, 1863.

Four score and seven years ago our fathers brought forth on this continent a new nation, conceived in Liberty, and dedicated to the proposition that all men are created equal.

Now we are engaged in a great civil war, testing whether that nation, or any nation so conceived, and so dedicated, can long endure. We are met on a great battle-field of that war. We have come to dedicate a portion of that field, as a final resting place for those who here gave their lives that that nation might live. It is altogether fitting and proper that we should do this.

But, in a larger sense, we cannot dedicate—we cannot consecrate—we cannot hallow—this ground. The brave men, living and dead, who struggled here, have consecrated it, far above our poor power to add or detract. The world will little note, nor long remember what we say here, but it can never forget what they did here. It is for us, the living, rather, to be dedicated here to the unfinished work which they who fought here have, thus far, so nobly advanced. It is rather for us to be here dedicated to the great task remaining before us— that from these honored dead we take increased devotion to that cause for which they gave the last full measure of devotion—that we here highly resolve that these dead shall not have died in vain—that this nation, under God, shall have a new birth of freedom—and that government of the people, by the people, for the people, shall not perish from the earth.

*   *   *

Reply to New York Workingmen's Democratic Republican Association. March 21, 1864.

Gentlemen of the Committee

The honorary membership of your Association, as generously tendered, is gratefully accepted.

You comprehend, as your address shows, that the existing rebellion, means more, and tends to more, than the perpetuation of African slavery—that it is, in fact, a war upon the rights of all working people. . . .

None are so deeply interested to resist the present rebellion as the working people. Let them beware of prejudice, working division and hostility among themselves. The most notable feature of a disturbance in your city last summer, was the hanging of some working people by other working people. It should never be so. The strongest bond of human sympathy, outside of the family relation, should be one uniting all working people, of all nations, and tongues, and kindreds. Nor should this lead to a war upon property, or the owners of property. Property is the fruit of labor—property is desirable—is a positive good in the world. That some should be rich, shows that others may become rich, and hence is just encouragement to industry and enterprise. Let not him who is houseless pull down the house of another; but let him labor diligently and build one for himself, thus by example assuring that his own shall be safe from violence when built.

*   *   *

From Address at Sanitary Fair in Baltimore.
April 18, 1864.

We all declare for liberty; but in using the same *word,* we do not all mean the same *thing.* With some, the word liberty may mean for each man to do as he pleases with himself and the product of his labor; while with others, the same word may mean for some men to do as they please with other men and the product of other men's labor. Here are two, not only different, but incompatible things, called by the same name—liberty. And it follows that each of the things is, by the respective parties, called by two different and incompatible names—liberty and tyranny.

The shepherd drives the wolf from the sheep's throat, for which the sheep thanks the shepherd as a liberator, while the wolf denounces him for the same act as the destroyer of liberty, especially as the sheep was a black one. Plainly, the sheep and the wolf are not agreed upon a definition of the word liberty; and precisely the same difference prevails to-day among us human creatures, even in the North, and all professing to love liberty.

*　　*　　*

From Speech to the 166th Ohio Regiment.
August 22, 1864.

It is not merely for to-day, but for all time to come that we should perpetuate for our children's children that great and free government, which we have enjoyed all our lives. I beg you to remember this, not merely for my sake, but for yours. I happen, temporarily, to occupy this big White House. I am a living witness that any one of your children may look to come here as my father's child has. It is in order that each one of you may have through this free government which we have enjoyed, an open field and a fair chance for your industry, enterprise, and intelligence; that you may all have equal privileges in the race of life, with all its desirable human aspirations. It is for this the struggle should be maintained, that we may not lose our birthright—not only for one, but for two or three years. The nation is worth fighting for, to secure such an inestimable jewel.

*　　*　　*

From Second Inaugural Address. March 4, 1865.

On the occasion corresponding to this four years ago, all thoughts were anxiously directed to an impending civil war. All dreaded it— all sought to avert it.... Both parties deprecated war; but one of them would *make* war rather than let the nation survive; and the other would *accept* war rather than let it perish. And the war came.

One eighth of the whole population were colored slaves, not distributed generally over the Union, but localized in the Southern part of it. These slaves constituted a peculiar and powerful interest. All knew that this interest was, somehow, the cause of the war. To strengthen, perpetuate, and extend this interest was the object for which the insurgents would rend the Union, even by war; while the government claimed no right to do more than to restrict the territorial enlargement of it. Neither party expected for the war, the magnitude, or the duration, which it has already attained. Neither anticipated that the *cause* of the conflict might cease with, or even before, the conflict itself should cease. Each looked for an easier triumph, and a result less fundamental and astounding. Both read the same Bible, and pray to the same God; and each invokes His aid against the other. It may seem strange that any men should dare to ask a just God's assistance in wringing their bread from the sweat of other men's faces; but let us judge not that we be not judged. The prayers of both could not be answered; that of neither has been answered fully. The Almighty has His own purposes. "Woe unto the world because of offences! for it must needs be that offences come; but woe to that man by whom the offence cometh!" If we shall suppose that American Slavery is one of those offences which, in the providence of God, must needs come, but which, having continued through His appointed time, He now wills to remove, and that He gives to both North and South, this terrible war, as the woe due to those by whom the offence came, shall we discern therein any departure from those divine attributes which the believers in a Living God always ascribe to Him? Fondly do we hope—fervently do we pray—that this mighty scourge of war may speedily pass away. Yet, if God wills that it continue, until all the wealth piled by the bond-man's two hundred and fifty years of unrequited toil shall be sunk, and until every drop of blood drawn with the lash, shall be paid by another drawn with the sword, as was said three thousand years ago, so still it must be said "the judgments of the Lord, are true and righteous altogether."

With malice toward none; with charity for all; with firmness in the right, as God gives us to see the right, let us strive on to finish the work we are in; to bind up the nation's wounds; to care for him who shall have borne the battle, and for his widow, and his orphan —to do all which may achieve and cherish a just and lasting peace, among ourselves, and with all nations.

*　　*　　*

(Spelling and punctuation in some of the foregoing quotations have been changed to conform to modern usage.)

LINCOLN WRITES

Handbill replying to Charges of Infidelity.
July 31, 1846.

To the Voters of the Seventh Congressional District.
Fellow Citizens:

A charge having got into circulation in some of the neighborhoods of this district, in substance that I am an open scoffer at Christianity, I have by the advice of some friends concluded to notice the subject in this form. That I am not a member of any Christian church, is true; but I have never denied the truth of the Scriptures; and I have never spoken with intentional disrespect of religion in general, or of any denomination of Christians in particular. It is true that in early life I was inclined to believe in what I understand is called the "Doctrine of Necessity"—that is, that the human mind is impelled to action, or held in rest by some power, over which the mind itself has no control; and I have sometimes (with one, two or three, but never publicly) tried to maintain this opinion in argument. The habit of arguing thus however, I have, entirely left off for more than five years. And I add here, I have always understood this same opinion to be held by several of the Christian denominations. The foregoing, is the whole truth, briefly stated, in relation to myself, upon this subject.

I do not think I could myself, be brought to support a man for office, whom I knew to be an open enemy of, and scoffer at, religion. Leaving the higher matter of eternal consequences, between him and his Maker, I still do not think any man has the right thus to insult the feelings, and injure the morals, of the community in which he may live. If, then, I was guilty of such conduct, I should blame no man who should condemn me for it; but I do blame those, whoever they may be, who falsely put such a charge in circulation against me.

*   *   *   A. Lincoln

To George P. Floyd

Springfield, Illinois,

Mr. George P. Floyd,   February 21, 1856
Quincy, Illinois.

Dear Sir: I have just received yours of 16th, with check on Flagg &
Savage, for twenty-five dollars. You must think I am a high-priced
man. You are too liberal with your money.

Fifteen dollars is enough for the job. I send you a receipt for
fifteen dollars, and return to you a ten-dollar bill. Yours truly,

A. LINCOLN

* * *

(Excerpt from a letter)

To Henry L. Pierce and Others

Springfield, Illinois

Gentlemen: April 6, 1859

. . . This is a world of compensations; and he who would *be* no
slave, must consent to *have* no slave. Those who deny freedom to
others, deserve it not for themselves; and, under a just God, can not
long retain it.

All honor to Jefferson—to the man who, in the concrete presence
of a struggle for national independence by a single people, had the
coolness, forecast, and capacity to introduce into a merely revolutionary document, an abstract truth, applicable to all men and all
times, and so embalm it there, that to-day, and in all coming days,
it shall be a rebuke and a stumbling-block to the very harbingers of
re-appearing tyranny and oppression. Your obedient Servant

A. LINCOLN

* * *

To Jesse W. Fell, enclosing autobiography

Springfield

J. W. Fell, Esq   Dec. 20, 1859

My dear Sir:

Herewith is a little sketch, as you requested. There is not much
of it, for the reason, I suppose, that there is not much of me.

If any thing be made out of it, I wish it to be modest, and not to go beyond the material. If it were thought necessary to incorporate any thing from any of my speeches, I suppose there would be no objection. Of course it must not appear to have been written by myself. Yours very truly

A. LINCOLN

I was born February 12, 1809, in Hardin County, Kentucky. My parents were both born in Virginia, of undistinguished families— second families, perhaps I should say. My mother, who died in my tenth year, was of a family of the name of Hanks, some of whom now reside in Adams, and others in Macon County, Illinois. My paternal grandfather, Abraham Lincoln, emigrated from Rockingham County, Virginia, to Kentucky about 1781 or 1782, where a year or two later he was killed by the Indians, not in battle, but by stealth, when he was laboring to open a farm in the forest. His ancestors, who were Quakers, went to Virginia from Berks County, Pennsylvania. An effort to identify them with the New England family of the same name ended in nothing more definite, than a similarity of Christian names in both families, such as Enoch, Levi, Mordecai, Solomon, Abraham, and the like.

My father, at the death of his father, was but six years of age, and he grew up, literally without education. He removed from Kentucky to what is now Spencer County, Indiana, in my eighth year. We reached our new home about the time the State came into the Union. It was a wild region, with many bears and other wild animals still in the woods. There I grew up. There were some schools, so called; but no qualification was ever required of a teacher beyond "readin', writin', and cipherin',", to the Rule of Three. If a straggler supposed to understand Latin, happened to sojourn in the neighborhood, he was looked upon as a wizard. There was absolutely nothing to excite ambition for education. Of course, when I came of age I did not know much. Still, somehow, I could read, write, and cipher to the Rule of Three; but that was all. I have not been to school since. The little advance I now have upon this store of education, I have picked up from time to time under the pressure of necessity.

I was raised to farm work, which I continued till I was twenty-two. At twenty-one I came to Illinois, and passed the first year in Illinois —Macon County. Then I got to New Salem, at that time in Sangamon, now in Menard County, where I remained a year as a sort of Clerk in a store. Then came the Black Hawk War; and I was elected a Captain of Volunteers—a success which gave me more pleasure than any I have had since. I went the campaign, was elated, ran for the Legislature the same year (1832), and was beaten—the only time I ever have been beaten by the people. The next, and three succeeding biennial elections, I was elected to the Legislature. I was not a candidate afterward. During this Legislative period I had studied law, and removed to Springfield to practice it. In 1846 I was once elected to the lower House of Congress. Was not a candidate for re-election. From 1849 to 1854, both inclusive, practiced law more assiduously than ever before. Always a Whig in politics, and generally on the Whig electoral tickets, making active canvasses. I was losing interest in politics when the repeal of the Missouri Compromise aroused me again. What I have done since then is pretty well known.

If any personal description of me is thought desirable, it may be said, I am, in height, six feet, four inches, nearly; lean in flesh, weighing, on an average, one hundred and eighty pounds; dark complexion, with coarse black hair, and grey eyes—no other marks or brands recollected. Yours very truly

A. LINCOLN

* * *

To William D. Kelley

Private

Springfield, Illinois

Hon. William D. Kelly   Oct. 13. 1860

My dear Sir:

Yours of the 6th. asking permission to inscribe your new legal work to me, is received. Gratefully accepting the proffered honor, I give the leave, begging only that the inscription may be in modest terms, not representing me as a man of great learning, or a very extraordinary one in any respect. Yours very truly

A. LINCOLN

* * *

(In answer to a letter written by a little girl of Westfield, New York, in which she told him that she was eleven years old and asked him "to let his whiskers grow." She added: "You would look a great deal better for your face is so thin.")

To Grace Bedell

Private

Springfield, Illinois

Miss. Grace Bedell

October 19. 1860

My dear little Miss.

Your very agreeable letter of the 15th. is received.

I regret the necessity of saying I have no daughters. I have three sons—one seventeen, one nine, and one seven, years of age. They, with their mother, constitute my whole family.

As to the whiskers, having never worn any, do you not think people would call it a piece of silly affectation if I were to begin it now? Your very sincere well-wisher

A. LINCOLN

(Not long afterwards, Lincoln let his beard grow. Happening to pass through Westfield, he asked for his little friend and said, "You see I let these whiskers grow for you, Grace.")

* * *

To Ephraim D. and Phoebe Ellsworth

To the Father and Mother of Col.

Washington, D. C.

Elmer E. Ellsworth

May 25. 1861

My dear Sir and Madam: In the untimely loss of your noble son, our affliction here, is scarcely less than your own. So much of promised usefulness to one's country, and of bright hopes for one's self and friends, have rarely been so suddenly dashed, as in his fall. In size, in years, and in youthful appearance, a boy only, his power to command men, was surpassingly great. This power, combined with a fine intellect, an indomitable energy, and a taste altogether military, constituted in him, as seemed to me, the best natural talent, in that department, I ever knew.

And yet he was singularly modest and deferential in social intercourse. My acquaintance with him began less than two years ago;

yet through the latter half of the intervening period, it was as intimate as the disparity of our ages, and my engrossing engagements, would permit. To me, he appeared to have no indulgences or pastimes; and I never heard him utter a profane, or an intemperate word. What was conclusive of his good heart, he never forgot his parents. The honors he labored for so laudably, and, in the sad end he so gallantly gave his life, he meant for them, no less than for himself.

In the hope that it may be no intrusion upon the sacredness of your sorrow, I have ventured to address you this tribute to the memory of my young friend, and your brave and early fallen child.

May God give you that consolation which is beyond all earthly power. Sincerely your friend in a common affliction—

A. LINCOLN

*   *   *

To John C. Fremont
Private and Confidential
Major General Fremont: Washington D.C. Sept. 2, 1861

My dear Sir: Two points in your proclamation of August 30th give me some anxiety. First, should you shoot a man, according to the proclamation, the Confederates would very certainly shoot our best man in their hands in retaliation; and so, man for man, indefinitely. It is therefore my order that you allow no man to be shot, under the proclamation, without first having my approbation or consent.

Secondly, I think there is great danger that the closing paragraph, in relation to the confiscation of property, and the liberating slaves of traiterous owners, will alarm our Southern Union friends, and turn them against us—perhaps ruin our rather fair prospect for Kentucky. Allow me therefore to ask, that you will as of your own motion, modify that paragraph so as to conform to the *first* and *fourth* sections of the act of Congress, entitled, "An act to confiscate property used for insurrectionary purposes," approved August 6th, 1861, and a copy of which act I herewith send you. This letter is written in a spirit of caution and not of censure.

I send it by a special messenger, in order that it may certainly and speedily reach you.

Yours very truly
A. LINCOLN

* * *

To George D. Ramsay

Executive Mansion
October 17, 1861

Majr. Ramsay

My dear Sir

The lady—bearer of this—says she has two sons who want to work. Set them at it, if possible. Wanting to work is so rare a merit, that it should be encouraged. Yours truly

A. LINCOLN

* * *

To Edwin M. Stanton

Executive Mansion
January 22, 1862

Hon Sec of War

My Dear Sir

On reflection I think it will not do as a rule for the Adjutant General to attend me wherever I go; not that I have any objection to his presence, but that it would be an uncompensating incumbrance both to him and me. When it shall occur to me to go anywhere, I wish to be free to go at once, and not to have to notify the Adjutant General, and wait till he can get ready. It is better, too, for the public service, that he shall give his time to the business of his office, and not to personal attendance on me. While I thank you for your kindness of the suggestion, my view of the matter is as I have stated. Yours truly

A. LINCOLN

* * *

To George B. McClellan

Executive Mansion,
Washington, Feb. 3, 1862.

Major General McClellan

My dear Sir:

You and I have distinct, and different plans for a movement of the Army of the Potomac—yours to be down the Chesapeake, up the Rappahannock to Urbana, and across land to the terminus of the

Railroad on the York River—, mine to move directly to a point on the Railroad South West of Manassas.

If you will give me satisfactory answers to the following questions, I shall gladly yield my plan to yours.

1st. Does not your plan involve a greatly larger expenditure of *time,* and *money* than mine?

2nd. Wherein is a victory *more certain* by your plan than mine?

3rd. Wherein is a victory *more valuable* by your plan than mine?

4th. In fact, would it not be *less* valuable, in this, that it would break no great line of the enemies' communications, while mine would?

5th. In case of disaster, would not a safe retreat be more difficult by your plan than by mine?

Yours truly
A. Lincoln

*   *   *

To Horace Greeley

Executive Mansion
Washington, August 22, 1862

Dear Sir: I have just read yours of the 19th, addressed to myself through the New York "Tribune." If there be in it any statements or assumptions of fact which I may know to be erroneous, I do not, now and here, controvert them. If there be in it any inferences which I may believe to be falsely drawn, I do not, now and here, argue against them. If there be perceptible in it an impatient and dicta-torial tone, I waive it in deference to an old friend whose heart I have always supposed to be right.

As to the policy I "seem to be pursuing," as you say, I have not meant to leave any one in doubt.

I would save the Union. I would save it the shortest way under the Constitution. The sooner the national authority can be restored, the nearer the Union will be "the Union as it was." If there be those who would not save the Union unless they could at the same time save slavery, I do not agree with them. If there be those who would not save the Union unless they could at the same time destroy slavery, I do not agree with them. My paramount object in this struggle is to save the Union, and is not either to save or to destroy slavery. If I could save the Union without freeing any slave, I would do it; and if I could save it by freeing all the slaves, I would do it; and if I could save it by freeing some and leaving others alone, I would also do that. What I do about slavery and the colored race, I do because I believe it helps to save the Union; and what I forebear, I forebear because I do not believe it would help to save the Union. I shall do less whenever I shall believe what I am doing hurts the cause, and I shall do more whenever I shall believe doing more will help the cause. I shall try to correct errors when shown to be errors, and I shall adopt new views so fast as they shall appear to be true views.

I have here stated my purpose according to my view of official duty; and I intend no modification of my oft-expressed personal wish that all men everywhere could be free.

Yours,
A. LINCOLN

*   *   *

To Fanny McCullough

Executive Mansion
Washington, December 23, 1862.

Dear Fanny

It is with deep grief that I learn of the death of your kind and brave Father; and, especially, that it is affecting your young heart beyond what is common in such cases. In this sad world of ours, sorrow comes to all; and, to the young, it comes with bitterest agony, because it takes them unawares. The older have learned to ever expect it. I am anxious to afford some alleviation of your present distress. Perfect relief is not possible, except with time. You can not now realize that you will ever feel better. Is not this so? And yet it is a mistake. You are sure to be happy again. To know this, which is certainly true, will make you some less miserable now. I have had experience enough to know what I say; and you need only to believe it, to feel better at once. The memory of your dear Father, instead of an agony, will yet be a sad sweet feeling in your heart, of a purer, and holier sort than you have known before.

Please present my kind regards to your afflicted mother.

Your sincere friend
A. LINCOLN

Miss. Fanny McCullough.

*   *   *

(Excerpt from a letter)

To the Workingmen of Manchester, England

Executive Mansion, Washington.
January 19, 1863

To the workingmen of Manchester:

I have the honor to acknowledge the receipt of the address and resolutions which you sent to me on the eve of the new year.

... I know and deeply deplore the sufferings which the workingmen at Manchester and in all Europe are called to endure in this crisis. It has been often and studiously represented that the attempt to overthrow this government, which was built upon the foundation of human rights, and to substitute for it one which should rest exclusively on the basis of human slavery, was likely to obtain the favor of Europe. Through the actions of our disloyal citizens the workingmen of Europe have been subjected to a severe trial, for the purpose of forcing their sanction to that attempt. Under these circumstances, I cannot but regard your decisive utterance upon the question as an instance of sublime Christian heroism which has not been surpassed in any age or in any country. It is, indeed, an energetic and reinspiring assurance of the inherent power of truth and of the ultimate and universal triumph of justice, humanity, and freedom. I do not doubt that the sentiments you have expressed will be sustained by your great nation, and, on the other hand, I have no hesitation in assuring you that they will excite admiration, esteem, and the most reciprocal feelings of friendship among the American people. I hail this interchange of sentiment, therefore, as an augury that, whatever else may happen, whatever misfortune may befall your country or my own, the peace and friendship which now exist between the two nations will be, as it shall be my desire to make them, perpetual.

ABRAHAM LINCOLN

*   *   *

To Joseph Hooker

Major General Hooker

Executive Mansion
Washington, January 26, 1863

General: I have placed you at the head of the Army of the Potomac. Of course I have done this upon what appear to me to be sufficient reasons, and yet I think it best for you to know that there are some things in regard to which I am not quite satisfied with you. I believe you to be a brave and skilful soldier, which of course I like. I also believe you do not mix politics with your profession, in which you are right. You have confidence in yourself, which is a valuable if not an indispensable quality. You are ambitious, which, within reasonable bounds, does good rather than harm; but I think that during General Burnside's command of the army you have taken counsel of your ambition and thwarted him as much as you could, in which you did a great wrong to the country and to a most meritorious and honorable brother officer. I have heard, in such a way as to believe it, of your recently saying that both the army and the government needed a dictator. Of course it was not for this, but in spite of it, that I have given you the command. Only those generals who gain successes can set up dictators. What I now ask of you is military success, and I will risk the dictatorship. The government will support you to the utmost of its ability, which is neither more nor less than it has done and will do for all commanders. I much fear that the spirit which you have aided to infuse into the army, of criticizing their commander and withholding confidence from him, will now turn upon you. I shall assist you as far as I can to put it down. Neither you nor Napoleon, if he were alive again, could get any good out of an army while such a spirit prevails in it; and now beware of rashness. Beware of rashness, but with energy and sleepless vigilance go forward and give us victories.

Yours very truly

A. LINCOLN

* * *

To Ulysses S. Grant

Major General Grant

Executive Mansion,
Washington, July 13, 1863

My dear General

   I do not remember that you and I ever met personally. I write this now as a grateful acknowledgment for the almost inestimable service you have done the country. I wish to say a word further. When you first reached the vicinity of Vicksburg, I thought you should do, what you finally did—march the troops across the neck, run the batteries with the transports, and thus go below; and I never had any faith, except a general hope that you knew better than I, that the Yazoo Pass expedition, and the like, could succeed. When you got below, and took Port Gibson, Grand Gulf, and vicinity, I thought you should go down the river and join Gen. Banks; and when you turned Northward East of the Big Black, I feared it was a mistake. I now wish to make the personal acknowledgment that you were right, and I was wrong.

Yours very truly
A. Lincoln

*   *   *

To James H. Hackett

Executive Mansion,
Washington, August 17, 1863.

My dear Sir:

Months ago I should have acknowledged the receipt of your book, and accompanying kind note; and I now have to beg your pardon for not having done so.

For one of my age, I have seen very little of the drama. The first presentation of Falstaff I ever saw was yours here, last winter or spring. Perhaps the best compliment I can pay is to say, as I truly can, I am very anxious to see it again. Some of Shakespeare's plays I have never read; while others I have gone over perhaps as frequently as any unprofessional reader. Among the latter are Lear, Richard III, Henry VIII, Hamlet, and especially Macbeth. I think nothing equals Macbeth. It is wonderful. Unlike you gentlemen of the profession, I think the soliloquy in Hamlet commencing "O, my offence is rank" surpasses that commencing "To be or not to be." But pardon this small attempt at criticism. I should like to hear you pronounce the opening speech of Richard III. Will you not soon visit Washington again? If you do, please call and let me make your personal acquaintance. Yours truly

A. Lincoln

James H. Hackett, Esq

*   *   *

(Excerpt)

To James C. Conkling

Executive Mansion,
Hon. James C. Conkling   Washington, August 26, 1863.

My Dear Sir.

. . . .

Peace does not appear so distant as it did. I hope it will come soon, and come to stay; and so come as to be worth the keeping in all future time. It will then have been proved that, among free men, there can be no successful appeal from the ballot to the bullet; and that they who take such appeal are sure to lose their case, and pay the cost. And then, there will be some black men who can remember that, with silent tongue, and clenched teeth, and steady eye, and well-poised bayonet, they have helped mankind on to this great consummation; while I fear, there will be some white ones, unable to forget that, with malignant heart, and deceitful speech, they strove to hinder it.

Still, let us not be over-sanguine of a speedy final triumph. Let us be quite sober. Let us diligently apply the means, never doubting that a just God, in His own good time, will give us the rightful result. Yours very truly

A. LINCOLN

* * *

To Edwin M. Stanton

Executive Mansion
Hon. Sec. of War—   Washington, March 1, 1864.

My dear Sir:

A poor widow, by the name of Baird, has a son in the Army, that for some offence has been sentenced to serve a long time without pay, or at most, with very little pay. I do not like this punishment of withholding pay—it falls so very hard upon poor families. After he has been serving in this way for several months, at the tearful appeal of the poor Mother, I made a direction that he be allowed to enlist for a new term, on the same conditions as others. She now comes, and says she can not get it acted upon. Please do it. Yours truly

A. LINCOLN

* * *

To Mrs. Lydia Bixby

Executive Mansion,
Washington, November 21, 1864.

Dear Madam,—I have just been shown in the files of the War Department a statement of the Adjutant General of Massachusetts, that you are the mother of five sons who have died gloriously on the field of battle.

I feel how weak and fruitless must be any words of mine which should attempt to beguile you from the grief of a loss so overwhelming. But I cannot refrain from tendering to you the consolation that may be found in the thanks of the Republic they died to save.

I pray that our Heavenly Father may assuage the anguish of your bereavement, and leave you only the cherished memory of the loved and lost, and the solemn pride that must be yours, to have laid so costly a sacrifice upon the altar of Freedom. Yours, very sincerely and respectfully,

A. LINCOLN

Mrs. Bixby

(If the original letter is still in existence, its whereabouts is shrouded in deep mystery)

* * *

(*In some instances in the letters given above the modern version of an older word form or usage has been adopted*)

LINCOLN, MAN OF WISDOM

The people know their rights, and they are never slow to assert and maintain them, when they are invaded.

(From a speech at Springfield, Ill., Jan. 1837)

* * *

There is no grievance that is a fit object of redress by mob law.

(Address before the Young Men's Lyceum
of Springfield, Ill., Jan. 27, 1838)

* * *

How miserably things seem to be arranged in this world. If we have no friends, we have no pleasure; and if we have them, we are sure to lose them, and be doubly pained by the loss.

(To Joshua F. Speed, Feb. 25, 1842)

* * *

The true role, in determining to embrace, or reject any thing, is not whether it have any evil in it; but whether it have more of evil than of good. There are few things wholly evil or wholly good.

(Speech in the U.S. House of
Representatives, June 20, 1848)

* * *

Let the past as nothing be. Go at it while you're young.

(From a letter to William H. Herndon,
July 11, 1848)

* * *

The better part of one's life consists of his friendships.

(To Joseph Gillespie, July 13, 1849)

*   *   *

Resolve to be honest at all events.

(Fragment; Notes for a Law Lecture,
July 1, 1850 ?)

*   *   *

Stand with anybody that stands right. Stand with him while he
is right, and part with him when he goes wrong.

(Speech at Peoria, Ill., Oct. 16, 1854)

*   *   *

As a nation we began by declaring that "all men are created
equal." We now practically read it "all men are created equal, except
Negroes." When the Know Nothings get control, it will read "all
men are created equal, except Negroes and foreigners and Catho-
lics." When it comes to this, I should prefer emigrating to some
country where they make no pretense of loving liberty,—to Russia,
for instance, where despotism can be taken pure, and without the
base alloy of hypocrisy.

(From a letter to Joshua F. Speed,
Aug. 24, 1855)

*   *   *

The plainest print cannot be read through a gold eagle.

(Speech at Springfield, Ill.,
June 26, 1857)

*   *   *

I believe each individual is naturally entitled to do as he pleases
with himself and the fruit of his labor, so far as it in no wise interferes with any other man's rights.

(Speech at Chicago, Ill., July 10, 1858)

*   *   *

As I would not be a slave, so I would not be a master. This expresses my idea of democracy. Whatever differs from this to the extent of the difference, is no democracy.

> (Definition of Democracy, supposed to have been written about August 1, 1858. Original manuscript formerly on deposit in the Chicago Historical Society. *The collected works of Abraham Lincoln,* Roy P. Basler, editor. Vol. 2, p. 532)

* * *

You can fool all the people some of the time and some of the people all the time, but you cannot fool all the people all the time.

> (Speech at Clinton, Ill., September 2, 1858)

* * *

Our reliance is in the love of liberty which God has planted in our bosoms. Our defense is in the preservation of the spirit which prizes liberty as the heritage of all men, in all lands, every where.

> (Speech at Edwardsville, Ill.,
> September 11, 1858)

* * *

That [morality] is the real issue. . . . It is the eternal struggle between these two principles—right and wrong—throughout the world. They are the two principles that have stood face to face from the beginning of time; and will ever continue to struggle. The one is the common right of humanity and the other the divine right of kings. It is the same principle in whatever shape it develops itself. It is the same spirit that says, "You work and toil and earn bread, and I'll eat it." No matter in what shape it comes, whether from the mouth of a king who seeks to bestride the people of his nation and live by the fruit of their labor, or from one race of men as an apology for enslaving another race, it is the same tyrannical principle.

> (Seventh and Last Debate with Stephen A. Douglas,
> at Alton, Ill., Oct. 15, 1858)

* * *

This is a world of compensations; and he who would be no slave, must consent to have no slave. Those who deny freedom to others, deserve it not for themselves; and, under a just God, can not long retain it.

(Letter to Henry L. Pierce and others,
Apr. 6, 1859)

*   *   *

Advancement—improvement in condition—is the order of things in a society of equals. . . . Free Labor has the inspiration of hope; pure slavery has no hope. The power of hope upon human exertion, and happiness, is wonderful.

(Fragment on Free Labor, Sept. 17, 1859)

*   *   *

I hold [that] if the Almighty had ever made a set of men that should do all the eating and none of the work, he would have made them with mouths only and no hands, and if he [had] ever made another class that he had intended should do all the work and none of the eating, he would have made them without mouths and with all hands.

(Speech at Cincinnati, Ohio, Sept. 17, 1859?)

*   *   *

It is said an Eastern monarch once charged his wise men to invent him a sentence to be ever in view, and which should be true and appropriate in all times and situations. They presented him the words: "And this, too, shall pass away." How much it expresses! How chastening in the hour of pride!—How consoling in the depths of affliction! "And this, too, shall pass away." And yet let us hope it is not *quite* true. Let us hope, rather, that by the best cultivation of the physical world, beneath and around us; and the intellectual and moral world within us, we shall secure an individual, social and political prosperity and happiness, whose course shall be onward and upward, and which, while the earth endures, shall not pass away.

(Address before the Wisconsin Agricultural
Society, Sept. 30, 1859)

*   *   *

I think very much of the people, as an old friend said he thought of woman. He said when he lost his first wife, who had been a great help to him in his business, he thought he was ruined—that he never could find another to fill her place. At length, however, he married another, who he found did quite as well as the first, and that his opinion now was that any woman would do well who was well done by. So I think of the whole people of this nation—they will ever do well if well done by. We will try to do by them in all parts of the country, North and South, with entire confidence that all will be well with all of us.

(Speech at Bloomington, Ill., 1860)

* * *

Let us have faith that right makes might, and in that faith let us, to the end, dare to do our duty as we understand it.

(Address at Cooper Institute, New York City,
Feb. 27, 1860)

* * *

I am not ashamed to confess that twenty-five years ago I was a hired laborer, mauling rails at work on a flatboat—just what might happen to any poor man's son! I want every man to have a chance.

(Speech at New Haven, Connecticut,
March 6, 1860)

* * *

Solomon says that there is "a time to keep silence," and when men wrangle by the month with no certainty that they mean the same thing, while using the same word, it perhaps were as well if they would keep silence.

(From an address to the
Indiana Legislature, Feb. 12, 1861)

* * *

The loss of enemies does not compensate for the loss of friends.

(To William Seward, June 30, 1862)

* * *

The severest justice may not always be the best policy.

(Message to the Senate and
House of Representatives, July 17, 1862)

* * *

I am conscious of no desire for my country's welfare, that is not in consonance with His [God's] will, and of no plan upon which we may not ask His blessing. It seems to me that if there be one subject upon which all good men may unitedly agree, it is imploring the gracious favor of the God of Nations upon the struggles our people are making for the preservation of their precious birthright of civil and religious liberty.

(Letter to Caleb Russell and
Sallie A. Fenton, Jan. 5, 1863)

* * *

The reasonable men of the world have long since agreed that intemperance is one of the greatest, if not the very greatest of all evils among mankind.

(Reply to Sons of Temperance,
Sept. 29, 1863)

* * *

I do the very best I know how—the very best I can; and I mean to keep doing so until the end. If the end brings me out all right, what is said against me won't amount to anything. If the end brings me out wrong, ten angels swearing I was right would make no difference.

(Francis B. Carpenter: *Six Months at the
White House with Abraham Lincoln*)

* * *

A man watches his pear-tree day after day, impatient for the ripening of the fruit. Let him attempt to *force* the process and he may spoil both fruit and tree. But let him patiently *wait,* and the ripe pear at length falls into his lap. . . . I have done what no man could have helped doing, standing in my place.

(Francis B. Carpenter: *Six Months at
the White House with Abraham Lincoln*)

* * *

The man who stands by and says nothing, when the peril of his government is discussed, can not be misunderstood. If not hindered, he is sure to help the enemy. Much more, if he talks ambiguously—talks for his country with "buts" and "ifs" and "ands."

> (Letter to Erastus Corning and others,
> June 12, 1863)

*   *   *

... You were convicted of two offences. One of them, not of great enormity, and yet greatly to be avoided, I feel sure you are in no danger of repeating. The other you are not so well assured against. The advice of a father to his son "Beware of entrance to a quarrel, but being in, bear it that the opposed may beware of thee," is good, and yet not the best. Quarrel not at all. No man resolved to make the most of himself, can spare time for personal contention. Still less can he afford to take all the consequences, including the vitiating of his temper, and the loss of self-control. Yield larger things to which you can show no more than equal right; and yield lesser ones, though clearly your own. Better give your path to a dog, than be bitten by him in contesting for the right. Even killing the dog would not cure the bite. In the mood indicated deal henceforth with your fellow men, and especially with your brother officers; and even the unpleasant events you are passing from will not have been profitless to you.

> (Letter to Captain James M. Cutts,
> Oct. 26, 1863)

*   *   *

Take hold with an honest heart and a strong hand. Do not let any questionable man control or influence you.

> (Letter to General Steele, Jan. 27, 1864)

*   *   *

If we do right, God will be with us, and if God is with us, we cannot fail.

> (*Complete Works of Abraham Lincoln*,
> Nicolay and Hay, editors. Footnote.
> July 7, 1864)

*   *   *

We better know there is a fire whence we see much smoke rising than could know it by one or two witnesses swearing to it. The witnesses may commit perjury, but the smoke can not.

(Letter to John R. Underwood and
Henry Grider, Oct. 26, 1864)

*   *   *

Human nature will not change. . . . In any future great national trial, compared with the men of this, we shall have as weak and as strong, as silly and as wise, as bad and as good.

(Response to a serenade, Washington, D.C.,
Nov. 10, 1864)

*   *   *

I cannot understand why men should be so eager after wealth. Wealth is simply a superfluity of what we don't need.

(To David R. Locke, 1864)

*   *   *

I believe I shall never be old enough to speak without embarrassment when I have nothing to talk about.

(*New York Tribune,* Dec. 8, 1864)

*   *   *

Important principles may, and must be inflexible.

(Last public address, Apr. 11, 1865)

*   *   *

It's a fortunate thing I wasn't born a woman, for I cannot refuse anything, it seems.

(William H. Herndon and Jesse W. Weik:
Herndon's Life of Lincoln)

*   *   *

I think the Lord must love the plain people, He has made so many of them.

(James Grant Wilson: *Recollections of Lincoln*)

* * *

A man has not time to spend half his life in quarrels. If any man ceases to attack me, I never remember the past against him.

(John Hay: *Lincoln and the Civil War in
the Diaries and Letters to John Hay*)

* * *

It is my pleasure that my children are free and happy, and unrestrained by parental tyranny. Love is the chain whereby to bind a child to its parents.

(Statement of Mary Todd (Mrs. Abraham Lincoln) to
William H. Herndon, September 4, 1866)

* * *

Die when I may, I want it said of me by those who knew me best, that I always plucked a thistle and planted a flower when I thought a flower would grow.

(Statement by Joshua F. Speed to
William H. Herndon)

LINCOLN, MAN OF HUMOR

Throughout his life, Lincoln bore the reputation of a man who enjoyed telling or hearing a pointed anecdote or a funny story. He once said that his love of humor was the "safety valve" by which he escaped from the sorrows of his office. His writings reveal his sense of humor and his ability as satirist.

Abraham Lincoln   *he will be good*

his hand and pen   *but god knows when*

(From Lincoln's childhood copybook, circa 1820)

*   *   *

Captain Lincoln was drilling his men during the Black Hawk (Indian) War, marching with a front of over twenty men across a field, when he found himself before a gap in the fence through which he wanted to go.

"I could not for the life of me," said Lincoln, "remember the proper word of command for getting my command *endwise,* so that it could get through the gate; so, as we came near I shouted: 'This company is dismissed for two minutes, when it will fall in again on the other side of the gate!' "

(Ida Minerva Tarbell: *The Life of
Abraham Lincoln*)

*   *   *

In an interview (held at Quincy, Illinois, in 1858) between Lincoln and Petroleum V. Nasby, the name came up of a recently deceased politician of Illinois, whose undeniable merit was blemished by an overweening vanity. His funeral was attended by a very large crowd.

"If General . . . . had known how big a funeral he would have," said Lincoln, "he would have died years ago."

(Allen Thorndike Rice: *Reminiscences of Abraham
Lincoln by Distinguished Men of His Time*)

* * *

Some simple remark would often prompt Lincoln to tell an apropos story. On one occasion Secretary of the Treasury Chase happened to remark to Lincoln: "I am so sorry that I had to write a letter to Mr. So-and-So before I left home." Lincoln promptly responded: "Chase, never regret what you don't write; it is what you do write that you are often called upon to feel sorry for."

(General Egbert L. Viele: "Lincoln as a Story-teller,"
in *The Independent,* 1895)

* * *

Judge Baldwin, of California, being in Washington, called one day on General Halleck and asked for a pass outside the Northern lines to see a brother in Virginia. "We have been deceived too often," said General Halleck, "and I regret I can't grant it." Judge Baldwin then went to Secretary of War Stanton, and was very briefly disposed of with the same result. Finally he obtained an interview with President Lincoln, and stated his case. "Have you applied to General Halleck?" inquired the President. "Yes, and met with a flat refusal," said Judge Baldwin. "Then you must see Stanton," continued Lincoln. "I have, and with the same result," was the reply. "Well, then," said Lincoln, with a smile, "I can do nothing; for you must know that I have very little influence with this administration."

(Henry Jarvis Raymond: *The Life and Public
Services of Abraham Lincoln*)

* * *

Once an Austrian Count applied to President Lincoln for a position in the army. Introduced to Lincoln by the Austrian Minister, he explained that he was a Count, that his family were ancient and highly respectable, etc. Lincoln, with a merry twinkle in his eye, tapped the Count on the shoulder, in a fatherly way, as if the man had confessed to some wrong, and interrupted in a soothing tone: "Never mind, you shall be treated with *just as much* consideration for all that."

(Francis F. Browne: *The Every-day Life of Abraham Lincoln*)

*   *   *

Told by Secretary of State Seward:

Lincoln never tells a joke for the joke's sake, they are like the parables of old—lessons of wisdom. Let me give you an instance. When he first came to Washington, he was inundated with office-seekers. One day he was particularly afflicted; about twenty placehunters from all parts of the Union had taken possession of his room with bales of credentials and self-recommendations about ten miles long. After a while Lincoln said:

"Gentlemen, I must tell you a little story I read one day. . . . A certain king had a minister upon whose judgment he always depended. . . . One day he took it into his head to go a hunting, and after summoning his nobles, he summoned the minister and asked him if it would rain. The minister told him it would not, and he and his nobles departed. While journeying along they met a farmer on a jackass. He advised them to return, 'For,' he said, 'it will certainly rain.' But they passed on. . . . Soon a heavy shower came up and they were drenched to the skin.

"When they had returned to the palace, the king reprimanded the minister severely and sent for the farmer. 'Tell me,' said the king, 'how you knew it would rain?'

" 'I did not know,' said the farmer, 'my jackass told me.'

" 'And how did he tell you?' asked the king.

" 'By pricking up his ears, your majesty,' said the farmer.

"The king sent him away, and procuring the jackass of him, put him (the jackass) in the place of his minister.

"And here," observed Lincoln, "is where the king made a great mistake."

"How so?" inquired his auditors eagerly.

"Why, ever since that time," said Lincoln, with a grin, "every jackass wants an office."

(*Frank Leslie's Illustrated Newspaper,*
Oct. 31, 1863)

*   *   *

Robert Dale Owen, the spiritualist, once read President Lincoln a long manuscript on an abstruse subject with which that rather erratic person loved to deal. Lincoln listened patiently until the author asked for his opinion. The President replied with a yawn: "Well, for those who like that sort of thing it is just about the sort of thing they would like."

(Anthony Gross: Lincoln's Own Stories)

* * *

(Lincoln said in 1862)
"Horace Greeley reminds me of the big fellow whose little wife beat him over the head without resistance. The man said to others, 'Let her alone. It don't hurt me and it does her a power of good.'"

(Carl Sandburg: Abraham Lincoln:
The War Years)

* * *

A Southern lady from Tennessee came to see President Lincoln about her husband, who was confined at Johnson's Island, a northern prison. She urged that her husband was a religious man and should be released. Lincoln said: "You say your husband is a religious man. Tell him when you meet him that I say I am not much of a judge of religion, but that, in my opinion, the religion that sets men to rebel and fight against their Government because, as they think, that Government does not sufficiently help *some* men to eat their bread in the sweat of *other* men's faces, is not the sort of religion upon which people can get to heaven." Lincoln ordered the release of the prisoner, and then later wrote down the little speech and added the caption, "The President's Last, Shortest, and Best Speech."

(Noah Brooks: Personal Recollections
of Abraham Lincoln)

* * *

At the White House one day some gentlemen were present, excited and troubled about the commissions or omissions of the administration. President Lincoln heard them patiently, and then replied:—
"Gentlemen, suppose all the property you were worth was in gold, and you had to put it into the hands of an acrobat to carry across the

Niagara River on a rope, would you shake the cable, or keep shouting out to him—'Stand up a little straighter—stoop a little more—go a little faster—lean a little more to the north—lean a little more to the south'? No, you would hold your breath as well as your tongue, and keep your hands off until he was safe over. The Government are carrying an immense weight. Untold treasures are in their hands. They are doing the very best they can. Don't bother them. Keep silence, and we'll get you safe across.

(Henry Jarvis Raymond: *The Life and Public Services of Abraham Lincoln*)

* * *

Lincoln was a very tall man, reaching a height of six feet, four inches. On his 56th birthday a tall New Englander was introduced to him. When the President saw the giant, lacking but two inches of seven feet, he was speechless with astonishment. As he surveyed him several times from head to foot, the well-known smile spread over his homely face, and his sad eyes sparkled with fun, as he said: "My friend, will you kindly permit me to inquire if you know when your feet get cold?"

(James Grant Wilson: *Recollections of Lincoln*)

* * *

Lincoln was his own bootblack, and is known to have continued so to be while in the White House. "In England, Mr. Lincoln, no gentleman blacks his own boots," is said to have been the surprised remark of an Englishman as he came upon Lincoln in the act of applying blacking to his pedal covertures. "Whose boots does he black?" inquired Lincoln as he spat on his brush.

(William Eleazar Barton: *The Life of Abraham Lincoln*)

* * *

In February 1861 Lincoln made a speech in Jersey City, New Jersey, and his remarks were received with demonstrations of applause and the waving of handkerchiefs. Loud cries were kept up for "Lincoln, Lincoln," and to quiet the crowd the President-Elect once more came to the front of the platform and said:

There appears to be a desire to see more of me, and I can only say that from my position, especially when I look around the gallery (bowing to the ladies), I feel that I have decidedly the best of the bargain, and in this matter I am for no compromises here.

(The Collected Works of Abraham Lincoln,
edited by Roy P. Basler)

* * *

When Daniel Pierce Gardner applied to Lincoln for a soap testimonial, the President-Elect complied with this letter:

Springfield, Illinois,
September 28, 1860.

Dear Sir:

Some specimens of your soap have been used at our house and Mrs. L. declares it is a superb article. She at the same time, protests that *I* have never given sufficient attention to the "soap question" to be a competent judge. Yours truly

A. LINCOLN

(The Collected Works of Abraham Lincoln,
edited by Roy P. Basler)

* * *

Lincoln remarked that very exaggerated accounts of the carnage in the Civil War had been produced by including among the killed large numbers of men whose term of enlistment had expired, and who had been replaced by others, or had reenlisted themselves. He told in illustration of this remark one of his characteristic stories:

"A Negro had been learning arithmetic. Another Negro asked him, if he shot at three pigeons sitting on a fence and killed one, how many would remain. 'One,' replied the arithmetician. 'No,' said the other Negro, 'the other two would fly away.' "

(Goldwin Smith: "President Lincoln,"
Macmillan's Magazine)

* * *

A gentleman was pressing very strenuously the promotion of an officer to a "Brigadiership." "But we have already more generals than we know what to do with," replied Lincoln. "But," persisted the visitor, "my friend is very strongly recommended." "Now look here," said President Lincoln, throwing one leg over the arm of his chair, "you are a farmer, I believe; if not, you will understand me. Suppose you had a large cattle yard full of all sorts of cattle,—cows, oxen, bulls —and you kept killing and disposing of your cows and oxen, in one way and another,—taking good care of your bulls. By-and-by you would find that you had nothing but a yard full of old bulls, good for nothing under heaven. Now, it will be just so with the army, if I don't stop making brigadier-generals."

(Francis Bicknell Carpenter: *Six Months at the White House with Abraham Lincoln*)

*   *   *

Lincoln disliked titles being tacked onto his name and he incurred the criticism of fashionable Washington circles by his use of his last name only, without the prefacing "Mr. President." To an intimate friend who addressed him always by his proper title he said: "Now call me Lincoln, and I'll promise not to tell of the breach of etiquette —if you won't—and I shall have a resting spell from 'Mr. President.'"

(Noah Brooks: "Personal Recollections of Abraham Lincoln" in *Harper's New Monthly Magazine*, 1865)

*   *   *

Office seekers worried the life out of President Lincoln, besieging him everywhere. Referring to this annoyance, he said: "I am like a man so busy in letting rooms in one end of his house, that he can't stop to put out the fire that is burning the other."

(Henry Jarvis Raymond: *The Life and Public Services of Abraham Lincoln*)

*   *   *

Lincoln, speaking of unjust newspaper attacks, said in 1864:
"A traveller on the frontier found himself out of his reckoning one night in a most inhospitable region. A terrific thunder-storm came

up, to add to his trouble. He floundered along until his horse at length gave out. The lightning afforded him the only clew to his way, but the peals of thunder were frightful. One bolt, which seemed to crash the earth beneath him, brought him to his knees. By no means a praying man, his petition was short and to the point,—'O Lord, if it is all the same to you, give us a little more light and a little less noise!' "

(Francis Bicknell Carpenter: *Six Months at the White House with Abraham Lincoln*

*   *   *

(*Some of these anecdotes have been condensed in the interest of brevity.*)

CHRONOLOGY OF ABRAHAM LINCOLN

February 12, 1809	Abraham Lincoln born to Thomas and Nancy Hanks Lincoln, in a log cabin near Hodgenville, Kentucky.
Fall of 1816	The Lincoln family moves to an unsettled wilderness near Pigeon Creek, Indiana.
Fall of 1818	Lincoln's mother dies.
December 13, 1818	Mary Todd born at Lexington, Kentucky.
December, 1819	Lincoln's father marries Sarah Bush Johnston, a widow with three children.
1828	Lincoln takes a flatboat trip to New Orleans. His sister Sarah dies.
March, 1830	The Lincoln family leaves Indiana and settles near Decatur in Illinois.
1831	Lincoln makes a second flatboat trip to New Orleans. He sees Negroes in chains and on the selling block.
Fall of 1831	Lincoln settles in New Salem, Illinois. He works as clerk in the store of Denton Offutt.
1832	Makes his first political speech in which he announces himself a candidate for the Illinois State Legislature.
April–July, 1832	Joins the Army and serves three months as Captain in the Black Hawk (Indian) War.
1832	Studies law. At the election in the fall, he is defeated.
May, 1833	Appointed postmaster of New Salem and serves until 1836.
1834	Makes his first survey as a deputy surveyor of Sangamon County. Continues his surveying until the end of 1836.

August, 1834	Elected to the Illinois State Legislature.
February, 1835	Returns to New Salem.
August, 1836	Re-elected to the Illinois State Legislature.
September, 1836	Licensed to practice law.
1837	Admitted to the bar in Illinois. Moves to Springfield to practice law in partnership with John T. Stuart.
1838	Elected to the Illinois State Legislature for the third time.
1840	Elected to the Illinois State Legislature for the fourth time.
1841	Becomes a law partner of Stephen T. Logan.
1842	Declines renomination to the Illinois State Legislature.
November 4, 1842	Marries Mary Todd of Lexington, Kentucky.
August 1, 1843	Birth of first child, Robert Todd Lincoln.
1844	Becomes a law partner of William H. Herndon.
March 10, 1846	Birth of second son, Edward Baker Lincoln.
August, 1846	Elected to U. S. House of Representatives.
October, 1847	Moves from Springfield to Washington, D.C., to serve congressional term.
December 6, 1847	Takes seat in Congress.
January 10, 1849	Introduces bill to free slaves in District of Columbia.
March, 1849	Gives up politics. Returns to Springfield and private law practice. Admitted to practice in the U. S. Supreme Court.
February, 1850	Edward Baker Lincoln, second son, dies.
December, 1850	Birth of third son, William Wallace Lincoln.
January, 1851	Lincoln's father, Thomas, dies.
1851–1853	Continues law practice.
April, 1853	Birth of fourth son, Thomas ("Tad") Lincoln.
1854	Re-enters politics. Elected to Illinois Legislature.
1855	Candidate for the U. S. Senate, but defeated by vote of Legislature.

June, 1856	Delegate to the first convention of the Republican Party, at Philadelphia.
1858	Engages in seven debates with Senator Stephen A. Douglas in various towns of Illinois, but is defeated in his candidacy for the Senate.
November, 1858	First mentioned in press for President.
May 18, 1860	Nominated for President of the United States by the Republican National Convention in Chicago.
November 6, 1860	Elected President of the United States.
February 11, 1861	Leaves Springfield for Washington. Farewell address at Springfield.
February 23, 1861	Arrival in Washington.
March 4, 1861	Inaugurated as President.
March 29, 1861	Orders relief of Fort Sumter.
April 15, 1861	Issues proclamation calling for 75,000 volunteers to serve in the militia, following the fall of Fort Sumter, at the outbreak of the War Between the States.
May 3, 1861	Proclaims martial law.
November 1, 1861	Appoints McClellan to command Union armies.
February 20, 1862	Death of third son, William Wallace Lincoln.
April 16, 1862	Signs act freeing slaves in District of Columbia.
September 22, 1862	Issues the preliminary Emancipation Proclamation.
January 1, 1863	Issues the final Emancipation Proclamation.
November 19, 1863	Delivers a great address at the dedication of the National Cemetery at Gettysburg, Pennsylvania.
March, 1864	Appoints Ulysses S. Grant commander in chief of the Northern armies.
July 18, 1864	Calls for 500,000 volunteers.
November 8, 1864	Re-elected President.
February 1, 1865	Approves the Thirteenth Amendment, abolishing slavery.
March 4, 1865	Delivers his Second Inaugural Address, "with malice toward none; with charity for all."
March 11, 1865	Issues proclamation, offering pardon to deserters.

April 9, 1865	End of War Between the States. General Robert E. Lee, commander of the Southern armies, surrenders to General Grant.
April 11, 1865	Delivers last public speech, in Washington.
April 14, 1865	Lincoln is shot at Ford's Theatre in Washington by the actor John Wilkes Booth.
April 15, 1865	Dies at the age of fifty-six, and the country goes into mourning.
April 21–May 3	The funeral train bears the remains of Lincoln on the journey to Springfield.
May 4, 1865	Lincoln is buried in Oak Ridge Cemetery in Springfield.
July, 1871	Death of Lincoln's fourth son, Thomas ("Tad") Lincoln.
July, 1882	Mary Todd Lincoln dies in Springfield at the age of sixty-four. She is buried in the Lincoln Tomb with her husband and three of their four sons.
July 26, 1926	Lincoln's first son, Robert Todd Lincoln, dies in Manchester, Vermont, at the age of almost eighty-three, and is buried in Arlington (Virginia) National Cemetery.

LINCOLN BIBLIOGRAPHY

It is estimated that more than 5,000 books and pamphlets about Lincoln have been published in the United States since 1837. The following list contains only some of the more important works published since 1900.

AGAR, Herbert   *Abraham Lincoln* (1952)

ANGLE, Paul M.   *"Here I Have Lived" A History of Lincoln's Springfield, 1821–1865* (1935)

A Shelf of Lincoln Books. A Critical Selective Bibliography (1946)

ANGLE, Paul M. (ed.)   *The Lincoln Reader* (1947)

ANGLE, Paul M., and MIERS, Earl Schenck (ed.)   *The Living Lincoln. His Mind, His Times and the War He Fought. Reconstructed from His Own Writings* (1955)

Poetry and Prose by Abraham Lincoln (1956)

BALLARD, Colin R.   *The Military Genius of Lincoln* (1952)

BARINGER, William E.   *Lincoln's Rise to Power* (1937)

A House Dividing: Lincoln as President Elect (1945)

Lincoln's Vandalia, A Pioneer Portrait (1949)

BARONDESS, Benjamin   *Three Lincoln Masterpieces* (1954)

BARTON, William E.   *The Paternity of Abraham Lincoln* (1920)

The Soul of Abraham Lincoln (1920)

The Life of Abraham Lincoln (2 vols., 1925)

The Lineage of Lincoln (1929)

Lincoln at Gettysburg (1930)

BASLER, Roy P.   *The Lincoln Legend. A Study in Changing Conceptions* (1935)

BASLER, Roy P. (ed.)   *Abraham Lincoln: His Speeches and Writings* (1946)

The Collected Works of Abraham Lincoln (9 vols., 1953–1955)

BEVERIDGE, Albert J.   *Abraham Lincoln, 1809–1858* (2 vols., 1928)

BISHOP, James A. (Jim)   *The Day Lincoln Was Shot* (1955)

BRUCE, Robert V.   *Lincoln and the Tools of War* (1956)

BRYAN, George S.	*The Great American Myth* (1940)
BULLARD, Frederick L.	*Abraham Lincoln and the Widow Bixby* (1946)
	Lincoln in Marble and Bronze (1952)
CANBY, Courtlandt (ed.)	*Lincoln and the Civil War* (1958)
CARMEN, Harry J., and LUTHIN, Reinhard H.	*Lincoln and the Patronage* (1943)
CARRUTHERS, Olive, and McMURTRY, R. Gerald	*Lincoln's Other Mary* (1946)
CATTON, Bruce	*Mr. Lincoln's Army* (1951)
	A Stillness at Appomattox (1953)
CHARNWOOD, Lord (Godfrey Rathbone Benson)	*Abraham Lincoln* (1917)
COMMAGER, Henry Steele	*The Blue and the Gray* (1950)
CRAMER, John Henry	*Lincoln Under Enemy Fire* (1948)
CURRENT, Richard N.	*The Lincoln Nobody Knows* (1958)
CUTHBERG, Norma Barrett	*Lincoln and the Baltimore Plot* (1949)
DAUGHERTY, James Henry	*Abraham Lincoln* (1943)
DAVIS, Burke	*To Appomattox* (1959)
DENNETT, Tyler (ed.)	*Lincoln and the Civil War in the Diaries and Letters of John Hay* (1939)
DEWITT, David Miller	*The Assassination of Abraham Lincoln and Its Expiation* (1909)
DODGE, Daniel Kilham	*Abraham Lincoln, Master of Words* (1924)
DONALD, David	*Lincoln's Herndon* (1948)
	Divided We Fought (1952)
	Lincoln Reconsidered (1956)
DONALD, David (ed.)	*Inside Lincoln's Cabinet: The Civil War Diaries of Salmon P. Chase* (1954)
DORRIS, Jonathan T.	*Pardon and Amnesty Under Lincoln and Johnson* (1953)
DRINKWATER, John	*Abraham Lincoln,* a play (1927)
EVANS, William A.	*Mrs. Abraham Lincoln, A Study of Her Personality and Her Influence on Lincoln* (1932)
GRAY, Wood	*The Hidden Civil War* (1942)
HARNSBERGER, Caroline Thomas (ed.)	*The Lincoln Treasury* (1950)
HARPER, Robert S.	*Lincoln and the Press* (1951)
HENDRICK, Burton J.	*Lincoln's War Cabinet* (1946)
HERNDON, William H., and WEIK, Jesse W.	*Herndon's Life of Lincoln: The History and Personal Recollections of Abraham Lincoln* (1949)

HERTZ, Emanuel — *The Hidden Lincoln: from the Letters and Papers of William H. Herndon* (1938)

HESSELTINE, William B. — *Lincoln and the War Governors* (1948)

HILL, Frederic — *Lincoln, the Lawyer* (1906)

HOFSTADTER, Richard — *The American Political Tradition and the Men Who Made It* (1948)

HOLDEN, Raymond Peckham — *Abraham Lincoln: The Politician and the Man* (1929)

JONES, Edgar Dewitt — *Lincoln and the Preachers* (1948)

JORDAN, Donaldson, and PRATT, Edwin J. — *Europe and the Civil War* (1931)

KIMMEL, Stanley Preston — *Mr. Lincoln's Washington* (1957)

LAIR, John — *Songs Lincoln Loved* (1954)

LANG, J. Jack — *The Wit and Worldly Wisdom of Abraham Lincoln* (1941)

LEARNED, Marion Dexter — *Abraham Lincoln, An American Migration* (1909)

LEECH, Margaret — *Reveille in Washington* (1941)

LEWIS, Lloyd — *Myths After Lincoln* (1929)

LINCOLN, Waldo — *History of the Lincoln Family: An Account of the Descendants of Samuel Lincoln of Hingham, Massachusetts, 1637–1920* (1923)

LINDSTROM, Ralph G. — *Lincoln Finds God* (1958)

LORANT, Stefan — *Lincoln: His Life in Photographs* (1941)
Lincoln, A Picture Story of His Life (1952)

LUDWIG, Emil — *Abraham Lincoln* (1949)

LUTHIN, Reinhard Henry — *The First Lincoln Campaign* (1944)

MASTERS, Edgar Lee — *Lincoln the Man* (1931)

McCARTHY, Charles Hallan — *Lincoln's Plan of Reconstruction* (1901)

McCLURE, Alexander K. — *Lincoln as a Politician* (1916)

MEARNS, David C. — *The Lincoln Papers: The Story of the Collection with Selections to July 4, 1861* (2 vols., 1948)

MESERVE, Frederick Hill, and SANDBURG, Carl — *The Photographs of Abraham Lincoln* (1944)

MIERS, Earl Schenck — *Gettysburg* (1948)
The Great Rebellion (1958)

MILTON, George Fort — *Abraham Lincoln and the Fifth Column* (1942)

MITGANG, Herbert (ed.) — *Lincoln as They Saw Him* (1956)
Noah Brooks: Washington in Lincoln's Time (1959)

MONAGHAN, Jay · *Diplomat in Carpet Slippers* (1945)

MORSE, John T., Jr. (ed.) · *The Diary of Gideon Welles* (3 vols., 1911)

NEVINS, Allan · *The Ordeal of the Union* (2 vols., 1947–1950)

NICOLAY, Helen · *Personal Traits of Abraham Lincoln* (1912)

PETERSEN, William F. · *Lincoln-Douglas: The Weather as Destiny* (1943)

PHILLIPS, Isaac Newton · *Abraham Lincoln by Some Men Who Knew Him* (1910)

POTTER, David Morris · *Lincoln and His Party in the Secession Crisis* (1942)

PRATT, Harry E. · *Lincoln 1840–1846; Being the Day-by-Day Activities of Abraham Lincoln from January 1, 1840 to December 31, 1846* (1939)
Lincoln 1809–1840; Being the Day-by-Day Activities of Abraham Lincoln from February 12, 1809 to December 31, 1839 (1941)
The Personal Finances of Abraham Lincoln (1943)

PRATT, Harry E. (ed.) · *Concerning Mr. Lincoln. In which Abraham Lincoln Is Pictured as He Appeared to Letter Writers of His Time* (1944)

RANDALL, James G. · *Constitutional Problems Under Lincoln* (1926)
Lincoln the President (4 vols., 1945–1955)
Lincoln the Liberal Statesman (1947)
Mr. Lincoln (1957)

RANDALL, Ruth Painter · *Mary Lincoln: Biography of a Marriage* (1953)
Lincoln's Sons (1955)

REDWAY, Maurine W., and BRACKEN, Dorothy K. · *Marks of Lincoln on Our Land* (1957)

RIDDLE, Donald W. · *Lincoln Runs for Congress* (1948)
Congressman Abraham Lincoln (1957)

SANDBURG, Carl · *Abraham Lincoln: The Prairie Years* (2 vols., 1926)
Abraham Lincoln: The War Years (4 vols., 1939)

SANDBURG, Carl, and ANGLE, Paul M. · *Mary Lincoln: Wife and Widow* (1932)

SHAW, Archer · *The Lincoln Encyclopedia* (1924)

SHERWOOD, Robert E. · *Abe Lincoln in Illinois,* a play (1939)

SILVER, David M.   *Lincoln's Supreme Court* (1956)
SMITH, T. V.   *Abraham Lincoln and the Spiritual Life*
                               (1951)

SPARKS, Edwin Erle (ed.)   *The Lincoln-Douglas Debates of 1858* (1908)
STAMPP, Kenneth M.   *And the War Came* (1950)
STEPHENSON, Nathaniel W.   *Lincoln, An Account of His Personal Life*
                               (1922)

STERN, Philip Van Doren   *The Life and Writings of Abraham Lincoln*
                               (1940)
                               *An End to Valor: The Last Days of the Civil
                               War* (1958)

STONE, Irving   *Love Is Eternal,* a novel (1940)
TARBELL, Ida M.   *The Life of Abraham Lincoln* (1900)
                               In the Footsteps of the Lincolns (1924)

THOMAS, Benjamin P.   *Lincoln's New Salem* (1934)
                               *Lincoln 1847–1853; Being the Day-by-Day Ac-
                               tivities of Abraham Lincoln from January 1,
                               1847 to December 31, 1853* (1936)
                               *Portrait for Posterity: Lincoln and His Biog-
                               raphers* (1947)
                               Abraham Lincoln, A Biography (1952)

TOWNSEND, William H.   *Lincoln and His Wife's Hometown* (1929)
VAN DOREN, Mark   *The Last Days of Lincoln,* a play (1959)
WARREN, Louis A.   *Lincoln's Parentage and Childhood* (1926)
WEIK, Jesse W.   *The Real Lincoln* (1922)
WHEARE, Kenneth Clinton   *Abraham Lincoln and the United States*
                               (1949)

WHITNEY, Henry Clay   *Life in the Circuit with Lincoln* (1940)
WILLIAMS, Kenneth P.   *Lincoln Finds a General* (1949)
WILLIAMS, T. Harry   *Lincoln and the Radicals* (1941)
                               Lincoln and His Generals (1952)

WILSON, Rufus Rockwell   *Lincoln Among His Friends* (1942)
  (ed.)

                               Intimate Memories of Lincoln (1945)
WILSON, Rufus Rockwell   *Lincoln in Caricature* (1945)
WOLDMAN, Albert A.   *Lawyer Lincoln* (1936)
                               Lincoln and the Russians (1952)

ZORNOW, William Frank   *Lincoln and the Party Divided* (1954)

MITS, WITS AND LOGIC

Books with text by Lillian R. Lieber
and drawings by Hugh Gray Lieber

The Education of T. C. Mits
 (W. W. NORTON & COMPANY, INC.)
The Einstein Theory of Relativity
 (HOLT, RINEHART & WINSTON)
Take a Number
 (RONALD PRESS COMPANY)
Galois and the Theory of Groups
 (GALOIS INSTITUTE PRESS)
Non-Euclidean Geometry
 (GALOIS INSTITUTE PRESS)
Good-bye Mr. Man, Hello Mr. NEWman
 (GALOIS INSTITUTE PRESS)
Mits, Wits and Logic
 (W. W. NORTON & COMPANY, INC.)
Infinity
 (HOLT, RINEHART & WINSTON)
Comedie Internationale
 (GALOIS INSTITUTE PRESS)
Lattice Theory: The Atomic Age in Mathematics
 (GALOIS INSTITUTE PRESS)
Human Values and Science, Art and Mathematics
 (W. W. NORTON & COMPANY, INC.)

MITS
WITS
and
LOGIC

Text by
LILLIAN R. LIEBER

Drawings by
HUGH GRAY LIEBER

Third Edition

NEW YORK
W. W. Norton & Company, Inc.

160
L 62

PRINTED IN THE UNITED STATES OF AMERICA

67890

This little book
is affectionately dedicated to

YOU

in the hope that
you CARE
and will
DO SOMETHING
about
all
this.

PREFACE

This is not intended to be
free verse.
Writing each phrase on a separate line
facilitates rapid reading,
and everyone
is in a hurry
nowadays.

PREFACE TO THE SECOND EDITION

In the main, this second edition is the same as the first –
some minor corrections were made, the situation with
respect to modern bombs has been brought up to date.
But, as regards the antiquated courses in Logic in most
colleges, they are still being given, and therefore this survey
of how they can be improved by the introduction of
Boolean Algebra, is still in order. And SAM is still
waiting to help us.

Since the book was first published, it has been read by
the great logician, Rudolf Carnap, who was good enough
to say: "Not only did I find 'Mits, Wits and Logic'
exceedingly well done and the drawings inspired and
charming, but I was highly gratified to find there the
impressive connection of the scientific material with
your Weltanschauung, and I am delighted that you too
are so deeply impressed with the necessity of avoiding
another war. That is just my feeling that in the present
situation the elimination of war is paramount to all the
other issues."

I trust the reader will agree that this not only holds
good in 1954, but it is imperative that this point of view
be EMPHASIZED at this time, in the hope that it will
become universal and really effective so that we may
eliminate not alone war itself, but also the threat and the
fear of war, and direct our energy and our wealth to the
many human needs all over the world. This is my prayer.

L. R. L.

PREFACE TO THE THIRD EDITION

Everything that was in the Preface to the
Second edition, still holds good now, in 1960!
Chapters II and III have been brought up to date.
But of course Part II on "Realism, Modern Style,"
and Part III on "Logic" are as good as ever.
And again I repeat, as in Part I, "The Emergency":

WAR MUST STOP HERE AND NOW!

Or else!
This is still my prayer.

L. R. L.

CONTENTS

ACKNOWLEDGMENT

I take pleasure in acknowledging my
thanks to Professor Ernest Nagel of the
Department of Philosophy of Columbia University
for reading this entire book in manuscript,
for his enthusiastic expression of approval of it,
and for making several valuable suggestions.

L. R. L.

PART I

THE EMERGENCY

I. INTRODUCING SAM

Those of you who
have met Mits before
know that he is
the celebrated
Man-In-The-Street.*

From which you can guess that
Wits
is the
Woman-In-The-Street.

Both of them are
anxious to meet
SAM,
who, they have heard,
can help them to
get along in this
Modern World.

Mits begs you
NOT to mistake him for
Mitts,
who believes that
MIGHT makes RIGHT!

And Wits does NOT want
to be mistaken for
one who "wittily"
tweaks his neighbor's nose,

* See "The Education of T. C. Mits"
  by Lillian R. Lieber,
  with drawings by
  Hugh Gray Lieber
  (W. W. Norton & Company, 1944).

15

saying,
"Whatsa matter,
ain't you got
no sense o' humor?"

Mits and Wits
are
merely the two billion
men and women
who want
TO LIVE AND LET LIVE,
and who would like to ask
SAM
the $64 question:
"HOW?"

But who is this character,
SAM?
And what makes them think
that he
can help us?

To say that his name
is derived from
Science,
Art and
Mathematics
may leave you cold,
for you may say:
"I grant that
  Scientists,
  Artists,
  Mathematicians
have done some wonderful things,
BUT
when it comes to getting us out of
the horrible mess in which

16

the whole world now finds itself—
they are
no wiser and no better
than the rest of us.
And so
if that is all you have to offer,
please count me out!"

And of course
you are quite right—
for you have probably
seen or heard of
some scientists and mathematicians
who are rational enough while
they are working on
one of their own problems,
but who,
as soon as they come away
from their desks and laboratories,
are as irrational as
the rest of us—
just as some
so-called "religious" people
are "good" on Sundays
and pirates on
all the other days of the week.

But SAM himself is
DIFFERENT.
For he is the
ESSENCE of
what is best in
Science,
Art,
Mathematics,
and therefore is
good and true and beautiful
on all the days of the week

and is always available
to guide and help us
if we would but
go to him.

But "HOW?"

II. A MESSAGE FROM SAM

Here is an illustration of
how SAM is trying
to help us,
if we would only listen!

Recently *
Einstein and
some Atomic Physicists
made the following statements:

(1) Atomic bombs can now be made
cheaply and in large number.
They will become MORE destructive.*

(2) There is NO military defense
against atomic bombs and
NONE is to be EXPECTED.†

(3) Other nations can rediscover
our secret processes
by THEMSELVES.

* This was written in the
first edition, 1947,
but is still of interest
because it shows how long ago
the Atomic Physicists foresaw and warned us
about our dilemma of TODAY, in 1960!
How long will it take us to find out that
SAM is not only competent
but has a profound understanding of
and love for
The Human Race!
He wants LIFE for the human race
in spite of all its failings!

(4) Preparedness against atomic war
    is FUTILE, and
    if attempted, will RUIN
    the structure of
    our social order.

(5) If war breaks out,
    atomic bombs WILL be used
    and they will SURELY DESTROY
    our CIVILIZATION.

(6) There is no solution
    to this problem
    EXCEPT
    the ELIMINATION of WAR.

And yet
some people are ignoring this
WARNING
and are advocating
"strong defense measures,"
more bombs,
biological means such that
a small bottle of the stuff
may be at least
as "strong" as an atomic bomb,
and can be made cheaply
in an innocent-looking "brewery,"
so that even international "control"
would be impossible.
Biological warfare has not received
as much publicity as
atomic-bomb warfare,

but SAM strongly advises you to
acquaint yourself with it!
Well, please read again
SAM'S SIX-POINT WARNING
given above,
and you will see how right SAM was.
For atomic bombs have indeed become more destructive—
there are now hydrogen bombs,
Intercontinental ballistic MISSILES (ICBM's)
(and there are no ANTI-missile missiles!).
Other nations have indeed got these now,
and more nations are getting ready to make them!
Everyone now agrees that
World War III would indeed
SURELY DESTROY CIVILIZATION,
if not the whole human race!
Indeed,
COMPLETE DISARMAMENT is even now
being discussed—
this is NOT an easy problem to solve
and will take much TIME and PATIENCE—
but the alternatives are so much worse that
even our President Eisenhower and
some of his own Generals
(like General Power, for instance, as well as others)
disagree among themselves as to whether or not,
for example,
to keep our bombers with the most terrible bombs,
up in the air around the clock,
twenty-four hours a day,
in case the Soviet Union
pulls a "Pearl Harbor" with ICBM's.
Power says yes, Eisenhower says no,
and the people are of course
terribly confused by all this!
And so, I say again,
let us listen to point (6) of SAM's warning (p. 21),

for SAM, as you have seen, is still
our best prognosticator! (see footnote on p. 20).
"But," you may say,
"why do you call this SAM's warning,
when it is really only the opinion of some scientists;
they are of course entitled to their opinion in a
Democracy,
but so am I entitled to my own opinion,
and I don't agree with them,
that's all."
To which the answer is of course:
This is NOT a matter of opinion,
but a matter of SCIENTIFIC FACTS,
a domain in which the scientists
KNOW what they are talking about,
and mere "opinion," like yours and mine,
has nothing to do with the case.

So you see that
in matters of SCIENCE
we MUST NOT take the
INCOMPETENT advice of anyone,
regardless of how we may value
his friendship and good sense in other things.
For here is a domain in which
SAM,
not Mother,
"KNOWS BEST!"

III. THE MODERN PAUL REVERE

"Well," you say,
"suppose we grant that
your ideal,
SAM,
is right in maintaining
that it would be wonderful
if war were eliminated.
But what can we,
Mits and Wits and
all the little Mits-Wits,
DO ABOUT IT?
Obviously nothing, for
war is just a part of
human nature—
there was always war,
and always will be.
So,
being helpless to stop it,
let's forget about the bombs, etc.,
and have us a good time
as long as we can.
And when the end comes,
it will all be over
in a few minutes anyway,
so why worry?"

To which SAM replies:
"What makes you think that
you will be
one of the lucky ones who
will die instantly?
Have you read the description of

what really happened in
Hiroshima? *

Do you know that
some of those people
are still alive and
suffering from hideous diseases,
some of the effects of which
will appear even in
their children and grandchildren?
No,
death is NOT the worst thing
that modern warfare brings!"

And therefore let us ask
SAM
what we CAN DO about it,
hoping that he will remember
that
we humans cannot
"take it"
as he can—
we need a little rest and recreation,
Mits representing the
tired businessman—
and Wits may have been
standing over a hot stove
all day!

SAM is of course
most sympathetic with Wits,
telling her that
she really need not
stand over a hot stove
these days,
for there are pressure-cookers

* See *Hiroshima* by John Hersey
(Alfred A. Knopf, 1946).

and all sorts of conveniences in
his gadget department
for her.
And,
as regards rest and recreation,
his staff of
physicians,
psychologists,
psychiatrists
and others
are fully aware of this,
and heartily agree that
they are essential for
Mits and Wits.
So we see that
SAM has a heart,
and is definitely
FOR us.
And it is exactly BECAUSE
he is our friend
that he is warning us that
the TIME HAS COME
for eliminating war—
or ELSE!

Furthermore,
he believes that YOU,
Mits and Wits,
CAN DO it.
That is why he got
the Atomic Scientists
not only to
announce the above-mentioned
six-point warning,
but to act as
the modern Paul Revere
to arouse the entire country
to an awareness of the

DANGER.
That is why
Professor Einstein sent the following
TELEGRAM TO THE PEOPLE:

Our world faces crisis
as yet UNPERCEIVED by those
possessing power to make
great decisions for good or evil.
Unleashed power of the atom
has CHANGED EVERYTHING
EXCEPT our modes of THINKING
AND WE THUS DRIFT TOWARD
UNPARALLELED CATASTROPHE.
We scientists who released this immense power
have overwhelming responsibility
in this world-wide life-and-death struggle
to harness atom
for BENEFIT of MANKIND
and NOT for humanity's destruction.
Bethe, Condon, Szilard, Urey and
Federation of American Scientists
join me in this appeal
and beg you to support
our efforts to bring realization to America
that mankind's destiny is being decided
TO-DAY, NOW, THIS MOMENT!
We need $200,000 AT ONCE †
for NATIONWIDE CAMPAIGN

† Since this was written, this money and more was raised
  and the people have become much better informed concerning
  Atomic Energy—
  its potentialities for PEACE as well as
  its overwhelming powers of DESTRUCTION (see p. 23).
  But as of now, 1960, we have new headaches of course!
  Strontium 90, fall-out, and all the rest.
  Furthermore, even for PEACEFUL uses,
  vital decisions must be made—
  where do we put the radioactive "garbage" which is
  a by-product of even peaceful Atomic Energy plants?!

TO LET THE PEOPLE KNOW
that
NEW TYPE OF THINKING IS ESSENTIAL
IF MANKIND IS TO SURVIVE and
move toward higher levels.
This appeal sent you
only after long consideration
of IMMENSE CRISIS we face.
Urgently request you send
immediate check to me,
as Chairman of
Emergency Committee of
Atomic Scientists,
Princeton, New Jersey.
We ask your help
in this fateful moment.
(Signed)
Albert Einstein.

And, believe me, brother,
SAM IS NOT FOOLING!

So,
according to SAM,
the first thing we CAN DO is:
to help the
Modern Paul Revere
to spread the warning of
the World's danger,
by sending money to the *
Emergency Committee
for their
EDUCATIONAL CAMPAIGN
and
by telling all our
friends and neighbors
that
we must

* No longer necessary—see p. 29.

STOP REPEATING
THE OLD SLOGAN that
"There always have been wars,
 there always will be wars"—
for we have reached a point
where

WAR MUST STOP HERE AND NOW!

We must demand that
our representatives in
the Government
understand this and
repeat it until
they
DO SOMETHING about it.
And we MUST NOT
follow any leader who,
like the Goat in
the slaughter houses,
leads the lambs up a ramp,
at the top of which
he is removed to safety,
but the lambs
who trustfully followed him
are slaughtered,
while he starts up again
at the head of a new flock!
And he looks so dignified
and respectable!

Thus the first point in the
NEW TYPE OF THINKING
which we must all learn
is that
we must STOP thinking that

WAR IS INEVITABLE,
and we must replace it by
the MODERN REALISTIC THOUGHT that
WAR MUST BE ELIMINATED
HERE AND NOW,
or we won't live to tell the tale.

Perhaps you are inclined to say:
"But, SAM,
  this may be easy for you,
  but we are only human,
  and much as we would like
  to go along with you
  on this,
  it is impossible for us—
  we are simply not built that way.
After all,
  you must understand that
  you cannot drive us humans
  beyond our strength.
You're a practical fellow
  when it comes to
  technical things,
  but
  you don't seem to understand that human beings are
  much more complex than
  the physical world
  and you cannot push us around
  even if it is for our own good—
  we just can't take it."

IV. OH, YES, YOU CAN TAKE IT!

We are told that
Abraham Lincoln said:
"God must like the common people,
  He made so many of them."
And SAM, too, is very fond of
Mits and Wits,
who are too modest
to know their own strength.
Many of them
surprised themselves
during the war
by doing things
they would have thought to be
impossible.
And SAM knows it
and that is why
he has so much faith in them.
Besides,
as we look back
through the ages,
we see various species
doing the "impossible"
again and again,
adapting themselves
to all sorts of conditions.
Do you think it was
EASY
to grow hands and feet
and brains
and become adapted
to various new environments
through the ages?!—
(as shown on pages 36 and 37)

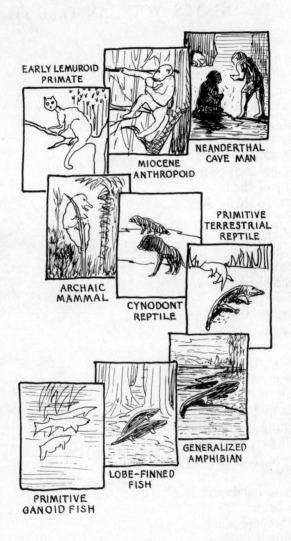

EARLY LEMUROID PRIMATE

MIOCENE ANTHROPOID

NEANDERTHAL CAVE MAN

PRIMITIVE TERRESTRIAL REPTILE

ARCHAIC MAMMAL

CYNODONT REPTILE

GENERALIZED AMPHIBIAN

PRIMITIVE GANOID FISH

LOBE-FINNED FISH

STUDENTS IN NATURE'S TRAINING SCHOOL

In the present and past ages of the earth Nature has kept a physical and mental training-school of many grades. Her examinations have always been practical ones, the prize of survival being awarded to the "fittest" in each successive grade.

In the primary school the lower grades were passed through under water. Here one learned to swim and steer in the currents, to lurk quietly, to strike successfully. A few grades further on the pupils were equipped with air-sacs, so that they could wriggle out on the banks and use their fore-and-hind paddles as limbs.

After acquiring the physique to withstand hardships of heat and cold, some of the more advanced candidates were admitted to the school of the forests and to the uncertainties of life in the trees, where a practical course in the care and feeding of infants was required of all mothers.

At last the most intelligent pupils ventured out into the open and went into training both for short sprints and cross-country runs. In their manual training schools they learned the art of making flint implements and weapons and with these, before they retired to their dormitories at night, they prepared for themselves their simple meal of bear's meat.

Thus they were trained for the degree of H. S. (Homo sapiens), which was eventually won by their descendants.

(Reprinted by permission of W. K. Gregory and The American Museum of Natural History)

Indeed,
even among plants,
"the same individual plant,
if transplanted,
will take on
a very different form
if grown near a mountain-top
or in a lowland valley;
Ranunculus will acquire
one appropriate shape
if grown in water,
another if grown in air." *

And, of course,
Man's brain,
YOUR brain,
has most miraculous potentialities
for adaptation,
and is certainly
NOT going to permit itself
to be destroyed
just because
it is called upon
to adapt itself to this
NEW, MODERN WORLD.
SAM merely reminds you that
you have done it before and
you CAN DO it again!
Thus,
let us follow SAM's lead
and trace through
the changes in our ideas about
REALISM,
and see how we can apply it
to understand

* See the article on Evolution
  in the *Encyclopaedia Britannica*,
  14th edition.

38

what IS most REALISTIC
in the modern world
and how the mind can
accept it,
adapt to it,
and reap the usual reward of
adaptation,
namely,
SURVIVAL.

V. REALISM

Take, for example,
an uneducated man,
out in his own back yard,
who sees the sun rise daily,
run its course through the day
and set in the evening.
He naturally thinks
that the sun
revolves around the earth.
His theory is:
"Seeing is believing."
And so,
the occurrences
in the outside world
plus his theory
create in him
a deep FEELING of confidence in
the REALITY of his experience.

Now, after a while,
along come other men,
who not only watch the sun
in its daily course,
but who, like the astronomers,
spend years of their lives
watching the course of
the planets,
and are driven to have
a more sophisticated theory
to explain
the more sophisticated observations—
namely, that
it is the earth

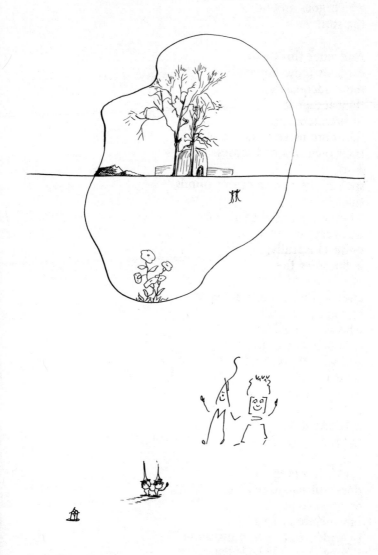

(as well as the other planets)
which goes around
the sun!

And since this theory
explains more observations
more adequately,*
they accept it
in preference to
the more naïve evidence of
their own unaided senses.
And
such is the nature of our minds
that
when we get used to an idea
we accept it
quite cheerfully;
it becomes the
NEW REALISM
and we FEEL quite superior
to the naïve fellow
who does not know
as much as we do,
and who thinks that
what he sees
with his own eyes
in his own back yard
is REALISM—
ha! ha!

SAM, however,
does not laugh at him
or at anyone,
but merely asks us
to widen our "common sense"
through more knowledge.

* See Chapter VII for a
   further discussion of this point.

Thus,
as new instruments
are developed,
telescopes,
microscopes,
spectroscopes,
cyclotrons,
etc., etc.,
more and more observations
are made,
and,
just as before,
the older theories
are less and less able
to account for them
adequately,
and we are driven
by these facts
to develop theories
more sophisticated and
more adequate to
include these facts.
Thus the people who
are right up to date
on the facts of science
and the mathematical theories
which account for them,
have accepted these
as being the new
MODERN REALISM,
far superior to
the naïve realism of
"seeing" and "common sense."
And they FEEL this
modern realism
just as intensely as the less informed person
FEELS and BELIEVES in
his more naïve

observations and theories—
except that
these more sophisticated people
have learned by experience
that this process
of growing sophistication
goes on and on
and they are therefore
not so "set" in their ways
as the more naïve ones,
being more
PREPARED FOR CHANGE
and more willing and able
to make
NECESSARY ADJUSTMENTS
in their ideas about
what is
REALISM!

And so,
SAM,
observing that
these people, these
Scientists,
Artists,
Mathematicians,
have succeeded in
accepting a
NEW REALISM
which fits the world
much better,
and which makes it
possible for them
to ADAPT themselves better,—
thus
SAM knows that
such adaptation is
entirely possible for

human beings,
and therefore for
YOU.
And that
all you need for this is
more EDUCATION
of a kind that
will bring you
UP TO DATE on
Science,
Art,
Mathematics,
and then
your own wonderful possession,
your human brain,
will accept this
NEW REALISM
which will help you, too,
to live in this
MODERN WORLD.

Perhaps you are willing
to accept SAM's guidance,
at least in connection with
Science
(which brings in the observations)
and Mathematics
(which helps construct the theories),
but are you wondering
about Art?
How does that fit into the picture?
What does SAM have to do with
MODERN ART?

Well, in the first place
you will agree that
whereas Science gives us
the observations

and Mathematics
helps construct the theories,
we need also
to FEEL good about it,
to ACCEPT it
with our intuitive sense of
the fitness of things,
which really belongs to
the domain of Art,
so that
every Scientist
and Mathematician
is, in this sense,
also an Artist.

But, more than this,
the Artist himself
views the world
at first
from his own back yard
and at first
acquires the naïve ideas of
REALISM
according to which
he draws what he "sees,"
houses, people,
landscapes, seascapes,
et al.
But, after a while,
he too becomes aware that
"seeing is believing" and
"common sense"
have to be modified
more and more,
and he finds himself,
in modern times,
just like
the Scientist and Mathematician,

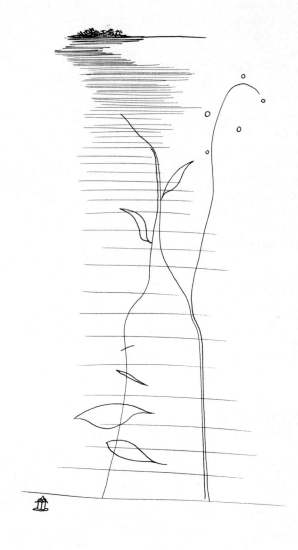

tending more and more
toward the
ABSTRACT
as the more adequate kind of
REALISM
needed for adaptation in
the MODERN WORLD.
Thus, in every way,
Art,
the A in SAM,
is an essential part of
his make-up,
and not an isolated part,
but right in his
blood stream
penetrating into
every corner of his
personality.

But what is this about the
"ABSTRACT"?
And how does it function in
Science,
Art,
Mathematics
to help create the
NEW REALISM
so needed for
ADAPTATION to the
MODERN WORLD?

VI. BE PRACTICAL THE MODERN WAY!

And so, apparently,
in order to survive,
the most PRACTICAL thing to do
is to accept
MODERN REALISM,
which implies
becoming familiar with the
ABSTRACT!

This sounds paradoxical to the NAÏVE mind,
but when we fully realize
that this is the only way to
SURVIVE,
we shall find
not only that we can
take it
all right,
but that it is such
FUN
to be SOPHISTICATED!

But
how is it possible
to become
sufficiently up to date in
Science,
Art,
Mathematics
to really appreciate their
MODERN REALISM and
to use it for our own
SURVIVAL and PLEASURE?
These are such vast domains!

Therefore SAM suggests
a twofold program:

(1) An EMERGENCY program:

    (a) To heed the
        WARNING of the
        MODERN PAUL REVERE,
        even if it means that
        we must get up from
        our nice warm beds
        and come to the rescue of
        not only America
        but the whole world by
        PREVENTING WAR,
        DEMANDING an
        INTERNATIONAL police force,
        DISARMAMENT of ALL NATIONS,
        (to include ALL the horrible
        modern weapons),
        and whatever
        SAM
        recommends! *
        Thus we can gain
        the time needed for
        the longer process of
        EDUCATION for the
        MODERN WORLD
        which SAM advocates.

    (b) To follow SAM's advice
        and nobody else's,
        even if we cannot yet
        quite understand
        all his reasons.

* You can subscribe to the
Bulletin of the Atomic Scientists
and keep yourself informed.

For he is our best friend!
He is trying so hard
to reach us.
We MUST keep ourselves
informed of his doings
and NOT follow
any of the Goats
up the ramp
to our DOOM
like the poor lambs in
the slaughterhouses!

(2) A long-term program of
EDUCATION,
starting in early youth
and continuing
as long as we live,
to become really acquainted
with SAM,
our best friend and guide.
For he will bring us
peace,
knowledge of
the world we live in,
the means to adapt ourselves
to this world,
resulting in
peace of mind,
plenty and
happiness.
For we must remember that
working for SAM,
to accomplish all these things,
are those who
can find
the peaceful uses of

atomic energy—
to cure disease,
to make food "out of the air"
(by photosynthesis),
to give us each
a home and garden,
to lengthen
youthful healthful life,
to think straight,
to have fun in
so many ways that
we can hardly imagine it!

And who stands in the way
of SAM's program?
Why, the ANTI–SAM–ITES of course!
Those who want to lead us
to believe that
World War III is inevitable,
who make us spend
most of our time and energy
and money
in preparing again
to destroy each other,
those who believe that
different races
must hate each other,
those who contradict
SAM's six-point warning!
Please refresh your memory on
these six points (page 20)
so that you can
not only
follow them yourself,
but help spread them,
and especially use them
as a means of recognizing
who ARE the Goats

leading us lambs
to the slaughter!

It is really a battle between
SAM's MEN and
the Goats,
and it is up to
Mits and Wits to
HELP SAM to
HELP MITS and WITS.

And now
let us ask SAM
to give us some idea of
ABSTRACT
MODERN
REALISM.

PART II

REALISM–MODERN STYLE

VII. MODERN REALISM IN SCIENCE

Even a naïve person
should admit that
"seeing is believing" is
rather a crude guide to
Reality,
for, after all, if
you see "pink elephants"
or hear "voices"
which no one else
sees or hears,
you would hardly call
these hallucinations
Reality!

Or,
if you look at an object
and see something like this:

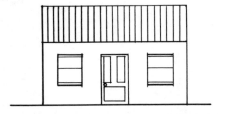

you may be seeing a house,
or perhaps just a billboard,
and it is not until
you look at it from
other points of view
that you can decide whether
it is a real house or not.

Thus you will agree that
a good way to describe
a "real" thing is
that which remains
INVARIANT
from different viewpoints,
or,
as a Scientist prefers to say:
INVARIANT under a given
TRANSFORMATION of axes.
For instance:

Suppose we are interested in
the distance from
A to B
and cannot measure it
directly,
because of some obstruction,
as shown:

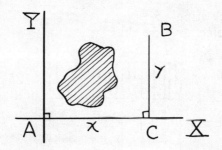

And suppose that
an ingenious gentleman,
Mr. K by name,
suggests the following:
Draw two lines, AX and AY,
perpendicular to each other,
and then draw
BC perpendicular to AX.

58

Then the distance from A to B
(call it d)
can be found by measuring x and y
and then calculating d,
by means of the well-known
Pythagorean Theorem:

$$d = \sqrt{x^2 + y^2}$$

Suppose, further,
that another gentleman,
Mr. K′,
equally ingenious,
suggests a similar method
but uses a different pair of
rectangular axes,
AX′ and AY′:

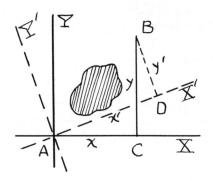

He therefore measures
x′ (= AD) and y′ (= BD)
instead of x and y as K did,
and yet,
by means of the
Pythagorean Theorem,
he too can calculate d by

$$d = \sqrt{(x')^2 + (y')^2}$$

Thus d is an
INVARIANT
under a ROTATION of the axes,
and therefore represents
what is "real" to
both K and K',
as against
the abscissa (x and x') and
the ordinate (y and y')
on which they do NOT agree.
Thus in Science
two observers,
K and K',
EMPHASIZE the INVARIANTS,
the "REALITY"
(in this case,
the distance between two points),
upon which they AGREE,
while, at the same time,
each allows the other
to have his own way in
measuring the
abscissa and ordinate,
agreeing to disagree on
these matters,
so long as they have
some common ground
where they can
do business together!
Is there not
a moral here
for human relations?

Similarly,
if the issue is
the distance between two points
in THREE dimensions,
you probably know that

the formula needed here is

$$d = \sqrt{x^2 + y^2 + z^2}$$

and

$$\sqrt{x^2 + y^2 + z^2} = \sqrt{(x')^2 + (y')^2 + (z')^2}$$

that is,
the distance between two points
is again an
INVARIANT
under a rotation of
the three axes.
It is important to note,
however,
that in three dimensions
$\sqrt{x^2 + y^2}$ $(= AC)$ represents
merely the "shadow" of d
upon the XY plane,
as shown in the following diagram:

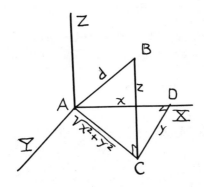

Hence, in this case, we have:

K and K′ AGREE on:

(1) the LENGTH of an object (d).
(2) The use of the Pythagorean Theorem.

K and K′ agree to DISAGREE on:

(1) the 3 co-ordinates:
$$x \neq x'$$
$$y \neq y'$$
$$z \neq z'$$

(2) the "SHADOW" of d:
$$\sqrt{x^2 + y^2} \neq \sqrt{(x')^2 + (y')^2}$$

since the shadow
changes in length
as the object, d,
changes its inclination
relatively to the 3 axes.
Thus the "shadow"
is NOT a "REALITY."

And so, again,
K and K′ have their
INVARIANTS,
their "REALITY,"
upon which they can agree
and do business,
while frankly admitting their differences,
WITHOUT starting a FIGHT over them!
And now,
let us see how this applies
in Modern Physics.
For reasons into which
it in inadvisable to go here,*
it has been found to be wise
to consider the world we live in
as a world of EVENTS,
instead of
a three-dimensional SPACE of

* See "The Einstein Theory of Relativity"
by Lillian R. Lieber,
with drawings by Hugh Gray Lieber
(Rinehart & Co., 1945)

POINTS,
with TIME coming in as
a separate consideration.
Now, to specify a certain event,
one would have to tell
the time and place of
its occurrence;
and since
it takes three numbers
to specify the place
(latitude, x, longitude, y, and altitude, z)
and one number for the time,
it thus takes in all
FOUR NUMBERS
to specify an event,
and therefore we may say that
the world of EVENTS
is FOUR-dimensional,
and hence,
in this sense,
we actually live in a
FOUR–DIMENSIONAL WORLD.
And, under a certain
rotation of axes,
the INVARIANT here is

$$d = \sqrt{x^2 + y^2 + z^2 + \tau^2}$$

where τ is related to the TIME
and where d is
the "space-time interval"
between two events
(instead of
the distance between 2 points,
as before);
and thus we now have:

K and K' AGREE on:

$$d = \sqrt{x^2 + y^2 + z^2 + \tau^2}$$

63

K and K′ agree to DISAGREE on:

(1)
$$x \neq x'$$
$$y \neq y'$$
$$z \neq z'$$
$$\tau \neq \tau'$$

(2)
$$\sqrt{x^2 + y^2} \neq \sqrt{(x')^2 + (y')^2}$$

(3)
$$\sqrt{x^2 + y^2 + z^2} \neq \sqrt{(x')^2 + (y')^2 + (z')^2}$$

Thus,
in our modern
FOUR–DIMENSIONAL
SPACE–TIME WORLD of EVENTS,
the length of an object
(namely $\sqrt{x^2 + y^2 + z^2}$)
is NOT an INVARIANT,
but is more like a "shadow";
whereas
the more ABSTRACT concept,
namely,
the SPACE–TIME INTERVAL
between two EVENTS,
is now the INVARIANT or
REALITY!
Thus the things
(like the length of an object)
which seem so real
to the naïve person
are NOT "real"
when all the data
are taken into account,
and the LESS OBVIOUS things
(like the space-time interval between two events)
become more "real." †

† If this sounds a little "mystical" to you,
  look it up in the book mentioned on p. 62,
  where it is clearly explained.

Thus we see that
MODERN REALISM,
which is BASED on
a vast amount of EXPERIMENTAL data,
leads us
(1) to accept
     ABSTRACT concepts
     as the more adequate
     REALITY
     and
(2) to accept these
     in spite of
     the differences which exist
     (and are freely acknowledged)
     between observers
     having different viewpoints
     (or co-ordinate systems).
This is how
the SOPHISTICATED HUMAN MIND
deals SUCCESSFULLY with
the complications of
the modern world.

Does it not behoove us
also in social relations
to find those basic
INVARIANTS (REALITIES)
like the
(1) DESIRE FOR PEACE
(2) NEED of FOOD and SHELTER
(3) Necessity of ELIMINATION of ALL
     WEAPONS of
     MASS DESTRUCTION
(4) CRAVING for JUSTICE and
     HUMAN DIGNITY,
     etc.,
the REALITIES for ALL NATIONS,
and to do business with

each other,
while agreeing to
let each one be
DIFFERENT in
language, customs, music, etc.,—
differences which,
if accepted,
will add color and variety
and enjoyment
to all our lives,
instead of being
a source of strife!
If anyone claims that
it is impossible for
the human mind
to adjust itself
to such an idea,
let him remember that in
MODERN PHYSICS
the human mind
has been able to accept
the seemingly fantastic ideas
that
things we actually see
are mere SHADOWS,
and that things which are
ABSTRACT,
like the
"space-time interval
between two events,"
or the ATOM
(which has never been seen or
even pictured by anyone)
are the REALITIES of the
MODERN WORLD!

These ideas were
NOT EASY to accept,

but your wonderful
human mind
CAN DO it.
Let no one claim that
he cannot accept the
NECESSARY ideas for
ALL NATIONS
to live together in
PEACE
on this ONE EARTH
without first
MAKING THE GREAT EFFORT
that
the Scientists have made
in accepting
the fantastic ideas of
modern science.
And, indeed,
when the resistance stops
the mind becomes
happier than ever
because it is then
so much better adjusted to
the modern environment,
and is then in contact
with the complexity of
the modern world
without being confused by it!

It is not the ABSTRACT that
the mind really dreads,
but rather the confusion
which comes from being
TOO NAÏVE!

VIII. CAN WE BE HAPPY WITH SAM?

Are you thinking that
if life is to be so difficult,
is the game worth the candle?

But if you examine SAM's personality
carefully,
you will find that
the A in SAM,
which is in his very heart,
and which is
the essence of life,
DEMANDS that
life bring "happiness."
Let us examine this remark
to see what it means.
The meaning of "happiness,"
as used here,
is:
the sense of joy which
an individual feels
at the moment when
he "unites" with
some other individual,
whether this latter is
another human being
(in love or friendship),
or a house
or a picture
or a tune
or an idea
or anything.
This intense desire
for union

is at the basis of
the "religious experience,"
of the desire for
ONE God,
for ONE theory embracing
the entire universe.
It may be called
"the aesthetic principle."
It is the basis
for the desire
to "smooth out"
the physical world
(which is made up of
discrete "quanta"),
thus resulting in the concept of
"continuity."
It makes us see
a "continuous" moving picture
even though we know
it is made up of
a series of
separate individual pictures.
It makes us want to
"glide,"
to dance,
to do anything which
gives this sense of
"smoothness" and "union" and
"oneness."
It is the essence of
happiness and life.

Now if you will accept
this lengthy description
of the A in SAM,
you will agree that
SAM wants you
to live and be happy,

and has an
enormous variety of ways
of being happy—
anywhere from
"swing" to
"religion,"
from skiing to
abstract mathematics,
anything with which
you can "unite."

Now,
suppose you grant this
for a moment,
and then ask:
"But is this 'happiness,'
  this variety of ways of
  'uniting' with others,
  this 'smoothing out'
  of the discrete into
  the continuous—
  is it good for us?"
And you will surely agree
that it depends on
WHAT you unite with,
and on
HOW MUCH uniting you do.
For instance,
if you "unite" with food,
it sustains your life
for you have
the magic ability
to transform the food into
YOU;
each one of us,
eating the same food,
magically converts it
into his own personality.

You are a magician
and you don't realize it!
But obviously
this need for food
can lead us astray,
a child must be guided away
from eating harmful things,
and even many adults
(gourmands and drunkards)
eat and drink
either harmful things
or more than they should,
thus allowing their
basic desire
to "unite" with food,
to mislead them.
Thus Hollywood and
your physician and
the insurance companies
all try to check
this desire to "eat"
and tell us where to stop.

Similarly,
the desire to "unite"
with material things,
to possess wealth,
goes on and on in some people,
until they want to
gather unto themselves
earthly possessions
not only beyond their own needs
but actually
to their own detriment.
Can Hollywood and
the psychiatrists
help SAM
by encouraging us

72

to put a wise limit on
the desire to "unite"
in this direction also?
Even in skiing
you have to watch out
for the trees,
and not give free rein
to the intense desire
to "glide,"
without caution.

If, then,
we are blessed with
this great desire
for "happiness"
and if it needs
curbing
to prevent us from
destroying ourselves,
what are we to do about it?
Well, SAM says
that we are lucky
in having
so many different ways
of achieving this "happiness"—
we do not have to
eat so much that we get
fatty degeneration,
or drink until we get
the D.T.'s,
or accumulate wealth until
we become overwhelmed
with our own greed.
For we can also
"unite"
with ideas!
Here, too, however,
we must carefully

"select" the ideas,
for some of them
are poison, too,
and can destroy us.
But we are still far from
having too many good ideas.
We are not yet
TOO fat with GOOD ideas,
which lead to
LIFE instead of death!
In the domain of ideas
we are still suffering from
malnutrition,
because we have been fed
too many poisonous ideas which
lead to
death and destruction.
Thus we have much "uniting" to do
in the immediate future,
to form the
"United Nations"
to make
"One World,"
to "join up" with
SAM
for peace and plenty
and happiness
for all.
For SAM can help us
to SELECT
the right kind and amount of
"food"
for our bodies and minds—
through his staff of
biologists,
physicians,
psychiatrists,—
indeed, all

Scientists,
Artists,
Mathematicians.
OUR job is
to "unite" with
all this knowledge,
not only because
we need SAM's guidance
to go toward
LIFE instead of death,
but,
this very act of
"uniting" with knowledge
will bring us
the very "happiness" we seek!
But, SAM reminds us,
this "happiness" itself
is NOT continuous
but comes in moments,
and between these moments
there is work to be done,
just as
in climbing a mountain,
the moments when we stop
to "unite" with the landscape
are intermittent,
each being followed by
further effort
to reach
a still "more beautiful" view,
with which we again
"unite" for a moment.

And so
let us follow SAM
a little way up
Mt. Mathematics
to see how the

ABSTRACT
can help us.
And if we "unite" with it
and let the magic of our minds
convert it into
our own personalities
(as we do with food),
we shall derive
both pleasure and profit
(as we do from food).

IX. A NEW VIEW FROM MT. MATH

As we saw in Chapter VII,
even in Science, which is
our closest contact with
the outside world,
modern "REALITIES"
are ABSTRACT!
And,
not only have we been
driven to this by
the EXPERIMENTAL data,
but we saw in Chapter VIII
that this is FORTUNATE
because
in the domain of IDEAS
there are
many opportunities
for satisfying
that aesthetic urge for
"union"
after having reached
a wholesome limit in
"union" on the
more naïve, physical level
(food, drink, etc.).
Of course
for those who do NOT YET
have enough food, etc.,
this craving comes first
and must be satisfied first—
and if those who do have enough
of these things
will "unite" with this "idea"
they will find "happiness"

in feeding the others.
But, in addition to that,
we need a domain for
"union"
in which there seems to be
no limit for "happiness"—
and that is
the ABSTRACT.

Thus let us try
to get a glimpse of
what has been done
in this respect in
Mathematics,
and see how it can help us.

We all know
from ordinary arithmetic
that
in multiplying two numbers
(say 7 and 11)
it does not matter which number
is written first:
thus $7 \times 11 = 77$ and
also $11 \times 7 = 77$,
giving us the same answer
either way.
Expressing this basic rule of
arithmetic
in more general terms,
as is done in algebra,
we write
$$a \times b = b \times a,$$
showing that this rule applies
for any pair of numbers
(not just 7 and 11).
Thus in going from
arithmetic to

algebra,
we find that
we gain in GENERALITY,
obtaining a relationship
$$a \times b = b \times a,$$
which then applies to
more cases than just
$$7 \times 11 = 11 \times 7.$$
Indeed,
when you stop to think of it,
even writing a number, like 7,
is already
more "abstract" than
"7 apples,"
which refers to concrete objects.
Thus, a child,
in learning arithmetic,
must first start
with actual concrete objects
to appreciate the meaning of
"addition," for instance.
Gradually, however,
he accepts the idea of
working with
the numbers themselves,
and,
later on, in algebra,
he abstracts still further
and learns to use
letters instead of numbers.

And please note that
each time
we go further into
the abstract
we GAIN in GENERALITY,
which makes the result
applicable to more cases

and therefore
MORE practical, NOT LESS!

But arithmetic and algebra
are of course
by this time
an old story.
For in MODERN mathematics
this process of
abstraction
has been going on and on,
with the result that
now
the letters need not even
represent numbers at all,
but may represent
ANY kind of "elements,"
and the word
MULTIPLICATION
need not represent
our old familiar friend in
arithmetic
(as in 7×11),
but may now mean
ANY "operation."
For instance,
suppose that
a and b represent "events,"
and suppose we take
multiplication to mean
"is followed by,"
then $a \times b$ would mean
that some event, a,
say, being born,
is followed by
some other event, b,
say, being married.
Now notice that

here
$a \times b$
does NOT equal
$b \times a$;
thus
$$a \times b \neq b \times a$$
under this interpretation
of a, b, and $\times$;
and thus
the old familiar
COMMUTATIVE LAW of MULTIPLICATION
(namely $a \times b = b \times a$),
which is so familiar to us in
arithmetic and algebra,
does NOT hold here.
Well, you might say,
so what is the use of it?
Is it not just going to
confuse us
after we have taken
so much trouble to learn
arithmetic and algebra?

NOT AT ALL!

For
all one needs to do
to keep from being confused
is to SPECIFY
the interpretation,
as on page 81,
and we then know that
we are not speaking of
ordinary arithmetic or algebra
but of some other domain
which makes just as much
SENSE,
but has DIFFERENT basic rules.

82

Thus we gain the
ADVANTAGE
OF BEING ABLE TO PUT
THE WONDERFUL MATHEMATICAL
SYMBOLISM
to NEW and IMPORTANT
USES,*
since arithmetic and algebra,
useful as they are,
are NOT adequate for
tackling the great VARIETY of
situations which we meet in life.
Later,
in Part III,
you will see how
a NEW "algebra,"
whose basic rules are
different from those
of our ordinary algebra,
is most useful in
LOGIC,
which we need
not only in
Mathematics and Science
but in ALL thinking
in our daily living!

And so you see
that
excursions into the
ABSTRACT,
far from being impractical,
are,
on the contrary,

* For instance, see
  "Theory of Games and Economic Behavior" by
  von Neumann and Morgenstern
  (Princeton University Press, 1944).

83

most rewarding in
giving us results
which can be applied
to more and more cases
and therefore become
more and more
USEFUL
to
more and more
PEOPLE
in more and more
SITUATIONS
we meet in life—
not just a device which
helps an accountant
to figure your income tax,
important as that may be.

Thus
the explorers of the
ABSTRACT in
Mathematics
have brought back to us
MANY
"arithmetics,"
"algebras,"
"geometries"
which are applicable
in LOGIC
(needed in ALL thinking),
in NON–EUCLIDEAN GEOMETRIES
(needed in MODERN PHYSICS),
in the THEORY of GROUPS
(valuable in the
Theory of Equations
so basic in ordinary algebra),
etc., etc., etc.
They have discovered

84

a veritable
TREASURE HOUSE,
with UNLIMITED treasure,
enough for all of us
to "unite" with,
without depriving anyone else
of his share!

X. THE ABSTRACT IN ART

Thus we have seen that,
in Science,
the ABSTRACT
is more REALISTIC
than the superficial
so-called realism of the
local yokel,
and that it has become
ESSENTIAL
in adapting our minds
to the experimental facts
of the physical world,
and is therefore most
PRACTICAL!

And,
in Mathematics,
the ABSTRACT
has enriched us
with so many new fields,
which have so many
NEW applications,
and so many more possibilities of
PRACTICAL applications
than ever before.

And now
let us take a look at
the ABSTRACT
in Art.
Here again
the naïve, unsophisticated
artist who

wishes to make
a portrait of you,
thinks that
he must copy
your features
as exactly as possible,
otherwise
it will not be
a good "likeness" of you,
it will not be
"realistic."
But you will admit that
if the artist is
a great portrait painter,
he will expect
to do better than that,
to put your "character"
(which is more "abstract"
than your face)
into the portrait.
And
a MODERN ARTIST
will go still further
and do
a "psyquaport" * of you,
which will show
your "human-ness,"
your love of
"gliding,"
"smoothness,"
"continuity,"
"happiness,"
"life,"
all different words
for the same urge

* A word invented by
  Hugh Gray Lieber
  to describe the drawings he makes.

to "unite" yourself
with all the world,
physical and mental.
The result is
an "abstract" portrait of you,
a "psyquaport,"
which,
by virtue of its
GENERAL human-ness,
is then a portrait
not of you alone,
but of all humanity,
and has therefore
more of the quality of
universality
than does a mere
snapshot of
your physical self.
Hence a psyquaport
appeals to many people,
who see in it also
their own "human-ness,"
just as
a symphony has
a more UNIVERSAL appeal
(to the sophisticated)
than a song with words,
which tells a concrete story
and which therefore
appeals to
the more naïve person.

And so we see that
the concrete objects,
the superficial "realities,"
the "common sense" of
the naïve, uninformed person,
have all given way

to more abstract
and deeper "realities"
of the modern world
in all domains.

We CAN and MUST
adapt ourselves to
this modern world,
and learn to
"unite" with the "abstract"
in order to
"live" and be "happy" in it.
And so,
in looking at
the psyquaports
on the next few pages,
do not look for
snapshots of concrete objects,
but look for
something to "unite" with,
to "enjoy,"
to "eat,"
to "absorb" into yourself,—
whether it be
grace of curve
or some associations
of your own,
or ideas,
or what have you.
It is like listening to
a symphony—
feel free to
think your own thoughts,
to make your own
applications to
your own needs—
just as
various scientists

make their own applications
to their own needs
of abstract mathematics.

That is why
a modern artist
does not, as a rule,
give names to his pictures.
And when he does,
he often gives them
different names at
different times,
showing that
they do not have
specific definite meanings
even for the artist himself—
any more than
Abstract Mathematics has for
the mathematician himself,
until it is "applied."

You may be interested
to know that
these psyquaports
are not sketched out first
but come "gliding" out of
the artist,
like oil out of a well,
or water in a stream,
without any effort—
a truly NATURAL phenomenon,
wonderful to behold!
You would probably
enjoy them even more
if you could see them
in the process,
as you watch
an expert dancer

or skier,
or listen to a great violinist.

And now look at
these drawings
and see if you can
find in them
something of
the magic
and beauty
of YOUR OWN
human spirit.†

† See also the book of drawings:
  "Good-bye Mr. Man, Hello Mr. NEWman"
  by Hugh Gray Lieber,
  with an Introduction by
  Lillian R. Lieber
  (Galois Institute Press, 1958).

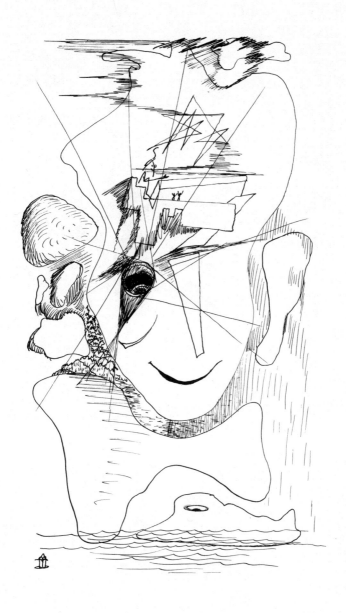

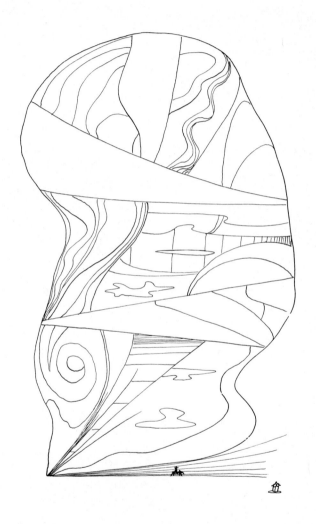

PART III

LOGIC

XI. THANK YOU, SAM!

Thus we see that:

(1) SAM is much more
POWERFUL and IMAGINATIVE
than "Superman" or
"Mighty Mouse,"
for he has all the
Scientists and Mathematicians
working for him
to help us,—
if we would only
avail ourselves of
all their wonderful inventions,
now ready for us,
and more to come!

(2) He is much more
KIND than "Robin Hood"
for he does not have to
rob one to pay another,
but has
ABUNDANCE for EVERYONE!

(3) He is much more
SANE than
a "Fairy Godmother,"
for she is only
an "escape mechanism,"
whereas he is a
REALISTIC IDEALIST!

(4) He agrees with
the great RELIGIONS,
which have long been telling us:
Thou shalt not kill.

(SAM too is for LIFE, against death!)
Thou shalt not steal
(no need to,
he has abundance for all).
And so on and so on.

(5) He is HONEST,
he will never double-cross you.

(6) He preaches love
(remember the A in SAM?)

Although he advocates
"uniting" with all the world
into ONE SOCIETY,
he does not forget
the need for "happiness" of
each INDIVIDUAL.
He is thus
for liberty and justice for all
regardless of race, creed or color.
He is for democracy
and can give us
some good, CLEAR ideas
about it.
For instance:
there is Freedom of Speech in
Science,
but freedom to say what?
Why, obviously,
to say something
INTELLIGENT and CONSTRUCTIVE,
not merely to heckle
or just to make a noise.
Similarly,
in considering VARIOUS issues
we can learn to ask
"What would SAM say about this,
or what would SAM do about that?"

It is surprising how,
when we form this habit,
he actually comes to the rescue
with excellent advice.

Try it and see!

For instance,
let us ask SAM about
LOGIC:
(1) What IS Logic?
(2) What is traditional,
     Aristotelian Logic?
(3) What is
     modern, streamlined Logic?
(4) How can it be of
     USE to us ALL?

XII. WHAT IS LOGIC?

One day
the following incident took place:
A high-school boy,
who had studied
Euclidean plane geometry,
and the school janitor, who
had once been a seaman,
were having an "argument"
about the shortest path
from New York to Paris.
The boy,
maintaining that
"A straight line is
  the shortest distance between
  two points,"
placed a ruler on the map
and drew a straight line
between New York and Paris,
claiming that
this is the shortest path.
The former sailor, however,
maintained that
the shortest path would be
along a curve!
And so the boy said:
"The trouble with you is
  that you never
  studied geometry,
  and therefore
  you make statements that
  are not logical!"

Now, as a matter of fact,
the sailor was right
and the high-school boy wrong.
But please do not
jump to the conclusion
that it is wrong to
study geometry!
The point is that
if the boy had known
MORE geometry
he would have agreed
with the sailor,
who picked up
this information from
his practical experience
but,
not having had
a good education,
was unable to
defend himself,
and so they argued and argued
without getting anywhere!
The fact is that
BOTH
education and experience—
and plenty of each—
are needed.

Now let us examine
what the fight was all about.

You will agree that
if you cut the surface
of a globe in half
along a meridian
and tried to lay one half
flat on the table,
it just would not lie flat,

but would look like a cup—
unless you stretched it
at the North and South poles,
stretching each of these points
into a line as long as
the equator.
Now, in doing so,
you would distort
the regions around the poles,
so that
on such a flat map
Greenland appears to be
the same size as
South America,
whereas
on the globe
you can easily see that
Greenland is really
very much smaller than
South America!
Similarly,
to get some idea of
the shortest path
from New York to Paris,
stretch a string right on
the globe,
between these cities,
and you will see that
the path goes through
Newfoundland and Ireland,
which does NOT agree
with the straight-line path
on your flat map!
Thus the sailor knew this
from experience,
whereas the boy
did not realize that
the geometry on

the surface of a sphere
is DIFFERENT from the
Euclidean Geometry which
he had studied.*

Nowadays,
with fast airplane travel
coming in,
we are becoming
more "globe"-conscious,
and therefore should be
more map-conscious,
realizing that
different maps are useful for
different purposes.†

But where does
the "logic" come in?

Well,
if you make a SINGLE statement,
it makes no sense to say
that it is either
"logical" or "illogical";
it is only when
from one statement
you "infer" a second one
(you "draw a conclusion"),
that you can call
the process
"logical" or "illogical":

* See "Non-Euclidean Geometry"
  by Lillian R. Lieber
  with drawings by
  Hugh Gray Lieber
  (Galois Institute Press, 4th printing, 1959).
† See "Military and Naval Maps and
  Grids" by W. W. Flexner and G. L. Walker
  (Dryden Press, 1942).

it is "logical" when
your conclusion is drawn
VALIDLY,
and "illogical" when
your conclusion is
NOT VALIDLY drawn;
in the latter case
the conclusion is sometimes
referred to by the Latin term
"non sequitur," which means
it does NOT FOLLOW
from your first statement
(called the "premise").
Thus our young friend (page 104)
was really being illogical, for
from the premise of having
a non-Euclidean surface (the globe)
he was falsely drawing
Euclidean conclusions
which do NOT FOLLOW for
the surface of the earth!

You have probably heard lawyers
use the term
"non sequitur,"
for, in their experience,
they often find
people being "illogical."
A common example of
a DANGEROUS non sequitur is:
(1) Your religion is
     different from mine. (Premise)
(2) Therefore you are no good! (Conclusion)

Thus lawyers and judges,
in order to serve justice,
are obliged to rule out
non sequiturs—

these are considered
a "foul"
in an argument.
And you can see that
all of us,
even outside of law courts,
should be obliged
to rule out
such "foul" arguments
if we want more
justice and peace,
so that we can all have a chance
to tackle
the ever-present problem of
adaptation to the modern world
and thus reap the benefit in
survival and happiness.
This will be hard enough to do
if we all work together,
but impossible for ANYONE
if we use up our strength
in getting "tough" with
each other, instead of
getting "tough" with
the PROBLEM itself!

A simple illustration of
a VALID conclusion is:

(1) From the premise:
    "If people live in
    New York State,
    they live in the
    United States of America"

(2) you can safely CONCLUDE:
    "Therefore
    if they do NOT live in the

United States of America
then they certainly
do NOT live in
New York State."

From the following diagram
you can easily see that
these two statements
are really saying
the SAME thing
using slightly different wording.

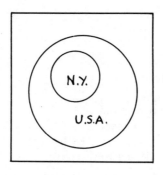

Since the circle representing
the N. Y. State dwellers
is entirely enclosed in
the larger, U.S.A., circle,
then it AUTOMATICALLY follows
that all those
outside of the larger circle
are certainly outside of
the smaller circle.

Such a simple inference
which follows directly
from a premise
without the mediation of
any other statement

is called an
"immediate" inference.
But more often
reasoning is not as simple
as this.
A common type of reasoning is
the "mediate" inference,
which requires a "middle" statement
before the conclusion can be drawn.
An example of this type is
the so-called
SYLLOGISM,
the study of which
dates way back to
Aristotle,
and is known as
Aristotelian Logic or
Traditional Logic.
It is still treated in most
college courses and texts,
although it is now known to be
only a very small part of
Modern Symbolic Logic,
which has become
a wonderful streamlined
mathematical machine,
but which has not yet replaced
the traditional methods
in many colleges!

Let us first take a look
at the old way,
so that you can better
appreciate
the "modern improvements."

XIII. ARISTOTLE AND BARBARA

Thus we see that
Logic is
the study of
HOW TO DRAW CONCLUSIONS VALIDLY.
As was stated at the end of
Chapter XII,
Traditional Logic,
though now known to be
only a tiny part of
Modern Logic,
is still studied in the old way,
and therefore
you may be interested to
get a glimpse of it
so you can somewhat appreciate
the following quotation: *

"Thousands of men,
  through thousands of years,
  have had millions of headaches
  over the valid and invalid
  combinations of these terms,
  arranging, relating and
  naming them.
  Symbolic Logic proves them all
  equivalent to
  just three forms of a
  much greater system."

* See p. 355, "Introduction to Symbolic
  Logic" by S. K. Langer
  (Houghton Mifflin Co., 1937).

114

Let us therefore proceed
to the study of
SYLLOGISMS:

A syllogism consists of
three and only three propositions:

(1) the major premise
(2) the minor premise
(3) the conclusion.

And the problem in the old
Aristotelian Logic was
to determine what must be
the GENERAL form (or forms)
of the two premises
in order that
the conclusion may be
validly drawn,
thus giving us a kind of
"thought-machine"
to help us to draw conclusions
VALIDLY,
and not jump at
non sequiturs
which are based on
mere personal prejudices,
mere "wishful thinking."

You must admit that
it took a great man
to conceive such an idea,
even if it does need
streamlining today.

Now an "argument" often
consists of a SERIES of
syllogisms,
not very clearly or completely

stated.
And it then behooves us
to clarify and complete them,
and then to test their validity
by Aristotelian Logic
(preferably, of course, using
the new symbolism,
which you will see in
subsequent chapters).

Let us therefore return to
the consideration of
the syllogism.

Each proposition of a syllogism
consists of two terms,
subject and predicate
(connected by a verb),
such that
there are only three distinct terms in
the entire syllogism,
each term therefore
occurring twice in
the syllogism.
For instance:
the following is a syllogism:

(1) All metals † are elements.
     (Major premise)
(2) All iron is metal. (Minor premise)
(3) Therefore iron is an element. (Conclusion)

† "Metal," as used here,
 is a technical term,
 as used in Chemistry,
 and not as used
 colloquially
 to include alloys,
 which are not "elements."

Here the terms are:
iron, metal, element.
Note that
each occurs twice in the
syllogism,
and the "middle" term
(metal, in this case)
does NOT occur in the conclusion.

Note further that
a proposition may be

(1) UNIVERSAL
     (if it applies to
     ALL members of a class,
     like
     "ALL metals are elements")

or

(2) PARTICULAR
     (if it applies to only
     SOME members of a class,
     like
     "SOME men are trustworthy.")
Also a proposition may be
AFFIRMATIVE or NEGATIVE.

Thus propositions may be
of four different kinds:

(1) UNIVERSAL AFFIRMATIVE   (A)
(2) UNIVERSAL NEGATIVE   (E)
(3) PARTICULAR AFFIRMATIVE   (I)
(4) PARTICULAR NEGATIVE   (O)

Notice that the letters A and I
occur in the Latin word
"affirmo"
and E and O occur in

"nego."
This helps to remember
which is which.

Now, since a syllogism
contains three propositions,
and since each of these may be
one of four kinds (A, E, I, O)
we can form
4 × 4 × 4 or 64
different kinds of syllogisms,
called "Moods."
Thus the syllogism on page 116
may be represented by
AAA.

Now
these 64 different "Moods"
are by no means all valid!
Indeed there are
RULES of validity: ‡

(1) The middle term must be
    distributed once at least
    (i.e., the whole of it
    must be referred to
    universally
    in one premise, if not both).
(2) No term must be
    distributed in the conclusion
    which was not distributed in
    one of the premises.
(3) From two negative premises
    nothing can be inferred.
(4) If one premise be negative,
    the conclusion must be negative;
    and vice versa:

‡ See any standard book on Traditional Logic.

to prove a negative conclusion
one of the premises must be
negative.
(5) From two particular premises
no conclusion can be drawn.
(6) If one premise be particular,
the conclusion must be
particular.

You may wish to try your hand
at using these rules
in order to select from
the 64 possible Moods
mentioned above,
those which are valid.
In order to do this,
it will help you
to write out
the 64 cases
in a systematic manner,
thus:

(1) AAA	(5) AEA	(9) AIA	(13) AOA
(2) AAE	(6) AEE	(10) AIE	(14) AOE
(3) AAI	(7) AEI	(11) AII	(15) AOI
(4) AAO	(8) AEO	(12) AIO	(16) AOO

etc.
The next 16 cases will of course
all have E down the
first column;
then the second column will have
A's in the first four
E's in the next four,
etc.,
and the third column will have
AEIO in each set.
Similarly,
the next 16 will have

all *I*'s in the first column,
etc.,
and the last batch of 16
will have all *O*'s in
the first column, etc.,
thus making 64 cases
in all.

You will now see that
some of the 64 Moods
do not satisfy the rules on pages 118 and 119.
Thus, *AIA* is not valid
according to rule (6),
which says that
if one premise be particular
(*I*, the minor premise, here),
the conclusion must be particular
(whereas here, the conclusion, *A*,
is universal).
Similarly show that
EEI, IEA, IOI, etc.,
are not valid.
If you examine all the 64,
you will find that
only 11 valid ones remain.

But this is not all!
For, in addition to Moods,
there are also
"Figures,"
four "Figures,"
and each Mood may be
expressed in each of the four
Figures,
so that we have
11 × 4 = 44 possible forms.
To understand what is meant by
"Figures,"

you must recall that
every syllogism has
three terms.
Let us represent them by
X, Y and Z,
Y being the "middle term,"
the one which does NOT appear in
the conclusion.
Thus the terms
can be arranged in
the following four ways or
"Figures":

	I	II	III	IV
Major premise	YX	XY	YX	XY
Minor premise	ZY	ZY	YZ	YZ
Conclusion	ZX	ZX	ZX	ZX

And so
we are back to 44 cases,
but, fortunately,
they too are not all valid.
Only 24 of these are valid,
and of these
5 are "weak,"
thus leaving only
19 which are
both valid and useful.
To see what is meant by
a "weak" conclusion,
consider the following syllogism:

All material substances gravitate,
All metals are material substances;
Therefore some metals gravitate.

You can see that
you could have concluded that
"All metals gravitate,"
and therefore
to say only that
SOME metals gravitate,
though valid enough,
is obviously
a weaker conclusion
than you would be entitled to.

But this is not all,
for consider
the following quotations from
Jevons, a well-known authority on
Aristotelian Logic:

"In order to facilitate
the recollection of
the 19 valid and useful moods
of the syllogism,
logicians invented,
at least six centuries ago,
a most curious system of
artificial words,
combined into mnemonic verses,
which may be readily
committed to memory.
This device, however ingenious,
is of a barbarous and
wholly unscientific character;
but a knowledge of
its construction and use
is still expected from
the student of logic, §

§ Though this was published in 1881,
  it still holds now, in 1960!—
  such is the tenacity
  with which many people cling to
  outmoded ways of thinking!

122

and the verses are therefore
given and explained below."
And
"Aristotle looked upon
the first figure as
a peculiarly evident and cogent
form of argument—
and he therefore called it the
PERFECT FIGURE.
The fourth figure was
never recognized by him,
and it is often called
the Galenian figure,
because the celebrated Galen
is supposed to have discovered it.
The second and third figures
were known to Aristotle as
the Imperfect Figures,
which it was necessary to reduce
to the first figure by
certain conversions and
transpositions of the premises,
for which directions are to be found
in the artificial words."
The "artificial words"
to which he refers
are given below,
followed by an explanation of
their meaning and use:

Barbara, Celarent, Darii, Ferioque, prioris;
Cesare, Camestres, Festino, Baroco, secundae;
Tertia, *Darapti, Disamis, Datisi, Felapton,*
Bocardo, Ferison, habet;
Quarta insuper addit
Bramantip, Camenes, Dimaris, Fesapo, Fresison.

You will notice that
the italicized words

are NOT real words
in any language,
but have been made up
so that each contains
THREE VOWELS,
representing one of
the remaining 19 Moods (see p. 121).
Thus Barbara represents
the Mood *AAA*, etc.
The words which are
not italicized,
like "prioris," "secundae,"
"Tertia," "Quarta,"
are real Latin words
indicating
which of these moods
are in the first figure,
the second figure,
the third and fourth figures.
Furthermore,
the initial consonant
of each artificial word
indicates to which one
of the four moods of
the first figure
it can be reduced:
thus all those beginning with *B*
can be reduced to Barbara,
those beginning with *C* can be
reduced to Celarent,
etc.
And, furthermore,
each artificial word
contains also
other consonants which show
just how the reduction
is to be made.

For instance,
s indicates that
the proposition denoted by
the preceding vowel
is to be converted "simply,"
which means that
YX is to be re-worded
so that X precedes Y,
thereby converting YX to XY;
thus, instead of saying
"All planets are not self-luminous"
you may say
"No self-luminous bodies are planets."
And m (which comes from
the Latin word "mutare,"
which means "to change")
indicates that
the major and minor premises
are to be interchanged.
You can see that
this does not alter
the meaning of
the syllogism,
but merely helps to change
the figure.

Thus,
to take a standard illustration:
Consider the syllogism:

(1) All stars are self-luminous.
(2) No planets are self-luminous.
(3) Therefore no planets are stars.

This is obviously
in the mood AEE,
and the figure may be
represented by

$$XY$$
$$ZY$$
$$ZX$$

(where X = "stars"
  Y = "self-luminous bodies"
  Z = "planets")
and is therefore in
the second figure (see p. 121).
Hence it is to be designated by
Camestres (see page 123).
Now this word indicates that
it can be reduced to
Celarent
(because it begins with a C)
by the following procedure:

(1) the m tells us to
  interchange the
  major and minor premises,

(2) the first s tells us to
  "convert simply"
  the proposition represented by
  the preceding vowel, e,
  namely,
  the minor premise,
  and

(3) the last s tells us to
  do the same with
  the conclusion.

Thus the syllogism becomes:

(1) No self-luminous bodies are
  planets.
(2) All stars are self-luminous.
(3) Therefore no stars are planets.

which is a syllogism in
Celarent.

Of course a little consideration
shows clearly that
the meaning of the syllogism
has not been altered,
but the form is now such
that its validity is
easily tested,
since it has now been reduced to
the "Perfect" figure.

For further details
and illustrations
of this process
see page 163.
Also see any standard book on
Traditional Logic.*

And now
where do we go from here?

* For instance,
  "An Introduction to Logic" by
  H. W. B. Joseph
  (Oxford University Press, 1925).

XIV. WHAT THEN?

The syllogisms discussed
in the previous chapter
are known as
"categorical,"
since all three propositions
in each syllogism are
categorical or unconditional ones,
like

$$A \text{ is } B.$$

And these are the only ones
treated in the original
Aristotelian Logic.
Since then, however,
many scholars have added
the "hypothetical" and
"disjunctive"
syllogisms, in which
at least one of the propositions is
"hypothetical" or conditional:
For instance,

(1) Hypothetical:

If A is B, then C is D. }
If C is D, then E is F. (Premises)
Therefore if A is B, then E is F. (Conclusion)

(2) Disjunctive:

A is either B or * C. }
But A is B. (Premises)
Therefore A is not C. (Conclusion)

* Here "or" means
one of the two alternatives,
but not both.

Later,
after learning
something of
Modern Symbolic Logic,
you will see how
this powerful new tool
boils down both the
categorical and the
hypothetical
syllogisms
to an essence
containing only
a few lines!

Right now, however,
let us look at
some of the
hypothetical syllogisms,
with their picturesque
Latin names which are
still in use;
and let us try to get
a bird's-eye view of
all this
Traditional Logic.

A hypothetical syllogism may be
"pure" or "mixed."
The "pure" ones may be either:

(1) Modus ponens: †

> If A is B, then C is D,
> If C is D, then E is F;
> therefore,
> if A is B, then E is F.

† "Ponens" is
the Latin word for
"asserting."

129

or

(2) Modus tollens: †
   If A is B, then C is D,
   if C is D, E is not F;
   therefore
   if E is F, A is not B.

You may easily make up for yourself
simple illustrations of
these forms of reasoning.

Furthermore, in a
"mixed" hypothetical syllogism
the major premise is
hypothetical, while the
minor premise and the conclusion
are categorical assertions;
and here also we have:

(1) Modus ponens:
   If A is B, C is D,
   but A is B,
   therefore
   C is D.

and

(2) Modus tollens:
   If A is B, C is D,
   but C is not D,
   therefore A is not B.

And, finally in
the disjunctive syllogism,
the major premise is
"disjunctive"
(i.e., it gives two possible

† "Tollens" is Latin for "denying"
  and applies here because of
  the word "not" in this syllogism.

alternatives)
whereas
the minor premise is a
categorical proposition,
which may be
affirmative or negative,
thus:

(1) Modus ponendo tollens: ‡
    A is either B or * C,
    But A is B,
    Therefore A is not C.

or

(2) Modus tollendo ponens: ‡
    A is either B or C,
    But A is not B.
    Therefore A is C.

But perhaps you are beginning
to get one of those
million headaches
referred to by Langer (p. 113),
and are anxious to see
the modern method which

‡ "ponendo tollens" means:
  "by asserting" (ponendo)
  something, like A is B,
  we are led to "denying" (tollens)
  something else,
  like A is not C.
  and
  "tollendo ponens" means:
  "by denying" (tollendo)
  something, like A is not B,
  we are led to
  "asserting" (ponens)
  something else,
  like, A is C.
 * Here "or" means
  one of the two alternatives
  but not both.

131

reduces all these words
to a few lines of
clear symbolism.
When you have seen that,
you will see in a nutshell
what syllogistic reasoning
accomplishes,
as well as
having a tool with which
you can go far beyond
the syllogism.

First, however, it will be
worth while to consider that
the study of
traditional logic
exhibited many "fallacies"
which are still being used on
innocent victims
many, many times daily;
and hence
we must still learn to
recognize and destroy them!

But the mere study of
the syllogisms
and the "fallacies"
is not enough.
Modern logic,
as it appears in
Science and Mathematics,
and in the formal study of
Symbolic Logic itself
is essential for
MODERN THINKING!

XV. BEWARE OF THE PITFALLS!

Many logicians have
followed all kinds of
arguments,
legal and otherwise,
and have observed patterns
that have occurred
again and again,
down through the ages,
and are still going on.
So let us look at a few:
The Latin designations for
some of them are:

(1) Argumentum ad hominem
    ("homo" means "man"),
    which refers to
    an appeal to purely
    personal prejudice
    rather than to reason.

(2) Argumentum ad populum
    is an appeal to
    the prejudices of
    a group of people
    rather than to reason.

(3) Argumentum ad verecundiam
    is an appeal to
    respect for some authority
    rather than to reason.

(4) Post hoc, ergo propter hoc,
    which means
    "After this, therefore
    because of this,"

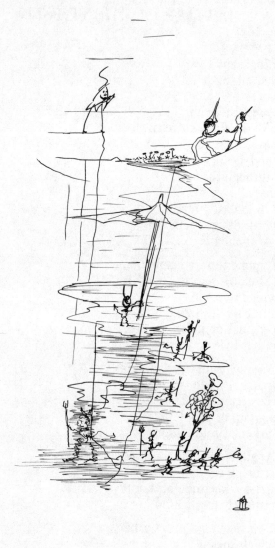

that is,
maintaining that
just because
one thing comes after another
therefore it is caused by it!
For instance,
in some advertising we read,
"She is engaged,
  she uses —— face powder,"
implying that
she is engaged
BECAUSE she uses
this brand of powder.
This type of appeal to desire,
not to reason,
is very commonly used.
And, believe it or not,
it actually influences people
unless they train themselves
to judge a product by
its worth
rather than by
false "arguments."

Another fallacy to be
particularly watched is
the fallacy of References,
in which a writer actually gives
"references" in support of
a statement
to passages which do NOT
really bear it out,
in the trust that
readers will not look up the
references
and discover this." *

* See "An Introduction to Logic"
  by H. W. B. Joseph (p. 574),
  published by Oxford Univ. Press, 1925.

This may seem to you like
a device so childish
that it would never be used by
serious grown-up people,
BUT IT IS,
and we must guard against it.
Recently a candidate for
a very important position
was supposed to have been
discredited in a letter
written by someone who
knew him well.
Subsequently the letter
was shown up as a fraud!
So you see these pitfalls
are not merely of
historical interest
but are being used against us
today.
And of course this applies
with even greater force
to speakers than to writers.
A more modern version of this
is to quote
unfounded "statistics"
which give an air of
Science and Mathematics
but are sometimes
mere frauds
and should therefore be
checked up!

All these things
we poor listeners and readers
have to watch for constantly,
follow up,
check up,
and be generally

awake to
the many types of
verbal frauds that have
come down to us
through the ages,
with new ones
always being added.
But fortunately,
there is a good deal of
repetition of the patterns,
so,
if we are not too gullible
and not too easily intimidated †
and keep our heads clear
and our hearts alive,
we CAN learn
to detect and conquer
these cheap tricks;
but naturally
it takes some training
and effort
on our part.
You can see that
such training and effort are
ESSENTIAL in a DEMOCRACY.
And it can even be FUN
to listen to
speakers on the radio
and elsewhere,
and to read

† Cf. the familiar illustration
  given in standard books on
  Logic:
  "An attorney for the defendant
  in a lawsuit
  is said to have handed
  to the barrister
  his brief marked:
  'No case; abuse the plaintiff's attorney' "
  (see Jevons: "Lessons in Logic").

articles in the papers
and elsewhere,
and look for
what we might call
logical "boners,"
and play the game of
seeing how many of them
we can detect,
either at once,
or after checking
the references and data.‡
You can get yourself
quite a liberal education
by playing this game.
And, if you already have one,
help yourself to another,
to bring you up to date,
for Education must march on
"until death do us part."

‡ This practice will be particularly useful in
  election campaigns and other speeches.

XVI. LET SAM BE THE JUDGE!

Sometimes some people say
that they are willing to grant
that the above-mentioned
fallacies
(as well as those in this chapter)
are unreasonable,
but they believe that
it is undesirable to
eliminate them,
because
sometime they may wish
to use them themselves
on somebody else!
Thus,
though they are annoyed
by the filibustering of
the opposing party
(that is, when the "opposition"
merely "hogs the floor,"
talking about all kinds of things
which are not relevant to
the subject under discussion,*
in order to keep others
from talking to the point!) —
still
they hope some day
to use this
"double-edged sword"
against the other party,
and are therefore opposed to
eliminating this practice!
But what does SAM say

* Non sequiturs in a BIG WAY!

139

about this view?
It is hardly necessary to say
that
this is definitely NOT
in the spirit of SAM!
For in Science and Mathematics
filibustering
is completely ruled out
AND YET
everyone must admit
that SAM's procedures
are ever so much more
SUCCESSFUL
than the
ANTI–SAM–ITIC
practice of
enduring the unreason of
the other fellow
in the hope that
you can get even with him
some day
by the same method!
SAM wants his men
to compete with each other
in being REASONABLE,
and thus
all move forward together,
instead of "opposite" sides
following a policy
of holding both of them back,
since under this scheme
the "winner" is the one
who can make the most noise or
who can "put over"
the "shrewder" scheme.
No wonder that
progress is so slow
and wars increasingly horrible!

While all the time
SAM keeps showing us
a way to
RAPID PROGRESS
and to the
ELIMINATION OF WAR.

And so
let us proceed to
examine some more of
the pitfalls
so that we may all
avoid them together.

Logicians have long
called attention to
the fallacy known as
Equivocation,
in which a word is used
in different senses
within the same syllogism—
"Double-talk"!
This of course
is done on purpose
to confuse,
but, in addition to this,
some people are beginning to
realize more and more
to-day,
that relatively FEW words
have clear, definite meanings,
even though
many people use them
quite confidently and innocently
WITHOUT REALIZING THIS! †

† See "Language in Action" by
  S. I. Hayakawa (Harcourt, Brace & Co., 1941).

Thus even the word
"Democracy"
is now being used
with such different meanings
that it might be wise
to avoid its use entirely
and to think
about specific issues
for the benefit of
all the people
rather than get side-tracked
in fighting over a word
and taking sides
on irrelevant grounds
instead of
striving for the good of
all the people
all over the world,
as SAM does!

And so, also,
with many, many
other words and phrases:
"freedom of speech"
"freedom of enterprise"
etc., etc.,
some of which
are now being
studied anew in
UNESCO,
with the realization
that we must
re-examine their meanings
in a rational manner.
And of course
we cannot leave
this important task
to members of

a particular organization alone,
but must,
EACH ONE OF US,
re-examine many
seemingly familiar words
and reconsider their meanings,
if this world is to be
one in which
we can ALL live and be happy
as SAM wants us to be!

And now let us look at
just one more well-known type
of fallacy,
known as "circular reasoning,"
not only because
it is a common type,
but also because
you will see here
how CAREFUL one must be
even in diagnosing it properly,
and how very helpful
a little ordinary algebra
can be!

Thus consider
the following situation:
A man promised his friend
a job on a commission basis
under the following terms:
"Your salary will be
  20% of the net profit,
  but the profit is to be
  considered net AFTER
  your salary
  (as well as all other expenses)
  has been deducted
  from the gross profit."

Now a young man who
had heard a little about
"circular reasoning,"
immediately jumped to the conclusion
that this problem is
"illogical"
because it involves
"circular reasoning,"
and therefore cannot be solved.
Let us examine this a moment.
In the first place
some people think of
"circular reasoning"
(or "Petitio Principii"
or "Begging the Question")
in the following way:
it is arguing that
A depends on B
and when asked
"But how do you know that
B is true?,"
giving the reply,
"Well, it follows from A"—
and thus neither A nor B
has been established.
Applying this idea to
the problem on page 144,
it APPEARS that
since the salary is to
depend upon the net profit,
and the net profit cannot
be determined until
AFTER subtracting this salary
(which is unknown!)
from the gross profit—
hence the problem seems to be
illogical and impossible!
But you will soon see

(1) how vague is this way of
describing circular reasoning,

(2) how easily the above problem
can be solved by algebra,
and

(3) how clear an idea of what
circular reasoning really is
we can get from
Mathematics.‡

Thus, let us first
solve the problem,
to show that it is
a perfectly reasonable one:

Let $x =$ the gross profit
Let $y =$ the salary in question
Let $z =$ all other expenses

Then the net profit
may be expressed by

$$x - y - z.$$

Therefore

$$y = .2(x - y - z)$$

which merely expresses
in algebraic language
the condition that
the salary (y) is equal to
.2 (or 20%) of
the net profit $(x - y - z)$.
Hence,
knowing the gross profit, x,
of the business, say $100,000,
and knowing that
all other expenses (rent, etc.)
amount to say $10,000,
we then have

$$y = .2(100,000 - y - 10,000)$$

‡ See page 184.

146

or

$$y = .2(90,000 - y)$$

or

$$y = 18,000 - .2y$$

Therefore

$$1.2y = 18,000$$

or

$$12y = 180,000$$

or

$$y = \$15,000$$

as any child knows from
elementary algebra.
In other words,
it is quite simple,
by means of algebra,
to put a problem in
the form of an equation
containing UNKNOWN quantities,
and yet
manipulate them
by simple, reasonable processes,
and soon,
almost mechanically,
arrive at the numerical value
of these quantities which
at first are unknown.§
And it is therefore
unnecessarily confusing to
worry about the above-mentioned

§ See "Take a Number: Mathematics for the Two Billion"
by Lillian R. Lieber
with drawings by
Hugh Gray Lieber
(Ronald Press Company).

147

FALSE idea of
what "circular reasoning"
really is.
So that,
to a person who,
in the course of his education,
has been confused with
VERBIAGE,
a little algebra will come
like a ray of sunshine!

Later, in Chapter XX,
you will find more
mathematical light
on the very meaning of
"circular reasoning" itself,
for this is a real danger
which we must learn to
guard against.
And so we see that
a LITTLE education is
a dangerous thing,
as we saw above
in the person who
had heard of
"circular reasoning" but
did not really understand it,
and went around
loudly proclaiming that
certain perfectly reasonable
problems
were illogical and unsolvable!
We must beware of
such HALF–EDUCATED DEFEATISM!
And SAM's advice of course is
NOT that we should therefore
go BACK to the good old days of
illiteracy,

but rather
go FORWARD to
MORE knowledge which
will help us
to SOLVE more and more of
our problems.

And now let us take
the old traditional logic
and eliminate from it
all the confusing verbiage,
boil it down to
a FEW LINES of
simple, mathematical symbolism
in order to see clearly
what it is all about
and
what it is good for,
as well as
to go forward
to more and better Logic
so desperately needed in
this MODERN world,
so that
we shall not continue
to be dragged down by
all the antiquated tricks
that have been used for
centuries—
verbiage, noise,
filibustering, fighting,
confusion, et al.

Let SAM take you
by the hand
and be
YOUR LEADER.

Is someone saying
"But can SAM
  eliminate difficulties
  that have been going on for
  centuries?"

To which the answer is:
"Why not give him a chance?
 He has done it many times before.
 Remember penicillin,
 and atomic energy,
 etc., etc.
 These are NEW and
 SAM believes that
 we can use them for our
 GOOD,
 for SAM is NO DEFEATIST!
 He has
 FAITH
 HOPE and
 CHARITY!
 It is in this spirit
 that he is now
 attacking the problem of
 CANCER,
 and will keep at it
 until he conquers it;
 and the problem of the
 ELIMINATION OF WAR
 and will conquer that too.
 But he needs YOUR backing
 in all these problems!
 You must help SAM
 to help YOU."

XVII. CLASSES

On page 111
you saw that
a diagram was helpful
in seeing the
VALIDITY of
an "immediate" conclusion.
And you will now find
that similar diagrams
will be helpful also
in connection with syllogisms.
But first
a little explanation is needed:

(1) It is necessary,
    in any discussion,
    to state explicitly
    what is to be
    the "universe of discourse,"
    that is,
    to say plainly
    what you are going to
    talk about.
    That is SAM's way,
    and avoids getting
    off the subject!
    Thus if we are going
    to talk about
    positive, whole numbers only
    (1,2,3, . . .)
    we must say so,
    and then we shall know that
    1½ is not included in
    this "universe of discourse."

ALGEBRA OF CLASSES

$aa = a$ $a + a = a$

(2) We may now "classify"
these numbers
in various ways:
we may form
the class of EVEN numbers,
containing 2,4,6, etc.;
or the class of ODD numbers,
containing 1,3,5, etc.;
or the class of numbers which
are less than 6,
containing only 1,2,3,4,5.
And so on, for other classes.
Of course the largest class
that can be formed here
will contain
ALL the positive integers,
and is called the
"Universe Class" of this
"universe of discourse."

(3) If we designate
by the letter e
the class containing
EVEN numbers only,
then the class containing
all the rest of this
"universe of discourse"
may be designated by e',
and is called
the "complement" of e.
Similarly,
if b is the class containing
only the numbers 1,2,3,4,
then b' is the class containing
all the numbers from 5 up.
The universe class
may be designated by 1.
And the class containing

NONE of the numbers
(the "null" class)
may be designated by o.
You will see that
the "null" class
is as important here
as our familiar o of arithmetic
without which you
could not even write
$1,000,000.

(4) In the following diagram
the rectangle represents
the universe class, 1, and

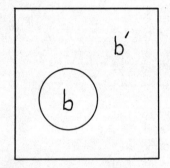

class *b*, with its complement *b'*,
may be represented as shown.

(5) If two classes, *b* and *e*, overlap,
as shown in the next diagram:

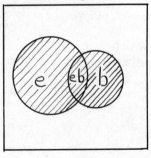

the "sum" * of classes b and e
will be understood to be
the class represented by
the entire shaded portion
as shown.
Thus if class b contains
only the numbers 1,2,3,4,
and class e contains
all even numbers,
then class $b + e$ includes
the numbers 1,2,3,4, and
all the even numbers,
because these are the numbers
which are in b or in e
or in both b and e.

(6) The part common to both
e and b
is called
their "product" * and
is represented by
$e \times b$ or eb.
Thus in our case
eb contains
only the numbers 2 and 4,
because these are the
only numbers which are in
BOTH e and b.

(7) Finally,
if from one or more premises, p,
we can draw
a valid conclusion, q,
it will be represented by

$$p \rightarrow q.$$

* For a justification of this use of
the words "sum" and "product"
see Chapter IX.

Now see if you understand
the following cases:

I.

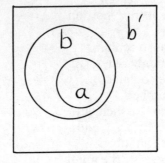

Here $ab' = 0$,
since a is entirely included in b
and obviously has
nothing in common with b',
and therefore their "product" is zero:
$ab' = 0$.

II.

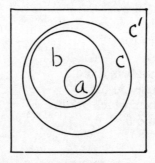

Here $ab' = 0$ again
since a is entirely
included in b.
Similarly $bc' = 0$ because
b is entirely included in c.
Hence you can easily see
the consequence of this,
namely,

    a must be entirely included in **c**

or

$$ac' = o.$$

In other words:

(1) $ab' = o$ ⎫
(2) $bc' = o$ ⎬ (Premises)
(3) Therefore $ac' = o$ (Conclusion)

Do you recognize
your old friend, Barbara? †
Or did it come on you
too suddenly
and startle you?!

III.

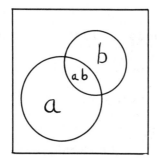

Here $ab \neq o$
since the two classes overlap
and therefore have
something in common;
hence their "product"
is NOT zero:
$ab \neq o$
which means that
SOME of the members of class a
also belong to class b.

† Since the two premises and the conclusion
  are universal affirmative statements
  and hence in the Mood AAA
  (or Barbara).

Suppose you now have

(1) $bc' = o$
meaning, as before, that
b is entirely within c,   (Premises)
(2) $ab \neq o$
as shown above,

(3) Therefore
$ac \neq o$ (Conclusion)
because if you
put class c so that
it includes b
(as demanded by
the major premise)
c will surely contain
SOME of a
(at least the ab part of a),
will it not?
Hence this conclusion is
obviously valid.
Surely you recognize
that this is another of
the syllogisms,
this one being in the mood
   AII ‡
and is in the first figure,§
and therefore in Darii.

Furthermore,
by means of these diagrams,
it is not necessary
to have any

‡ All members of b are in c (A)
  SOME members of a are in b (I)
  Therefore
  SOME members of a are in c (I)
  (See page 117).
§ The figure here is:
      bc ⎫   ⎧ yx ⎫
      ab ⎬   or   ⎨ zy ⎬ p. 121
      ac ⎭   ⎩ zx ⎭

158

negative statements at all,
because
every negative statement
may easily be changed to
a positive one, thus:
Instead of saying that
NONE of a certain type of thing
is in class a,
you may say that
they are ALL in class a',
as shown in the following diagram:

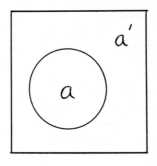

Thus *E* may always be changed to *A* (see page 117).
And instead of saying
"SOME members of *b* are NOT in *c*,"
you may obviously say:
"SOME members of *b* ARE in *c'*,"
as shown in the diagram below:

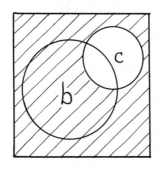

Here the shaded portion
represents c',
which obviously has
in common with b
the very part that is
NOT common to b and c.
Thus
O may be replaced by I (see p. 117),
eliminating
Celarent and Ferio (p. 123)
entirely,
leaving us with
Barbara and Darii only,
which may be briefly written,
as explained above:

(1) $ab' = 0$ and $bc' = 0 \longrightarrow ac' = 0$
$\qquad\qquad$ (Barbara)
(2) $bc' = 0$ and $ab \neq 0 \longrightarrow ac \neq 0$
$\qquad\qquad$ (Darii)

where the symbol $\longrightarrow$
merely means
"validly leads to,"
as in (7) on p. 155.

And so you can see that
all the VALID syllogisms
can be boiled down to
these two lines (1) and (2) above!
For
it is not even necessary
to perform any "conversions"
since ab is the same as ba
(both expressions representing
the common part of
the same two classes, a and b),
and, of course,
reversing the order of

the two premises is unnecessary,
since this does not
change the meaning
in any way.

There is only one further point
that must be made
in order to hand you
the entire subject of
categorical syllogisms
in that promised nutshell.
And that is
that since traditional logic
did not allow for
the "null" class,
whereas the modern study of classes
does include this class * (see p. 154)
one more statement must be made
to rule out the null class
from the new class notation
if we wish to see
exactly how to express
Aristotelian Logic
in the modern notation.
Hence,

(3) $a \neq 0$ and $ab' = 0$ and $bc' = 0 \longrightarrow ac \neq 0$.

Here, as usual,
$ab' = 0$ means that
a is entirely within b,
and similarly
$bc' = 0$ means that

---

* For otherwise we could not
  so conveniently write $ab = 0$,
  which says that
  the product of classes a and b
  is equal to the "null" class,
  and which merely means that
  a and b have no members in common.

b is entirely within c;
but, in addition,
in order to draw
the conclusion $ac \neq 0$,
namely that
a and c actually have
SOMETHING in common
(as in Barbara)
it is necessary to
include the premise $a \neq 0$,
namely,
that class a itself
is not empty.

THUS THE ENTIRE SUBJECT OF
CATEGORICAL SYLLOGISMS
IS SUMMED UP IN:

(1) $ab' = 0$ and $bc' = 0 \longrightarrow ac' = 0$
(2) $bc' = 0$ and $ab \neq 0 \longrightarrow ac \neq 0$
(3) $a \neq 0$ and $ab' = 0$ and $bc' = 0 \longrightarrow ac \neq 0$.

As Langer says: ¶
"For a true Aristotelian,
  this exhausts the abstract system
  of logic.
  Later generations of scholars,
  however,
  have added to the
  Aristotelian structure
  the two syllogisms of
  compound propositions,
  known respectively as
  the hypothetical and the disjunctive."
(discussed above on page 128 ff).
These will be
quite easily streamlined
in Chapter XXIII.

¶ See page 113.

But first you may wish to see
in a specific illustration
how neatly this
new symbolism works,
by comparison with
the old way.

Take the following syllogism:
(1) All P is M
(2) Some S is not M
(3) Therefore some S is not P.
The problem is to find out
whether the conclusion is valid.

Let us do it the old way first:

You can see that
this syllogism is in the mood AOO,
and is therefore in Baroco,
is it not?
Now the c in Baroco
(which stands for the Latin
"conversio syllogismi")
"indicates that we must employ **
the process of
Indirect Reduction.—
Indirect Reduction, or
Reductio per impossibile,
consists in showing,
by a syllogism in the
first figure,
against which no objection can
be taken,
that the falsity of the conclusion

** From "An Introduction to Logic" by
H. W. B. Joseph (pp. 291 ff).
By permission of Oxford University Press, New York.

163

in the original syllogism
is inconsistent with
the truth of its premisses.
This is done as follows:
Baroco is of the form

All *P* is *M*	All negroes have curly hair.
Some *S* is not *M*	Some natives of Africa have not curly hair.
∴ Some *S* is not *P*.	∴ Some natives of Africa are not negroes.

Now if this conclusion is false,
its contradictory will be true,
i.e., that
All natives of Africa are negroes.
We can then combine this with our
original major premise to form a
syllogism in Barbara, thus:

All *P* is *M*	All negroes have curly hair.
All *S* is *P*	All natives of Africa are negroes.
∴ All *S* is *M*	∴ All natives of Africa have curly hair.

But the conclusion thus obtained
contradicts the original
minor premiss;
hence if the original premisses
are true,
the conclusion we drew from them
cannot be false,
and our original syllogism
is therefore valid."

Let us now examine the problem
the new way,
using the following diagram:

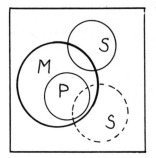

Here:

(1) $PM' = 0$ (Major premise)
(2) $SM' \neq 0$ (Minor premise)
(3) ∴ $SP' \neq 0$ (Conclusion)

Hence the conclusion is valid.

Now, candidly,
don't you like the new way better?!

†† Note that
   although S may be placed
   in various ways,
   still, in any case,
   SOME S is outside of M
   (in accordance with the minor premise)
   and therefore surely outside of P,
   which is briefly expressed by
   $SP' \neq 0$

XVIII. SOME FUN

The diagrams in
the previous chapters
were supposed to have been
first used by
the celebrated mathematician
Euler,*
in his letters to a princess
(sometime during the
eighteenth century).
And more extensive use of them
was made by
Venn †
toward the end of the
nineteenth century,
so that they are now called
Venn diagrams.‡

As you have already seen,
they are very simple to use;
and, since a good, easy
familiarity with them
will make the rest of this book
so intelligible to you,
it would be advisable
for you to express
each side of

* See "Lessons in Logic"
  by W. S. Jevons (Macmillan, 1881).
† "Symbolic Logic"
  by John Venn (London, 1894).
‡ "A Survey of Modern Algebra"
  by Garrett Birkhoff and
  Saunders MacLane
  (Macmillan, 1941).

each of the following equations
in the form of a
Venn diagram
and thus actually see that
both sides of each equation
really represent the
SAME class,
and that is why
it is legitimate to write
an = sign between them.

This will be
at least as much fun as
crossword puzzles or
jigsaw puzzles,—
and so practical besides,
since it will lead you
by an easy path
to a knowledge of
Modern Logic!

And so,
have a little fun
with yourself.

If you have studied
ordinary algebra,
you may think that
you can test these equations by
substituting numbers
in place of the letters,
but this is NOT so,
at least NOT for ALL the
equations.
You must test them by
the use of Venn diagrams!

Now try your skill:

(1) $a + a = a$
(2) $a \times a = a$
(3) $a + b = b + a$
(4) $a \times b = b \times a$
(5) $(a + b) + c = a + (b + c)$
(6) $(a \times b) \times c = a \times (b \times c)$
(7) $a + (b \times c) = (a + b) \times (a + c)$
(8) $a \times (b + c) = (a \times b) + (a \times c)$
(9) $a + ab = a$
(10) $a \times (a + b) = a$
(11) $a \times 1 = a$
(12) $a + 1 = 1$
(13) $a + 0 = a$
(14) $a \times 0 = 0$
(15) $a + a' = 1$
(16) $a \times a' = 0$
(17) If $a = b'$, then $b = a'$
(18) $a = (a')'$
(19) $ab + ab' = a$
(20) $(a + b) \times (a + b') = a$
(21) $(a + b)' = a' \times b'$
(22) $(a \times b)' = a' + b'$

And now that you have had
some fun with
Venn's diagrams,
let us see
what SAM did with them.
That boy not only
has fun with everything,
but
his games turn out to be
so practical
that they will lead us to
SURVIVAL and HAPPINESS
if we play along with him.

The main point is
NOT TO LISTEN TO
THE "EVIL ONE"
who tells people to
fight each other
and destroy this
lovely world!

Who shall be our
LEADER,
SAM or the EVIL ONE?
THAT is the question!
And the answer is
so easy:

If we want LIFE
then the ONLY LEADER is SAM.
And anyone who
REALLY believes that
the EVIL ONE is stronger
and that
destruction of the human race
is inevitable,
would do well for himself if
he would just
lie down and die peacefully
right now,
instead of waiting for
the horrible death and destruction
that he thinks are so inevitable.
Incidentally,
the rest of us,
who are NOT such defeatists,
could say
"Good riddance"
and get to work to
make this the fine world that
SAM has in mind for us.

Do you not think that
the very fact
that these defeatists
do NOT commit suicide
means that
deep down in their hearts
they too think there is some
HOPE,
and, to that extent at least,
there may be a chance
to convert even them
to SAM's philosophy!
Perhaps it is this very
confusion in
their own minds
which makes them
"throw fits"
like Pavlov's
poor confused dogs (see p. 172).
Or do they believe
that they alone
can be spared,
contrary to the opinion
of SAM's men, who
know the modern facts
better than anyone else!
(See Part I of this book.)

XIX. POSTULATIONAL THINKING

To see how
SAM further improved and enriched
Logic,
you must become familiar with
"postulational thinking,"
which you will love
for its clarity and power!

As you probably know,
before Euclid (300 B.C.)
quite a little geometry
was known,
but it was just
a lot of isolated bits of
information,
not connected until
Euclid put it into a
"system."
This he did by
first listing
what he considered to be
"self-evident truths,"
and then deriving from these,
by logic,
the "consequences"
or "inferences"
or "conclusions"
or "theorems."
The advantage of such a system
is obvious,
for,
in the first place,
a system shows

the interrelationships of
various bits of knowledge
and makes it easier
to understand and remember them.
But, more than this,
it enables us to make sure
that
at least in the basic ideas
(of which there are not many)
there are no contradictions—
for contradictions are
abhorrent to SAM.

You see he knows about
those experiments by
Pavlov,*
on the "conditioned reflexes" in dogs,
in which a dog was "conditioned"
to react pleasantly at
the sight of a circle,
and unpleasantly at
the sight of an ellipse,
and then
when the dog was shown
an ellipse that was
so nearly like a circle that
he could not tell
which it was,
the poor dog had
a violent fit!
Living creatures cannot bear
to be in a state in which
they are pulled
in opposite directions

* See "Conditioned Reflexes"
  by I. P. Pavlov
  (Oxford Univ. Press, 1928).

physically or mentally.
And SAM knows it!

And so
if we do not even know
a person's BASIC ideas
in a certain discussion
(or our own BASIC ideas
for that matter),
we cannot tell whether
they are contradictory or not
and therefore whether
his conclusions
are drawn validly or not.
He may be just
going around in "circles,"
never really proving anything,
and all we can do is
just to listen helplessly,
trying to make
a bit of sense here and there,
but not really knowing
what he is driving at.
You can see that
this kind of discussion
is fertile ground for
confusion and strife.
And, if our "friend" happens
to use a "fighting word,"
we suddenly feel
"That does it!"
and the fight is on.
Have you not heard
many discussions
of this kind?
But SAM does not care for it!
(DO YOU?)
That is why he insists that

his Mathematicians,
Logicians and Scientists,
EXPLICITLY state their
BASIC ideas,
and WRITE them down,
for otherwise
we forget them and
start contradicting ourselves
and creating confusion.
Many a worthless "argument"
could be eliminated by
this device alone.

Furthermore,
in the course of time,
the Mathematicians realized
that the BASIC ideas
were not really
"self-evident truths,"—
for in 1826,
Lobachevsky
(as well as Gauss and Bolyai,
quite independently of him)
made a new "system" of
geometry,
in which
all but one of
Euclid's basic ideas
were retained,
but that ONE was changed;
and he found that
he could,
by means of logic,
derive the consequences
of this new basic set of ideas,
which turned out to be
quite different from Euclid's,
resulting in

a "Non-Euclidean Geometry" †
now known to be
extremely important and useful.

Thus it was realized that
a set of BASIC ideas
is merely a collection of
ASSUMPTIONS or
POSTULATES,
and one can reason validly
from any set!
Thus you can say:
"If I were a king,
  then . . ."
Here your BASIC idea is
your being a king
(which may not be true at all),
and from this
certain consequences would follow.
And so
Mathematicians realized that
all that they were really doing
was
to study how to find out
what ARE the consequences
that follow from
ANY given set of POSTULATES.
And, by this time,
they have examined
many different postulate sets,
and created many different
"systems,"
some of which have
already found
practical applications,
and others will undoubtedly

† See the book referred to on p. 108.

find more.
But
the Mathematician is
not really concerned with
these applications
(that is the job of
the Scientists or
of anyone whose business it is
to apply the Mathematics
to something)—
the Mathematician's business is
merely
to DRAW CONCLUSIONS VALIDLY;
that is his specialty,
and that is why
he has built up,
in modern times,
so many systems which
are waiting for us
to use and apply them
to various needs.

You might say,
"How do you know that
  anyone will ever find
  any uses for them?
  Are they not perhaps
  just games
  that the Mathematicians
  are playing with themselves?"
SAM's answer is that
since, in the past,
many of these systems
HAVE found applications,
the probability is very high
that they will do it again.
Note that
SAM does **not arrogantly say**

"Yes, they surely will!"
He always talks in terms of
PROBABILITY—
merely that some things are
more probable than others.
He is cautious and modest,
and altogether
the gentleman,
don't you think?
(But please do not mistake him
for a Goat in a
"stuffed shirt";
on the contrary,
he is natural and at ease,
and loves music and dancing,—
remember?)

Furthermore,
SAM points out that,
even if some of the systems
do not find applications,
still they are very practical
because they show us
HOW TO THINK STRAIGHT,
and what can be
more practical than that?
"But," you may say,
"surely the Scientists also
  have to think straight,
  and how can they use
  Postulational Thinking
  when postulates are
  mere assumptions?!
  Surely they have to
  start with
  TRUE basic ideas,
  or they would not work!"

To which SAM replies that
it would be wonderful
if we could know
the TRUE basic ideas,
but since we cannot,
the next best thing is
to make assumptions
that seem to fit the observations
in the best and simplest manner,
and then
derive the consequences
(by mathematical methods)
and TEST them!
Thus it takes a GENIUS
    (like Einstein or Newton)
    propose assumptions
    which are adequate to
    the data of the times—
    and of course
the more observations
the assumptions have to satisfy,
the harder it is
to find adequate ones,
so that a MODERN Scientist
has to be
super-sophisticated
and wise!
Hats off, please!

And so
the pattern for thinking is:

(1) Start with
    ASSUMPTIONS
    which seem adequate
    for your purpose.

(2) State them EXPLICITLY
(Write them out!
and have VERY FEW of them!)

(3) Make sure they
DO NOT CONTRADICT
each other! ‡

(4) Derive the consequences
which logically follow
from these.

(5) TEST the consequences.

Try this on some problem,
and do it
conscientiously and calmly.
Do not expect too much
at first.
It takes time
to do a good job.
Studying with SAM
will certainly help!
If we would start this
in early childhood,
on simple problems,
we would become
quite good at it,
for SAM's achievements
are certainly
the "success story"
of all time!

But where does
LOGIC come in?

‡ For a discussion of
how this can sometimes be done
see J. W. Young's
"Fundamental Concepts of Algebra and Geometry"
(Macmillan, 1920).

Ah, that is
the essence of (4) above,
which says
"Derive the consequences."
LOGIC shows us
HOW to
"derive the consequences"
BEFORE
they really happen to us!
It shows us
HOW to FORETELL
WHAT the consequences will be!
If they are good,
let us go on,
by all means.
But,
if they are bad,
let us avert them
and PREVENT trouble.
Thus SAM's MEN and WOMEN
now FORESEE
the CONSEQUENCES of
using atomic energy
for the making of bombs
instead of for
the BENEFIT of mankind! §
Read again
Einstein's historic
TELEGRAM TO THE PEOPLE
(meaning YOU)
on page 29—
and BE SURE to
DO SOMETHING
about it!!!!

§ We must follow the advice of
  the Atomic Scientists in this matter
  (Subscribe to their Bulletin,
  mentioned on p. 50).

You are not just reading a book—
This is URGENT!

DO IT NOW,
OBEY THAT IMPULSE!
before you continue reading
this book.

XX. BOOLEAN ALGEBRA

Are you learning how
To follow SAM's advice?

This is your best
INSURANCE
against
CATASTROPHE.

If you realize that
part of your
daily business
from now on
is to
convince everyone you know
that
WAR MUST BE STOPPED,
that
ONE WORLD
has now become
IMPERATIVE,
that
we MUST join up with
SAM,
our friend and guide,—
then
you may wish to read more about
LOGIC,
for you will need it

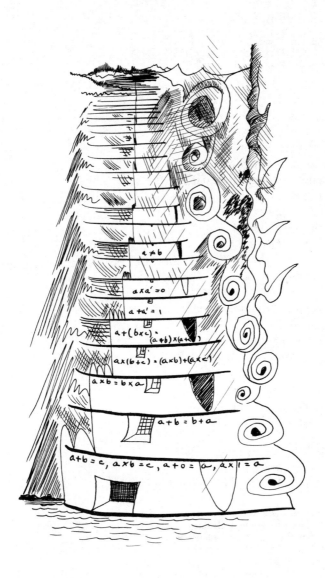

$a \neq b$

$a \times a' = 0$

$a + a' = 1$

$a + (b \times c) = (a+b) \times (a+c)$

$a \times (b+c) = (a \times b) + (a \times c)$

$a \times b = b \times a$

$a + b = b + a$

$a+b=c, \ a \times b=c, \ a+o=a, \ a \times 1 = a$

183

if you are here
"to tell the tale."

Thus you have seen that
every "system,"
like Euclidean Geometry,
has a certain definite set of
postulates.*
Before telling you
what is meant by
"Boolean Algebra"
and its connection with
Logic,
let us see first how
the very idea of
a postulate set
throws light on the question of
"circular reasoning" (see p. 146).
Thus
suppose you are asked
to PROVE
a certain geometric proposition, A,
and suppose you prove it
by means of another
geometric proposition, B
(that is, you show that
A follows from B).
Now,
if B has been previously
established from the
POSTULATES of the system,

* As a matter of fact
  there are various such sets,
  but they can be shown to be
  "equivalent" to each other
  so long as we stay
  within the boundaries of
  one system, say,
  "Euclidean Geometry."

then your proof of A
is VALID.
But, if B has NOT been
so derived,
and if you then proceed
to prove B by means of A,
which has also NOT been
derived from the
POSTULATES,
then you are using
"circular reasoning,"
making A depend upon B
and B upon A,
without having established
the validity of either one,
because
the VALIDITY of any proposition
means that
it follows from the
POSTULATES themselves
(either directly or
via some other propositions which
have themselves been shown to be
VALID,
in the sense described above).

And so,
whereas the Venn diagrams
are helpful,
SAM is not satisfied UNTIL
we clearly exhibit
the set of
POSTULATES
of the system which we are
considering here,
so that we may be sure
that we are not just
going around in "circles."

This will be done in
the present chapter,
and you will find that
the system in question here
is known as
"Boolean Algebra." †
You will find also that
the equations on page 168
all belong to this "algebra,"
which is UNLIKE
ordinary algebra in many respects,
although there are points of
likeness, too.

You can of course
compare and contrast
these two algebras
by substituting
NUMBERS for the letters
in the above-mentioned equations,
to see which of these equations
hold good in
ordinary algebra,
whereas
the letters represent
CLASSES (NOT NUMBERS)‡
in Boolean Algebra.

And so,
let us examine a set of

† First suggested by
  George Boole:
  "An Investigation of the
  Laws of Thought"
  (Macmillan, 1854).
‡ CLASSES are not the ONLY
  possible interpretation of
  the letters in
  Boolean Algebra,
  as you will see in
  Chapters XXII and XXIV.

POSTULATES for Boolean Algebra,
or the "Algebra of Classes":

Here, as explained in
Chapter XVII,
a, b, c, a', etc. represent
classes,
1 represents the
universe class,
o represents the null class,
+ and × having the meanings
given in that chapter.

Following are the Postulates:

(1) If a and b are any two classes,
    then their sum, $a + b$,
    is a certain definite class
    of the system.

(2) Similarly for the product:
    $a \times b$ is a
    certain definite class
    of the system.

(3) $a + o = a$,
    which says that
    if the null class is added
    to any class,
    it leaves that class
    unchanged.

(4) $a \times 1 = a$,
    i.e., the part which is common
    to any class, a, and
    the universe class, 1,
    is the class, a, itself.

(5) $a + b = b + a$,
    i.e., when adding two classes,
    it is immaterial which one

is taken first.
In other words,
Addition here is Commutative
(just as in
ordinary algebra).

(6) Similarly for Multiplication:
$a \times b = b \times a$,
i.e., Multiplication is also
Commutative
(as it is also in
ordinary algebra).

(7) Similarly
$a \times (b + c) = (a \times b) + (a \times c)$,
which says that
Multiplication is
distributive over Addition
(which also holds in ordinary
arithmetic and algebra).

(8) $a + (b \times c) = (a + b) \times (a + c)$,
which says that
Addition is "distributive" over
Multiplication
(which does NOT hold in
ordinary arithmetic and
algebra—
try it and see).

(9) $a + a' = 1$,
that is, any class when
added to its own complement
gives the universe class
(see Chapter XVII).

(10) $a \times a' = 0$,
which says that
any class has nothing in common with
its own complement.

(11) There are
AT LEAST two different classes
in the system,
though of course
there may be more.

You can easily see that
all these postulates
EXCEPT (8), (9) and (10)
hold also for numbers in
ordinary algebra,
whereas of course
they ALL hold for CLASSES in
Boolean Algebra.

Among the "exercises" on p. 168
you will find some of these
POSTULATES,
namely,
you can find among those exercises
the following postulates:
(3), (4), (5), (6), (7), (8), (9),
and (10).

And all the remaining exercises
would have to be
PROVED,
that is,
one would have to show that
each of them can be
derived from the postulates.

It is not necessary to do that here,
since, if you are interested,
you can find such proofs
in books on

Symbolic Logic.*
But,
to get the spirit of "proof,"
it will interest you
to see a few of these,
especially, in particular,
the proofs of
Barbara and Darii.

And it might be helpful
to arrange these proofs
as we have all been
brought up to do in school
in studying Euclidean Geometry—
namely,
writing the statements and
the reasons for them
clearly,
next to each other,
remembering of course that
the only legitimate "reasons"
are the basic rules (postulates)
themselves
(or "theorems" which have
previously been so proved).

Thus let us prove first that

$$a \times 0 = 0.$$

Since this is NOT among
the eleven postulates,
it must be PROVED,
no matter how reasonable
it may seem to your

* A very readable book is
  "Introduction to Symbolic Logic"
  by S. K. Langer
  (Houghton Mifflin, 1937).

"intuition."
Note that
in Chapter XVII,
all conclusions were drawn
"intuitively,"
and that was
acceptable as a tentative start,
but SAM demands
that results
must be derived by
meticulously showing
that they follow from the
BASIC POSTULATES,
and that nothing else
"sneaks in,"
either through carelessness
or by deliberate intent!

That is how
HONEST and CAREFUL
SAM is!

I. And so let us

PROVE $a \times o = o$ (or $a \cdot o = o$)

Proof

Statements	Reasons	
(1) $(a \cdot o) = (a \cdot o) + o$	Postulate	(3)
(2) $= o + (a \cdot o)$	Postulate	(5)
(3) $= (a \cdot a') + (a \cdot o)$	Postulate	(10)
(4) $= a(a' + o)$	Postulate	(7)
(5) $= a \cdot a'$	Postulate	(3)
(6) $= o$	Postulate	(10)

And so it has been
PROVED
that $a \cdot o = o$

II. Here is another one:

To prove $ab' = o \longrightarrow a = ab$
That is:
If we have given that $ab' = o$
we can PROVE from it that
$a = ab$:

Proof

	Statements	Reasons
(1)	$ab + o = ab$	Postulate (3)
(2)	$ab' = o$	Given
(3)	$\therefore\ ab + ab' = ab$	Since $ab' = o$
(4)	$\therefore\ a(b + b') = ab$	Postulate (7)
(5)	$\therefore\ a(1) = ab$	Postulate (9)
(6)	$\therefore\ a = ab$	Postulate (4)

If this result seems
"strange,"
please remember that
a and b are NOT numbers,
but CLASSES,
and what you have just proved
is shown in
the following diagram:

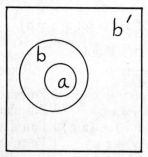

Here the rectangle is
the boundary within which
are all the classes of the set;
among them are a and b,
b' being the complement of b

(that is, the class containing
all the classes not in b);
hence $ab' = 0$ merely
expresses the fact that
a and b' have no classes in common
(and hence a is entirely within b).
And it has been proved
that the consequence of this is
that $a = ab$,
which simply means that
the part common to a and b
(represented, as usual, by ab)
is the class a itself,
a result which is
easily verified from
the diagram on p. 192.

Perhaps you are thinking that
you follow the argument better
from the diagram
than from the formal proof
written out on page 192.
But of course you must realize that:

(1) "intuitional" ideas
     require "checking";
     the "feeling" that
     we are right
     may be misleading!

(2) whenever we are trying
     to learn to use
     any new machine,
     we are a little unhappy about it
     at first.
     Thus when learning
     to drive a car
     you can no doubt
     walk around the block

more easily than
you can drive around,
but nevertheless,
if you learn to drive,
you will then have
a means of
"going places"
that you could never have if
you stuck to walking.
And so, here,
you are learning to use
Boolean Algebra,
basing all your arguments
on its postulates
and not on
any other consideration,
such as diagrams, etc.,
though whenever such
diagrams help you,
you may use them to guide you,
though they are NOT acceptable
in a formal proof—
since strict reliance on
the postulates
has been found to be
the safest method.
And, indeed,
in more difficult problems,
you will find that
these diagrams
are no longer so helpful,
so the wise thing is
to practice
and get skill
in formal proofs.

And now let us PROVE
Barbara and Darii.

XXI. BARBARA AND DARII

As you already know,
in a formal proof of
any proposition
(like Barbara or Darii),
each statement made
must be derived
either
directly from the postulates
or
via other propositions which
have already been
so derived.
Now,
in the proof of Barbara,
we shall need (6) on page 168,
namely,
$(ab)c = a(bc)$,
which
has not yet been proved here.
Now since the proof of (6)
is rather long,
and since you can easily
look it up,*
let us now proceed with
the proof of Barbara,
which may be stated
as follows
(see p. 160):

* See Appendix B in
"Introduction to Symbolic Logic"
by S. K. Langer,
previously mentioned.

Given: $ab' = 0$ and $bc' = 0$
To prove: $ac' = 0$

Proof

Statements	Reasons
(1) $ab' = 0$	Given
(2) $\therefore a = ab$	Proved on p. 192
Similarly, from $bc' = 0$ (which is also given) we can get $b = bc$	
(3) $\therefore$ (2) becomes $a = a(bc)$	By substitution
(4) But $a(bc) = (ab)c$	See †
(5) $\therefore$ (3) becomes $a = (ab)c$	By substitution
(6) But $ab = a$	See (2)
(7) $\therefore$ (5) becomes $a = ac$	By substitution
(8) $\therefore ac' = acc'$	Since a is the same as ac from (7)
(9) But $cc' = 0$	Postulate (10)
(10) $\therefore a(cc') = 0$	Proved on p. 191
(11) $\therefore (ac)c' = 0$	See step (4)
(12) $\therefore ac' = 0$	Substituting in (11) a for ac from (7).

And so
Barbara has been
rigorously justified!

And now let us do as much
for Darii:

† See footnote, p. 195.

Darii may be stated thus
(see page 160):

Given: $bc' = 0$ and $ab \neq 0$
To prove: $ac \neq 0$

Proof

Statements	Reasons
(1) $ab \neq 0$	Given
(2) $\therefore$ $a \neq 0$ and $b \neq 0$	For, if either of these were equal to zero, ab would have to equal zero (see p. 191)
(3) $bc' = 0$	Given
(4) $\therefore$ $b = bc$	Proved on p. 192
(5) $\therefore$ replacing b by bc in (1), it becomes $a(bc) \neq 0$	By substitution
(6) or $a(cb) \neq 0$	Postulate (6)
(7) $\therefore$ $(ac)b \neq 0$	See p. 195
(8) $\therefore$ $ac \neq 0$	See step (2) above.

And so
both Barbara and Darii
are now
firmly established
in fine modern style!

Let us now briefly
take stock of
what has been accomplished
and where we go from here:

I. Aristotelian Logic
has been
BOILED DOWN
and put on a
FIRM, MODERN BASIS.‡

II. The scope of the
Algebra of Classes,
simple as it is,
is much more inclusive than
the categorical syllogism,
which is summed up in
ONLY THREE THEOREMS
of this Algebra!—
See the proofs of
Barbara and Darii (pp. 196 and 197)
and (3) on page 162.

III. The model for
clear, modern thinking
has turned out to have
the same "pattern" as
a GAME,
namely,

   (1) We must first
       state clearly
       what the "equipment" is to be—
       that is,
       the things or "elements"
       with which we shall "play"
       (whether "numbers" or "classes,"
       or what have you).

‡ So far this has been done here
for categorical syllogisms only.
For the hypothetical and
disjunctive ones
see Chapter XXIII.

(2) We must then
state clearly
what we are supposed
"to do" with the equipment,
that is,
what are the "operations"
which we are to perform
upon the elements.

(3) Finally, we must
state clearly
what are the "rules" or
"postulates"
that govern the game.

Now isn't that simple?

And besides,
SAM's games
are not only
more fun than
other games
(to which you will
surely agree,
if you play some of them),
but also turn out to be
so PRACTICAL besides,
as you will soon see in
some Applications.

XXII. ANSWER "YES" OR "NO"

Before going into these
Applications,
let us take one more look at
Boolean Algebra
and compare it with
ordinary Algebra.
In the latter, as you know,
we may write

$$2^3 = 2 \times 2 \times 2 = 8$$

where the little number (^{3}),
(called the "exponent")
shows how many times
the large number (2)
(called the "base")
is to be used as a factor;
similarly

$$5^2 = 5 \times 5 = 25$$

etc.
And therefore, in general,

$$x^n \neq x$$

But, in the
Algebra of Classes
(Boolean Algebra)

$$x^2 = x \cdot x = x$$

since here the "product" of
two classes
is their common part,
and obviously the part
common to x and x
is x itself.

Hence, also,

$$x^3 = x \cdot x^2 = x \cdot x = x$$

and, in general,

$$x^n = x$$

so that here,
no matter how many x's
are multiplied together,
the answer is always x,
thus making
exponents unnecessary
in this Algebra!

The children would like
this Algebra,
don't you think?

Furthermore,
in ordinary Algebra

$$x + x + x = 3x \text{ and}$$
$$x + x + x + x + x = 5x$$

etc.,
the number in front of the x
(like the 3 or 5),
called the "coefficient" of x,
shows how many x's
were added together.
But, in the Algebra of Classes,

$$x + x = x$$

(see the definition of
"addition" of classes on p. 155),
and therefore

$$x + (x + x) = x + x = x$$

Thus, no matter how many x's

202

are added together,
the answer is always x,
so that
coefficients are also unnecessary!

Do we hear another cheer
from the children?
Do they like this new Algebra?
No doubt about it!

However,
they must of course
NOT get the idea that
they can now throw away
ordinary Algebra,
the Algebra of numbers which
we all study in school,
since they will still need it
for doing accounts and
figuring income taxes and
solving all the ordinary
algebraic problems.
But,
for the study of LOGIC,
which is just as practical
for daily life,
it is the NEW, EASY
Boolean Algebra
that we need!
You will soon see that
one of the many Applications
of this Algebra
is in the study of
electrical circuits in
a telephone company—
now what can be more
"practical"
than that?

But first
let us take
the eleven postulates of
Boolean Algebra (page 187 ff.)
and add one more,

(12) $a = 1$ or $a = 0$,

thus limiting the Algebra to
ONLY TWO CLASSES,
the universe class (1)
and the null class (0),
and of course
retaining all the other
eleven postulates.
This special type of
Boolean Algebra
is, as you see,
even simpler than
the one discussed before.
Perhaps you may think that
this is too simple
to be of any use.
But, as a matter of fact,
this super-simple Algebra,
which has only
TWO elements in it,
is the very one used in
the study of electrical circuits,
as well as in
other applications,
as you will see!

Not only that—
it is also this
super-simple Algebra
which is applicable to
what is called
"The Algebra of Propositions,"

which exhibits clearly
what is the very nature of
the kind of thinking
that has been employed here
so far,
including what are known as
"the Laws of Thought"
in Traditional Logic,
namely:

(1) the Law of Contradiction
(2) the Law of
    "Excluded Middle"
(3) the Law of Identity.

Let us therefore
take a look at
"the Algebra of Propositions":

(1) The "elements" in
    this "universe of discourse"
    are "propositions"
    (designated by p, q, r, etc.),
    where a "proposition" is
    a categorical statement.
    Also,
    p' is the negative of p;
    thus,
    if p is the proposition
    "All numbers are even,"
    then p' is the proposition
    "Not all numbers are even."
    Further,
    1 represents "truth" and
    0 represents "falsity."
    And $(p')'$ is the same as p.

(2) The "operations" are
    disjunction (represented by ∨) and

conjunction (represented by $\cdot$).
$p \vee q$ is to be read
"p or q or both."
$p \cdot q$ is to be read
"p and q."

(3) The postulates are
the following twelve
and will be presently discussed:

1. $p \vee q = r$
2. $p \cdot q = r$
3. $p \vee o = p$
4. $p \cdot 1 = p$
5. $p \vee q = q \vee p$
6. $p \cdot q = q \cdot p$
7. $p \cdot (q \vee r) = (p \cdot q) \vee (p \cdot r)$
8. $p \vee (q \cdot r) = (p \vee q) \cdot (p \vee r)$
9. $p \vee p' = 1$
10. $p \cdot p' = o$
11. $p \neq q$
12. $(p = 1) \vee (p = o)$

You cannot help noticing that
these twelve postulates
are very reminiscent of
the twelve postulates for
the Algebra of Classes,
eleven of which are
given on pages 187–189
and
postulate (12) on page 204.
Indeed,
either of these sets of
postulates
may be "translated"
into the other

with the aid of
the following "dictionary":

Language of Classes	Language of Propositions
a, b, c, · · ·	p, q, r, · · ·
+	v
×	·
o	o
1	1
a'	p'

Thus,
the statement that
class a is entirely included
in class b,
as shown in the diagram:

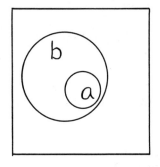

can be "translated" into
the Language of Propositions
by saying:
The proposition (p) that
"Something is a member of class a"
would "imply" *
the proposition (q) that
"It is also a member of class b."

* "Implication" will be discussed further
  in Chapter XXIII.

Furthermore.
the class $a + b$
is represented by
the shaded portion in the diagram:

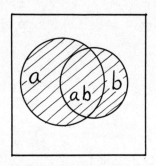

and refers to members which are
either in a or in b or in both,
and therefore you can
express this,
in the Language of Propositions,
by

$$p \vee q$$

(see p. 206 for the description of
the symbol v).

Similarly
the class "product" ab
refers to the class containing
members of BOTH a and b
as shown in the diagram above,
and therefore,
when translated into the
Language of Propositions,
becomes

$$p \cdot q$$

(see page 206).

Remember that
the addition of Postulate (12)
(page 204)
limited the system to
TWO classes ONLY,
so that class a can have
only two possible "values,"
either the universe class, 1, or
the null class, o.

Similarly
in this Algebra of Propositions,
Postulate (12) on page 206
says that
p can have
only two possible "values,"
either "truth," 1,
or "falsity," o.
This means, of course,
that any propositions
which are
"doubtful" or "ambiguous"
or have to be qualified in any way
are ruled out in
this "universe of discourse."

Furthermore,
Postulate (10) (page 206):

$$p \cdot p' = 0$$

says that
a proposition, p,
and its negative, p′
cannot BOTH be true,
which is really
the Law of Contradiction
mentioned on page 205.

And Postulate (9):

$$p \vee p' = 1$$

says that
either p or p' †
MUST be true,
which is the
Law of "Excluded Middle."

The third one of
"The Laws of Thought" (p. 205)
is not included in
this set of postulates,
but can be easily PROVED from them,
as a theorem,
in the following way:

To prove that $p = p$:

(1)		$p \cdot 1$	$= p$	Postulate	(4)
(2)	$\therefore$	$p\,(p \vee p')$	$= p$	Postulate	(9)
(3)	$\therefore$	$p \cdot p \vee p \cdot p'$	$= p$	Postulate	(7)
(4)	$\therefore$	$p \cdot p \vee 0$	$= p$	Postulate	(10)
(5)	$\therefore$	$p \cdot p$	$= p$	Postulate	(3)
(6)	$\therefore$	$p \vee 0$	$= p$	By substituting in Step (4)
(7)	$\therefore$	p	$= p$	Postulate	(3)

And so on;
you can interpret
the other postulates
and various theorems
derived from them.

---

† You remember that
  $p \vee q$ means
  either p or q or both (p. 206),
  but in $p \vee p' = 1$
  the case of BOTH p and p'
  being true (i.e. $= 1$)
  is ruled out by
  Postulate (10) on p. 206.

Thus we see that
the Algebra of Propositions
is really analogous to
the two-valued
Algebra of Classes or
a two-valued
Boolean Algebra,
and we see clearly that
by means of it
we can handle only
a "universe of discourse" whose
propositions are either
strictly "true" or
strictly "false,"
as in Aristotelian Logic,.
in which
to the question
"Is this true?"
you must answer strictly
ONLY "YES" or "NO"!
Later you will see that
MODERN Logicians are now
going much further
and developing systems in which
you will no longer be limited to
Yes or No,—
undoubtedly you can even now
appreciate what a boon this can be!

You are now also in a position to
summarize briefly the
"hypothetical" and "disjunctive"
syllogisms,
since these belong to
the Algebra of Propositions,
as you will see in
the next chapter.

XXIII. STREAMLINING "MODUS PONENS," *ET AL.*

Since, in Logic,
we speak of
one proposition "implying" another,
it is important that
you know clearly
how the term "implication"
is related to the
Algebra of Propositions.
In order to express
this relationship,
we must use what is known as
"material implication"
(designated by the symbol ⊃)
instead of the well-known
ordinary "implication" of
traditional Logic,—
the new term including
the old one.
For instance,
under the old meaning,
to say that "*p* implies *q*"
means that
from *p* you can INFER *q*,
that is,
if you know *p* to be true,
and if *p* implies *q*,
then you can infer that
q is also true.
Whereas

$$p \supset q$$

is DEFINED TO MEAN

$$p' \vee q$$

as used in the
Algebra of Propositions.
Now

$$p' \vee q$$

has, as you know,
a perfectly definite meaning
in the Algebra of Propositions,
whereas for the
ordinary "implication"
there is no operation here
corresponding to it;
but, fortunately,
these two kinds of
"implication"
are related,
so that we can,
by means of this Algebra,
see clearly what is involved in
the old meaning of
"implication" or "inference."
In order to do this,
let me introduce to you
what is known as
the "truth-table,"
a very useful and simple device:

Suppose we have
two propositions, p and q,
each of which may of course
have the value 1 or 0
(that is, it may be true or false).
Then the proposition

$$p' \vee q$$

formed from these
will of course also be
either true or false (1 or 0)

Let us therefore
tabulate all the possibilities
as follows
(remembering that
$p \supset q$ has been defined
to mean $p' \vee q$)—see p. 212.

see p. 212.

p	q	p'	$p' \vee q$	$p \supset q$
1	1	0	1	1
1	0	0	0	0
0	1	1	1	1
0	0	1	1	1

Here the "truth-values" (1 or 0)
for p and q
are listed in all four
possible combinations:

p true and q true
p true and q false
p false and q true
p false and q false;

p', being the negation of p
(see page 205),
is false whenever p is true
and vice versa.
Now, by the definition of

$$p' \vee q$$

we know that it will be true
either if p' is true or
if q is true or
if both p' and q are true;
hence the values in
the column headed $p' \vee q$

214

are easily supplied
when the columns q and p'
have been previously filled in.
And, finally,
since $p \supset q$ has been
defined to mean $p' \vee q$ (p. 212),
these two columns
(those headed $p' \vee q$ and $p \supset q$)
will have the same values
all the way down.
And now note that
the old definition of
"implication,"
namely, that
"If p is true, and
 if it is true that
 p implies q, then
 q must be true"
is completely satisfied by
the first row of the table on p. 214.
And, furthermore,
the second row claims that
if p is true and q is false,
then it is false to say that
p implies q.
Hence,
the first two rows of the table
are consistent with the
old idea of implication,
and therefore
the new "material implication"
includes the old idea.
Do not worry too much about
the last two rows in the table,
which say that
when p is false,
it can "materially imply" that
q is either true or false!

215

For remember that
"material implication"
does NOT mean the same thing as
"implication" in the ordinary
sense of this word.
No doubt you are now
sufficiently sophisticated
to accept this new meaning,
just as you have already
accepted new meanings of
"addition," "multiplication," etc.
For this is
a modern device which has
proved to be
extremely useful,
as you know.

And we can now proceed to
express the
"hypothetical" and "disjunctive"
syllogisms,
by means of this Algebra,
as promised.

Thus,
take the pure hypothetical
syllogisms in

(1) Modus ponens (page 129).
    It is of the form:

    $p \supset q$ and $q \supset r$,
    therefore $p \supset r$,
    where p stands for
    the proposition A is B, etc.
    Let us make out
    the following "truth-table": *

* Remember that $p \supset q$ means $p' \vee q$, etc.

p	q	r	p'	q'	$p \supset q$	$q \supset r$	$p \supset r$
1	1	1	o	o	1	1	1
1	o	1	o	1	o	1	1
1	1	o	o	o	1	o	o
1	o	o	o	1	o	1	o
o	1	1	1	o	1	1	1
o	o	1	1	1	1	1	1
o	1	o	1	o	1	o	1
o	o	o	1	1	1	1	1

Note that wherever
$p \supset q$ and $q \supset r$ are both true (1)
then $p \supset r$ is also 1.
Hence this syllogism (p. 216)
is merely a statement of
the fact that
"material implication" is
TRANSITIVE:
this means that
any relationship, R, between
three elements (a, b, c)
such that
a R b and b R c gives a R c
is called "transitive."
For instance,
the relationship "equality"
is transitive because
if $a = b$ and $b = c$, then $a = c$.
But, if R represents
the relationship "is the father of,"
then
a R b and b R c
does NOT give a R c,
since in this case
a is NOT the father of c
but his grandfather.

Thus
some relationships are transitive
and some are not.
And, as you see from
the table on page 217,
MATERIAL IMPLICATION
IS TRANSITIVE,
since
whenever $p \supset q$ and $q \supset r$ are
both 1,
then
$p \supset r$ is also 1;
and thus
the pure hypothetical
"modus ponens"
is merely an illustration of
this statement.

Let us next look at

(2) Modus tollens (see top of p. 130).
It is of the form:

$p \supset q$ and $q \supset r'$,
therefore $r \supset p'$.

Here it will be necessary
to show first that

$$(p \supset q) \supset (q' \supset p').$$

Since $p \supset q$ means $p' \vee q$
and $q' \supset p'$ means $q \vee p'$,
we see that these
both mean the same thing
by Postulate (5) (page 206).
Thus
$q \supset r'$ may be replaced by $r \supset q'$
and $q' \supset p'$ may replace $p \supset q$.
Hence the premises of

218

this syllogism
may be written
$q' \supset p'$ and $r \supset q'$
or
$(q' \supset p') \cdot (r \supset q')$
or (by Postulate (6) on p. 206)
$(r \supset q') \cdot (q' \supset p')$.
Consequently,
by the transitive property (p. 217),
we get the conclusion:

$r \supset p'$

the required result.

Also for
the mixed hypothetical syllogisms:

(1) Modus ponens (p. 130) is:

$p \supset q$ is true $(= 1)$
and p is true $(= 1)$,

therefore
from the table on p. 214
we get q is true.

(2) Modus tollens (near the bottom of p. 130):

$p \supset q$ is true and
q' is true.

Now since $p \supset q$ is equivalent to
$q' \supset p'$ (see p. 218)
we really have here

$q' \supset p'$ is true and
q' is true,
therefore p' is true
just as in
Modus ponens above.

Similarly for the other
hypothetical and disjunctive
syllogisms,
which you can work out
for yourself,
if you are interested.
Suffice it to say that
all of them can be done
by the use of
the same TWO principles:

(1) The transitive property of
material implication:

$p \supset q$ and $q \supset r$ gives $p \supset r$

and

(2) the fact that
the "negative converse" of
any proposition
has the same "truth-value" as
the proposition itself,
that is,

$p \supset q$ is the same as $q' \supset p'$

as shown on page 218.

And so,
if to the three lines on p. 162
(which summarize the original
categorical syllogisms)
you now add
these two principles, given above
(which summarize the
hypothetical and disjunctive
syllogisms),
you have,
in these five lines,

the entire subject of
traditional Logic,
as promised!
And you see that
they constitute only
a few of the theorems
which are possible in
Boolean Algebra!

And now let us
take a brief look at
the application to
electrical circuits,
that you may
further appreciate
the possibilities of
these
POWERFUL and SIMPLE
NEW METHODS!

XXIV. TURN ON THE LIGHT, SAM!

This is not the place
to describe
any applications of
Boolean Algebra to
"business";
anyone interested can
look them up.*
They are extremely interesting
and useful,
and,
as has happened so many times
in the course of
SAM's experience,
his games turn out to be
both ENTERTAINING and PRACTICAL.
Suffice it to say a little here
about C. E. Shannon,†
who made the application of
the two-valued Boolean Algebra
to electrical circuits.
He realized that
such a circuit is
"two-valued,"
since it can be only
either "closed" or "open";
and
back in his student days
he had studied

* See "Elementary Topics in Mathematical Logic"
  by A. Church (Galois Inst. Press, Long Island Univ.).
† Trans. of the
  Amer. Inst. of Elect. Eng.,
  vol. 57 (1938).

the two-valued Boolean Algebra.
Now, the connection between these two domains,
apparently so widely separated,
"clicked" in his mind,
and he became interested
in seeing whether
he could carry through successfully
this analogy.
And sure enough
he did it as follows:

He let the "elements" be
the switches, x, y, z, etc.,
and defined

$$x + y$$

to mean that
the switches x and y are
connected "in series," thus:

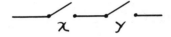

whereas

$$x \cdot y$$

is to mean that
they are connected "in parallel,"
like this:

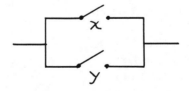

He then let o mean "closed"
and 1 mean "open."

You can see how
the following combinations
would affect the circuit.

SUMS

(switches "in series")

$$
\left.\begin{array}{l}
x \quad y \quad x+y \\
0+0= \quad 0 \\
1+0= \quad 1 \\
0+1= \quad 1 \\
1+1= \quad 1
\end{array}\right\} \begin{array}{l}
\text{according to} \\
\text{Boolean} \\
\text{Algebra.}
\end{array}
$$

That is,
if the switches are
connected "in series,"
the entire circuit $(x+y)$
is "closed" $(=0)$ only if
BOTH switches are "on" $(=0)$.

PRODUCTS

(switches "in parallel")

$$
\left.\begin{array}{l}
x \quad y \quad x \cdot y \\
0 \cdot 0= \quad 0 \\
1 \cdot 0= \quad 0 \\
0 \cdot 1= \quad 0 \\
1 \cdot 1= \quad 1
\end{array}\right\} \begin{array}{l}
\text{as per} \\
\text{Boolean} \\
\text{Algebra.}
\end{array}
$$

Here, where the switches are
"in parallel,"
the circuit is "closed" $(=0)$
(i.e. the current can flow)
in ALL cases except only
when BOTH switches are
"open" $(=1)$;
that is,.

224

$x = 1$ AND $y = 1$

is the only case in which

$$x \cdot y = 1.$$

Similarly,
he found that there was
a complete
"one-to-one correspondence"
between these circuits and
the two-valued Boolean Algebra,
so that by means of
the theorems in this Algebra
he was able to
solve problems like:

If there are four switches
(w, x, y, z) and
a motor
in a circuit,
what electrical connections
must be made so that
the motor will be "on" if

(1) any ONE of the switches is "on"
(2) any THREE of them are "on";

and so that
the motor will be "off" if

(3) any TWO of the switches are "on"
(4) all FOUR switches are "on."

You can easily believe that
this type of problem
would come up in a
telephone company's life!
But who would have thought that
it would be solved by
that funny little, abstract
Boolean Algebra?!

Naturally it took
one of SAM's men
to have the
IMAGINATION
to connect up his
SOPHISTICATED knowledge of
the ABSTRACT
with problems that
confront him in
his practical daily living.

Similarly,
another of SAM's men,
John von Neumann,‡
began an application
of other branches of
modern abstract mathematics
to the field of
Economics
(in collaboration with
an economist,
Oskar Morgenstern).

And of course
the great Einstein
derived the
atomic energy formula

$$E = mc^2$$

with the aid of
abstract mathematical
considerations,
and he now sees
the marvelous possibilities of
atomic energy

‡ See "Theory of Games and Economic Behavior"
 by von Neumann and Morgenstern
 (Princeton University Press).

for the BENEFIT of mankind—
do you wonder that
he is so anxious that
YOU
know about it,
so that you and your children
for generations
may have
a wonderful and abundant
LIFE!
Are YOU going to let the
ANTI–SAM–ITES
destroy you,
or are you going to follow
SAM
and be
HAPPY?!

XXV. GOOD–BYE FOR NOW

Thus you have learned
something about
the wonders of the
ABSTRACT
via Boolean Algebra.
You have seen it
simplify traditional Logic
and lead to
practical applications.

Undoubtedly
your own imagination
must have asked you:
But what about cases
in which
you cannot say just
"Yes" or "No,"
"True" or "False,"
"Closed" or "Open,"
as in the
Two-valued System?
And indeed
this IS a very
IMPORTANT question,
especially when you consider
how many problems
are erroneously FORCED
into this two-valued set-up.
Thus the opposing ideas of
"freedom of speech" or
"no freedom of speech,"—
"freedom of enterprise" or
"no freedom of enterprise,"

etc., etc.,
are NOT really just TWO-valued,
(all or none!),
but should be treated
as SAM handles the ideas of
"hot" or "cold":
thus,
if you perform the
following experiment,
much light will be shed for you
on this subject:

Take three vessels of water,
one (A) in which
the water is
as hot as you can stand it,
another (B) in which it is
as cold as you can stand it,
and the third (C) containing
lukewarm water at
room temperature.
Now put your right hand into A,
and your left into B,
and keep them there for a while.
If you then transfer
your right hand into C,
this water will seem
"cold" to you;
whereas if you transfer
your left hand into C,
this same water will seem
"warm" to you.
Thus our senses are
NOT
the best way to make
a "judgment."
And therefore
SAM prefers to use

a thermometer,
and not to bother with
the indefinite words
"hot" and "cold,"
but to express the temperature
in "degrees,"
thus allowing for
a great variety of
possible temperatures
instead of the two too naïve
"hot" and "cold."

And may it not be the same
with "freedom of enterprise"?
Might not either extreme
be undesirable for society?
And may there not perhaps
be an "optimum" point
somewhere along the line
which would be better than
either "all" or "none,"
as shown in the following diagram:

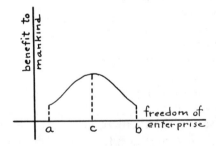

Might not too little
freedom of enterprise,
as at point a,
as well as too much,
as at b,
both be of less benefit

to mankind
than
at some intermediate point c?
No one really knows
where this optimum point is,
and it is therefore
a problem to be considered by
SAM
in the spirit
in which he always works,
and not by
arguments full of
all the old fallacies of
"ad hominem" (page 133),
ad this and
ad that
("odds buds")—
anything but
ad SAM, as they should be!

Thus SAM,
although he uses
the two-valued system
where it applies,
and there uses it expertly,
also realizes that
where such a two-valued system
does NOT apply,
he is the first to admit it
and to encourage
his Scientists and Mathematicians
to use the "function concept,"
which allows for
a large range of values,
(as in temperature measurements,
mentioned on page 231),
instead of only two.
Indeed,

even in Modern Logic itself,
new systems are
now being developed
which allow not only for
the two values
"true" or "false"
but also for
various degrees of
"probability"!
Of course
this is not the place
to go into
this new and important branch of
Logic.
Those interested
may wish to look up
"Symbolic Logic" by
Lewis and Langford.

And so,
till we meet again
let us all go back to
Part I of this book,
"The Emergency,"
and see to it that
there will be a world at all,
for,
as H. G. Wells so wisely observed,
there is a RACE on between
EDUCATION and CATASTROPHE!

But
if we go into it
with SAM at our side
to LEAD us,
we shall tackle it
in his spirit of

FAITH,
HOPE,
CHARITY,
JUSTICE,
MERCY,
HUMILITY,
INTELLIGENCE,
IMAGINATION,
MODERN REALISM,
MODERN ABSTRACT TOOLS—
in short,
with the essence of
what is best in
human nature.
This will restore
a well-justified faith in
human nature,
and will stop our
"knocking ourselves out"
with the slanderous views
about "human nature" which
make it a mere synonym for
hatred and greed.
Even granting that
there is in each one of us
a "bit of a stinker,"
still
why emphasize it out of all proportion?
Do you ever hear
anyone say on the radio,
right after the playing of
a Beethoven symphony,
"Isn't that a beautiful
  illustration of
  human nature?"
No! no one ever says that!
But when speaking of
thievery and murder and war,

THEN we hear
"There it is again—
  HUMAN NATURE!"
I ask you,
is that fair?!

Let us rather go along with
SAM
in his assertion that
greed, etc.,
are PATHOLOGICAL DISTORTIONS
of the legitimate desire to
"eat" (see Chapter VIII),
and that
the NORMAL functioning
of this urge
is in the direction of the
ABSTRACT
(after we have had
"enough" on the physical level)
for it is in the
ABSTRACT,
in creative
Science, Art, Mathematics,
that our urge to
"unite with" or
"love" or
"eat"
the whole world,
can go on and on
without our interfering with
each other.

XXVI. THE MORAL

As you have seen,
this little book
is an attempt to see what
MODERN REALISM
demands of us
in order to reward us with
SURVIVAL and HAPPINESS.

It therefore concerns itself with:

(1) An EMERGENCY program
(2) a long-term program of
     EDUCATION.

Obviously the EMERGENCY program
must consider the
ELIMINATION of WAR
(for otherwise
we just won't be here
to get educated!)
And since
modern warfare is
a matter of
WEAPONS of MASS DESTRUCTION,
we must consult SAM (p. 74)
in order to get the
FACTS,
without which
we cannot think
REALISTICALLY!
Here, then,

236

we MUST follow him,
the modern Paul Revere (p. 25),
who is trying to arouse us
to an awareness of
the DANGER—
and we must NOT follow
the lead of the
grossly uninformed,
who have the audacity
to say that
the modern weapons
have been
overrated!!

Then, if the human race
succeeds in
eliminating war,
it will
have to consider
what shall be our
ORIENTATION
in the future.
What kind of
philosophy of education
shall we need for
SURVIVAL and HAPPINESS?
What guide to
MORALITY,
and not to mere MORES?!

Those who are
truly religious
already have such a guide.
But those who do not follow
this guide,
as well as those
who merely use their creed

as a WEAPON to fight
other creeds,—
for all these
a guide,
an orientation,
a LEADER,
is desperately needed—
for NONE of us is safe
so long as there are
SOME who
either lead us to
destruction and death,
or who are
so CONFUSED
that they too drive us to
death and destruction.

Now,
NO PERSONAL LEADER
can fill the bill,
for no personal leader
knows enough or
lives long enough
to do the job.
And that is why
it has been here proposed
to follow
a character named SAM,
who is the ESSENCE of
what is best in
the human race itself.
And this little book
has tried to show, by
DOCUMENTARY EVIDENCE
from Science, Art, Mathematics
how we can actually
get help from
SAM

and how he can teach us to
recognize,
and protect ourselves from,
ANTI–SAM–ITES,
and how to
LIVE and be HAPPY!

While the name
SAM
is derived from
Science, Art, Mathematics,
its significance is wider than that: *
The S represents our contact with
FACTS,
with the
OUTSIDE WORLD;
the M represents
the REASONING power of our minds,
and
the A represents
our INTUITION,
which,
being between the S and M
is thus prevented from
going wild
(like Hitler's "intuition"),
but is checked by both
FACTS and REASON.
Thus,
if we follow
SAM,
we are led,
in the consideration of
any problem
to bring to bear upon it

* For further clarification of SAM
see "INFINITY" by Lillian R. Lieber, with
drawings by Hugh G. Lieber (1953).

S and A and M
in an INTEGRATED manner,
and stop being
the kind of
"split personality"
that, like the Nazis,
ignores facts and reason
and peddles lies,
or that,
like the defenders of
mere gadgets,
ignores the deep significance
of SAM's "A"
in "fundamental science."
It is interesting to test
SAM
in confused discussions,
for he really
can guide us through
the barrage of words
now attacking us
from every direction.

Let therefore
SAM,
who gets his inspiration
from the Lord Himself,
be
OUR LEADER.

DATE DUE

MY 09'88			
		·	

DEMCO 38-297